# THE LOST
# FIFTY-SEVEN

# THE LOST
# FIFTY-SEVEN

*A Genealogical Journey of Discovery,
Deception, Secrets and Scandal*

Ron Williams

To learn more about this author, visit
ronwilliamsmemoirs.com

*Some of the names in this book have been changed to
protect the privacy of certain individuals.*

*Dedicated to my dad,
Donald Roy Williams*

# TABLE OF CONTENTS

**PART III – TRUTH AND DISCOVERY (2022-2023)**

# Introduction

"Dear Alfred, I think I got one of the pleasantest shocks of my life, when I was handed your letter yesterday, as I had long given you up for dead. I thought perhaps you had been killed in the last war." These lines comprise the opening of a letter my grandfather received from his older brother, Charles. The letter continues, "I have made many enquiries but could not contact you, and your last letters which I still possess were postdated from the U.S.A. I have taken thousands of Canadian troops across the country, but of course it was no use trying to get information, as I had so little to go on." Near the end of the letter, Charles urges, "well Alfred, I expect you are like me, now settled down and finished with roaming, so we must not again lose touch with each other."

Reader, I present to you a missing person story. It's my own personal, missing person story, focusing on my efforts to discover the unknown, lost years of my grandfather, Alfred Victor Williams. I learned early in my research that he left his home in England as a young man - a boy, really - chasing fortune in a new world. Exactly how he chased that fortune during the majority of his adult life makes up the mystery. He had no contact with his family, including his cousins, his siblings, and even his parents. He missed his mother's funeral. In fact, he wasn't aware she had passed. Same with his father.

But then, suddenly, he wasn't missing anymore.

Just as quickly as he disappeared, my grandfather reemerged, in short succession re-connecting with his England family, meeting and marrying my grandmother and becoming parent to my father and aunt.

He was fifty-seven years old.

This is the story of my long, drawn-out search for what my grandfather was doing during his first fifty-seven years. He kept it a guarded secret, never discussing those years with anyone, including my father and aunt. The search proved difficult, even frustrating at times. I loved every minute of it. Like I said, above all else, it's a missing person story. But it also includes a long-lost inheritance, an ancient English castle and a kidnapping.

I pursued this missing person case on my own, more or less. I definitely had help from some very good people including my family. I wouldn't call myself a genealogist, however. I wouldn't even call myself an expert researcher. I'm just a regular guy who was determined to use genealogical tools to solve my own personal missing person case.

A genealogical hobbyist, if you like.

In fact, if there are any professional genealogists reading, they'd probably have a thing or two to say about my flawed research or missed opportunities. What can I say? I tried to be as proficient as possible.

You might be wondering if the mystery is solved, "is there a solution to the mystery?" Well, I can't give a simple straightforward answer. That would destroy the suspense. And I do want to keep you in suspense. I can tell you, I'm very satisfied I was able to solve the mystery, as are my wife, my mother and father, and my aunt. However, at this time, all I can do is to sincerely promise that you won't feel robbed, tricked or disappointed. With that in mind, I invite you to join me in my almost decade-long quest to account for the missing, first fifty-seven years of my paternal grandfather, Alfred Victor Williams.

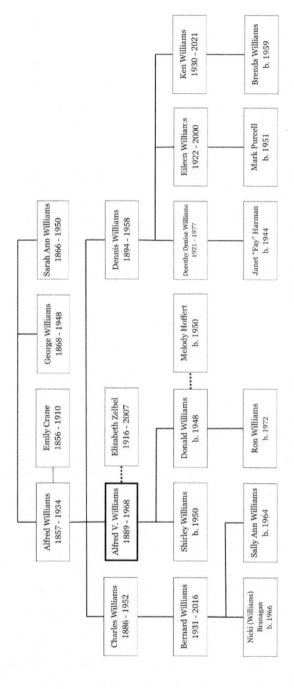

# Williams Family Tree

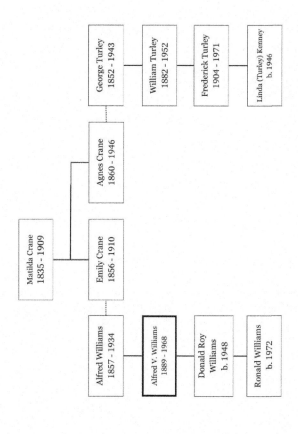

**Turley Family Tree**

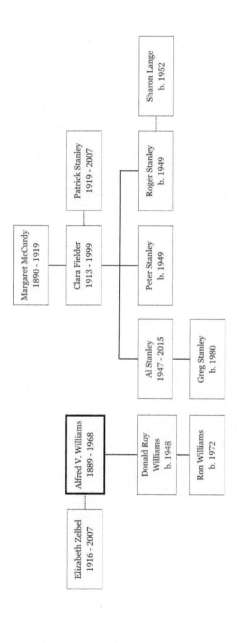

**Stanley Family Tree**

# PART I – HIDDEN REVELATIONS (2005-2015)

# In the Company of Mrs. Blake

**Saturday, October 23, 1880, 11:56 p.m. #18 House, Dog Lane, Bewdley, Worcestershire, England.**

*At twenty-three years old, Emily Crane is finally beginning the life of a married woman. Her early years were spent in the Chaddesley Corbett home of her grandparents, Thomas and Mary Crane. It was there that her unmarried mother, Matilda, raised Emily along with her younger siblings, William and Agnes. When Emily was six it all changed with twenty-nine-year-old Matilda taking the three children to the nearby home of her newly acquired groom, the recently widowed, forty-eight-year-old William Perry. There, Emily did her best to fit in with her many new stepsiblings, that is before a handful of half-siblings emerged. With a house so crowded, it was a welcome relief when Emily, then thirteen, left to become a servant for Ms. Elizabeth Shyles and her two young children in their Bromsgrove home almost five miles away. Compared to the chaos at Emily's home, looking after the Shyles' household seemed a breeze. Now, some ten years later, Emily is a married woman. No, she and her husband, Alfred Williams, don't yet have a place of their own. The newlyweds will reside at the Williams' family home on Dog Lane in Bewdley, consisting of her in-laws, George and Mary Williams, as well as her new husband's younger siblings, Annie, Thomas George, Edward and Lizzie.*

*The wedding earlier in the day was beautiful, if not modest, Emily's grandfather, Thomas, giving her away to her groom. It wasn't perfect, but it did mark a welcome, fresh beginning even if her new family did present some challenges.*

I f there's one thing you should know about me – aside from loving a good mystery – it's that I have a flair for the nostalgic. Whenever I'm in the area, I'll always detour to drive past one of my former houses. Going for a walk? Let's head to the old neighborhood. At over fifty years old, I still visit my childhood schools semi-regularly. I'm that guy.

It's with that spirit that I made a request of my father one day. "Hey Dad, could we spend the day exploring your old haunts? Places you hung around in your childhood and young adult years?" My dad's young life was not what you'd call "ordinary" or better yet, "stable." Without venturing too far ahead of myself, his teens were filled with fistfights, homelessness, reform schools, tattoo parlors and several minor brushes with the law. Let's just say his upbringing was in sharp contrast to my sheltered development. Who wouldn't be excited at a personal tour of the dark side of 1960s

Vancouver? The day was supposed to be about my dad, but it was my grandfather's legacy that stole the show.

In 2005 on a rainy, late December weekday morning, my mother and father arrived at my Maple Ridge home. My mother would spend her time on a task that was both natural and pleasurable, helping my wife, Lana, take care of the kids. And with that, my dad and I were off for a day of nostalgia for him and discovery for me.

I can't fully explain the feeling of anticipation and curiosity I held as we made our way west into the Vancouver area. I was aware that my father and his younger sister, my Aunt Shirley, had spent considerable time away from home, in "foster care," it was referred to. Before immersing myself in this research, I was always puzzled about this. I knew my grandfather and grandmother had separated soon after my aunt was born, but my grandmother, whom I affectionately referred to as "Oma," seemed like she would have been fully capable of raising two kids as a single parent. True, my father had always self-confessed that he was somewhat a handful growing up. My aunt couldn't have been that much trouble though. At least, that's what I figured. Eventually, my research helped me paint a much clearer, more sympathetic, picture. In addition to better understanding why my grandfather couldn't always take care of my dad and aunt, I'd learn why Oma wasn't always able to either. I'll save both for later.

As we crawled along the rainy Lougheed Highway connecting my Maple Ridge home with the city of Vancouver, I was a little tentative, even afraid of what I was about to learn. My dad did an excellent job as a father. Along with my mother, he gave myself and eventually my younger brother a spoiled upbringing, safe from danger and drama. The idea that he, himself, suffered was troublesome to me. I felt as if I was in some way responsible for protecting him as a youth, that same way he protected me. Writing this, I realize the misguidedness, but I suppose it was the instinct recently born in me as a young parent that made these feelings real, if not out of place.

I was aware that he'd predominantly called two houses "home" at various times, one in Vancouver and one in the bordering city of Burnaby. In the Marpole area of Vancouver, at 8168 Hudson Street, we discovered the place my father knew best. The home he'd occupied on and off between the years of 1955 and 1968, as I'd eventually learn, had been long torn down. Peeking inside the front gate of this newer structure, the current owner emerged to provide a brief background of his time of habitation and a few interesting notes about the neighborhood. Not much to see there.

Turning right onto Granville Street, we spied the location of the original White Spot Restaurant, a one-hundred-year mainstay in the Vancouver family dining scene. It was also where my father as a youth raised havoc by reaching into the take-out window and grabbing french fries, and also circled the aisles in the dining hall soliciting the day's copy of the *Vancouver Sun* newspaper, the very same that I'd eventually hock some twenty-years later. An impressive junior entrepreneur, my dad developed his signature sales pitch: "if I can guess your age, will you buy a paper?" he'd plead, bright-eyed and innocent.

"Okay, you've got a deal," the amused suit would snap back only now taking his eyes from his enticing, gravy-soaked Salisbury steak or possibly his somewhat more enticing dinner date.

"Well, you're the same age as your nose and a little older than your teeth," my father would retort, proud and confident in both the wittiness of his pitch and also the surety of a sale. And more often than not, the entire thirty-second interaction would end enjoyably for both parties, my father walking away victorious, a shiny dime added to his meager profits.

The nostalgic warmth of these stories was sadly juxtaposed with other more haunting realities. "I remember having no place to go and sleeping under that overpass one night. It was raining hard, but I was warm. I was okay," my dad offered, tentative, but smiling, maybe even a little proud that he'd persevered, survived.

"Hey, see that apartment building? I lived there with Gordon Hoy and Tom Hulbert for a while. We used to buy a bag of Chinese food for fifty cents and a bottle of rum for two dollars. That didn't last long, but they were good times." I envisioned a medium helping of cold "chop-suey" crudely scooped into a brown, paper sandwich bag.

Next, we doubled back east to the historic Astoria Hotel on the seven-hundred block of East Hastings Street, a run-down, homelessness and poverty-stricken Vancouver thoroughfare, serving as a sad, even horrific, central vein running through the city. I supposed it was once a part of a vibrant, new urban scene, ripe with expansion, vision and promise. This was not the case on this day, in 2005, as it hadn't been for some time. "That's where your grandparents met. Oma was working as a chambermaid and my dad rented a room." The tale sounded familiar and failed to inspire any follow-up questions. I took notice and filed the puzzle piece away for future reference, only to be properly followed up at the west-end office of the official Vancouver archives some years later.

In truth, my mind was somewhat preoccupied as we galivanted our way through the forgotten landmarks. The most profound experience of the day that paralyzed me with emotion and ultimately motivated me to research this story had occurred much earlier, during our first stop.

"4141 Yale Street was my first house," my dad reminisced with a tentative smile. "Let's begin there." The name evoked images of the ivy league school the street was named for, suggesting prestige and honor. Knowing my dad's history, it was somewhat at odds with the memories I assumed the address would evoke.

Turning off Boundary Road, which separates the city of Burnaby from the larger, Vancouver, I spied a typical dreary suburban street, host to single-dwelling family homes of

*The Yale Street home of Mrs. Blake where an uncomfortable visit sparked my long journey.*

various eras and maintenance states. Some seemed remnants of years past, likely constructed in the early twentieth century or thereabouts. Other Spanish or Italian-style houses seemed products of the 1970s or even 1980s, as the trends were. Still, other dwellings looked more modern, with stained wood and prominent glass suggesting construction in the 2000s.

It took my dad a couple minutes before realizing, much like the Hudson Street house, that 4141 Yale as he may have remembered it, no longer existed. Again, our luck was fortuitous, as a middle-aged man of South Asian descent emerged from a side door, taking confident strides up the cement walk on the side of the house. Rather than approach us with demand or annoyance, he was welcoming, but also expecting to discover why we were perched on the road staring quizzically at his home. "Hi. I used to live here," my dad offered. "But not this house. 4141 Yale was smaller, a one-floor home."

"Okay, well, yes, we live in this house for ten year maybe now," was the man's informative response in thoughtful, broken English. There was a little small talk, but it was clear he hadn't immersed himself into either the history or current

8

state of the neighborhood. My dad offered a few names, but it was essentially useless. In fairness, it had been some sixty years since my father lived there.

As the conversation wrapped up, I could spy my dad's gaze moving farther up the road, a few houses anyway. Saying our "goodbyes," my dad's curiosity led him up the slight hill as if he was possessed by some inner force guiding him. He unintentionally ignored a couple of my inquiries before offering out loud, mainly for his own benefit, "I wonder if Mrs. Blake still lives there."

It was then that I spied the early twentieth-century raised rancher. Positioned somewhat proudly on a large lot, the house contrasted the newer built structures that surrounded, but it didn't look out of place. Rather, the house stood strong, ascertaining its position, its seniority cementing its presence. It wasn't run-down, but it wasn't necessarily in good shape either. In fact, offering someone a photo they may have guessed the date to be the 1960s rather than 2005. I suppose the correct term is "anachronism," which is exactly how this house appeared: belonging to a different time period than which it exists.

Tentatively, somewhat bewildered, I followed behind my father up the front walk, but I'm sure his eyes sparkled with possibility and wonder. Approaching the faded, antique door, he offered a few hesitant knocks on the pale brown wood, the numbers 4149 fastened on the post beside.

Moments later, "Hello, Mrs. Blake? Do you remember me? I'm Don Williams and I used to live a few doors away."

I swear to God, the frail woman looked to be in her nineties but managed to display acceptable posture as she squinted her left eye in a bid to better recognize the two younger men in her doorway. "Yes, hello Don, please come in," she offered, turning her back to us and retreating to the inner house. My dad and I stole a knowing glance, each sharing the uneasy thought: this woman doesn't know who we are, and we shouldn't be in her house. With the advantage of knowing our motives were purely innocent, we tentatively followed into the home.

Minutes later, now uncomfortably stationed in her pre-1970s decorated living room, my father began the small talk, asking about the houses and of course throwing out the old names, "Neverosky" being one that I remember. My dad enquired about her son, Ronny, to which the woman perked up and explained that he lived in the nearby city of Surrey. At times, Mrs. Blake seemed to nod comprehendingly likely attempting to convince us that she remembered the details my dad shared. I wasn't confident she understood any of it.

In fact, the more my dad spoke, the more my unease grew. This woman, if she even was Mrs. Blake, wasn't familiar with what my dad was talking about and – I was convinced – had no recollection of my father.

Offering my dad a series of signals, delivered with both body language and eye contact, the conversation came to an end, and I stood up wanting to escape the small house and relieve the uneasy feeling of trespass. As we made our way back to the entrance, Mrs. Blake finally spoke up, taking the lead of the conversation for the first time.

"Donny, I remember the day your mother left. She put on her overcoat and stepped out with two suitcases. She marched up that hill to a taxicab that was waiting. Shirley wasn't there, but you were following ten feet behind, matching her step for step and you were crying all the way."

It was the first time I'd heard the story. Years later my dad would confirm the events so engraved in his mind, justifying his mother's actions as a result of the cruel treatment by her husband, my grandfather – Alfred Victor Williams – the very subject of this book. Eventually, my dad would offer some follow-up memories on future reunions and breakups between his two parents. If I wanted to gain a better understanding of my dad's life before I knew him, this story certainly helped. Hours later we'd hit our final stop of the day,

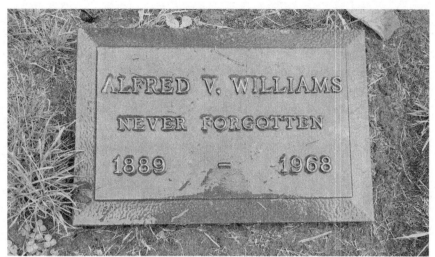

*The final earthly reminder of my grandfather - our last stop
for the day - created a paradox in my mind.*

Mountain View Cemetery. My dad had a clear recollection
that there was a marker with my grandfather's name
somewhere, although his body had been cremated in 1968
when he died. My father hadn't been to the cemetery in
decades, if ever at all, and it took the sales representative some
twenty minutes or so to locate his plaque before handing us a
map that would help guide us. To be fair, a large portion of
her twenty minutes seemed to focus more on her sales pitch
than directions.

After around fifteen minutes of purposeful wandering, we
located the eight-inch by fourteen-inch brass plaque secured
in a section of soggy, green sod. "Alfred V. Williams, Never
Forgotten, 1889-1968." Although it had been several hours
since the interaction at Mrs. Blake's, my mind couldn't help
but fantasize about the horrific events at the hands of my
grandfather that would have caused my grandmother to walk
out on her house, her marriage, her young son and daughter.
In truth, I was somewhat numb attempting to organize my
thoughts on this man. One thing I knew for sure: I wanted to
learn more about him.

Paradoxically, my father was crystal clear in his view. With the same horrific story fresh in his mind, having the far more traumatizing experience of living through the event as a child, my father remained unaffected.

He dropped to his denim-clad knees onto the wet grass, bent down and offered a kiss to the cold, metal, burial marker.

"Thanks for the gift of life, Dad. Rest in peace."

# A Gift from a Grandmother

**Saturday, November 23, 1889, 12:12 p.m. 64 Stourport Road, Wribbenhall, Kidderminster, Worcestershire, England.**

*Nine years married and in a place of their own, Alfred and Emily anxiously await the birth of their second child. Emily hasn't slept in days, her mind consumed with fear and worry. It's true she's rued the thought of giving birth once again, the traumatic pain of her firstborn, Charles, still fresh in her mind after almost three years. She also fears miscarriage, accepting it is her expectancy, or destiny, to provide a large family, especially considering the young age at which she was married, twenty-three. Emily's own mother, Matilda, has given birth to ten children.*

*Now, this morning, after another sleepless night, this*

*one mainly due to labor pains, Emily is sure this is the day. Her husband, Alfred, with three-year-old Charles, has retreated to his parents for a couple of days to allow Emily to recover in peace. Charles will receive quite the surprise when he returns home two or three days from now to discover he has a baby brother or sister.*

*Mrs. Elizabeth Maurice, a neighbor and local midwife of sorts looks over the birth for a modest fee of three shillings. She is assisted by Mrs. Malcolm and Mrs. Dickens who agree to stay in Emily's home for a few days to perform childcare and a few chores until the mother is back on her feet.*

*Emily lay in pain as the three women huddle around her bed. Finally, after some hours, the birth begins, Emily writhing and calling out in pain. Some hours later, Emily's second son, red and crying loudly, enters the world. Mrs. Malcolm goes on foot to alert Alfred that he now has a second healthy son and namesake, Alfred Victor Williams.*

M y experience at Mrs. Blake's and also the cemetery provided much of the catalyst that would eventually motivate me to mobilize my efforts to learn about my grandfather's life. However, it would take some time. At present, I'd like to begin this book on a personal level. Get to know one another before we fully delve into the mystery of my grandfather's secret life. If we were face-to-face, I'd lead you to my quiet den where, with a chilled pint of an Indian Pale Ale (IPA), we'd relax into conversation amidst the muted sounds of soft jazz and the backdrop of a natural fire warming the room. But, alas, we are at a distance, and you'll have to settle in with the copy you hold in hand...and your own beverage of choice.

*All together and dressed up. (From left to right) Ben, Tom, myself, Lana, Scott and Jack.*

I was born in St. Paul's Hospital in the heart of Vancouver, British Columbia, Canada in late 1972. It was the same hospital my father, Donald Roy Williams, was born in some twenty-four years earlier. Currently, I'm a fifty-year-old happily married father of four living in Maple Ridge, British Columbia, a small suburb about thirty miles east of Vancouver.

I've been married to Lana for about twenty-four years, a number made convenient by the fact that we were married in the last year of the twentieth century. Together, we're very proud of our four boys. Jack, born in 2001, is a skilled musician, busy recording and performing on drums, guitar, keyboards and vocals. Man, is he talented. Ben, born in 2002, is more focused on athletics, currently playing both college field lacrosse and junior box lacrosse. Tommy, born in 2004, is our hockey player, competing in the local junior ranks. All three are attending Simon Fraser University, where I somehow graduated in 1997. Our youngest, Scott, was born in 2006. Still in high school, he looks to be following Ben's path in continuing his educational and lacrosse career. All have far exceeded my humble academic, musical and athletic prowess.  Of course, the cornerstone of the family is Lana, every part as beautiful and intelligent as when we first met.

It's easy to throw out various cliches about one's wife. "She's my rock." "She's my best friend." "I'd be lost without her." I prefer to be a little more specific in my adoration.  If I had to say what Lana means to me and the boys, I'd say she forms the structure that drives our family and keeps us close. She pushes me to travel, reflect on priorities and always stretch my boundaries.  For the most part, she sets my social calendar.  Quite simply she's responsible for creating the life I enjoy so much...and she's also a lot of fun to be around, most of the time.

I enjoyed a typical family upbringing in another close suburb of Vancouver: Port Coquitlam.  The city itself is infamous for being home to one of Canada's most prolific mass murderers.  Thankfully, Port Coquitlam is better known for being home to Canada's most renowned hero, Terry Fox, a courageous, young cancer patient who ran upwards of twenty-six miles a day on a prosthetic leg, all in a bid to raise awareness and funding for cancer research.  I remember the Sunday morning when I was eight years old.  My friend called and broke the news that Terry Fox had died.  I cried.  In fact, my eyes still well up when I think about him.

Early on, it was rock stars and pro athletes whom I dreamed of becoming.  Upon graduating Terry Fox Secondary in 1990, I enrolled at Douglas College, then Simon Fraser University, until eventually I found myself teaching English at the same Terry Fox Secondary that I'd left some years earlier. I recently received my pen for twenty-five years' service, and I can truthfully say that the teaching career has been a good one for me.  Although, if I could earn a living pursuing my other interests, like brewing IPA's or toiling in the kitchen, my teaching days would be behind me.  Accepting my limited potential, the notion of writing professionally fails to enter my thoughts.

*My parents, Melody Hoffert & Don Williams, on their 1969 wedding day.*

Perhaps it's a little ironic that I've spent the better part of the past decade immersing myself in family research and my grandfather's missing years. The truth of the matter is that for most of my life, I was ashamed of how very little I knew about my family history. I used to marvel at friends who celebrated their family heritage with Scottish flags, German cooking, or Ukrainian traditions. I really didn't know what my family heritage was. As a boy, I was aware that my maternal grandmother was Scottish, and I assumed that she was born there, as she often mentioned, "the old country." Similarly, I was aware that my Oma was German, which was her first language. It was strange some years later when I discovered that she was actually from Russia. Somehow, I had learned that my maternal grandfather was from Birmingham, complicated by the fact that he wasn't actually my mother's birth father. Then there was the case of my paternal grandfather, which – well – that's the subject of this book.

I really was brought up in an idyllic household with loving parents. Both my mother, Melody Hoffert, and my father, Don Williams, in their own ways, took excellent care of myself and my brother. As for cultural traditions? My Oma cooked a couple of German dishes, a pork and rice masterpiece she simply called, "Pilau," and a German cake she referred to as "Streuselkuchen," the latter of which I indulgently picked-off the moist sugary balls on top. I can still taste both today and have tried to replicate on occasion, well the "Pilau" at least. Over the years, I'd ask my mother to cook the dish. I remember it being so rich in fat with fragrant carrots to cut through the taste. However, my Oma would never pass on the recipe, maintaining that it "would take an entire day to share." Other than that, I can't recall any Scottish, German or other cultural influences in our house. If pressed, I'd call myself "Canadian," although even at fifty-years of age, I am still not one hundred percent sure what that means.

By far, I was closest to my mother's parents, Grandma and Grandpa Fryer. Margaret Ann McGillivary was born in New Aberdour, Scotland in 1917. Along with her mother, father and an older brother, she immigrated to Canada just after World War I in 1924. First, working as farmhands in Saskatchewan, the family eventually made their way west, settling in the city of Burnaby. By the time my grandmother arrived in Burnaby she was already married to her first husband, my biological maternal grandfather. However, when my mother was born in 1950, her father was long gone, chasing another woman whom he'd eventually drive into poverty and alcoholism.

The man I consider my maternal grandfather, not to be confused with my paternal grandfather who is the subject of this book, was a good one. No, he was a great one. Albert Henry Fryer, or "Papa," as I called him, was born in 1907 in Birmingham, England. He too immigrated – also with his parents and siblings – to Canada in 1908. A pioneering Burnaby family, he dealt with the death of his mother at an early age and remained a dedicated son, living with and taking care of his father until the early 1950s. He lived on Francis Street in Burnaby down the road from my grandmother and at some point, their neighborly relationship became more, and they married. From what I understand, my Papa not only saved the life of my grandmother but her entire family. Again, my eyes tear up.

Fortunately, I was close to both as a youth, punctuated by frequent visits, outings and sleepovers. I remember, vividly, one day as a child my Grandma Fryer sat me down with a serious tone. "Ronny. I want to talk to you for a few minutes about something very important." There was a long pause as she put down her Players cigarette and composed herself. Taking a sip of her tea, she continued, "I'm not going to be around forever and want you to have something." She reached down and presented a dark, emerald green, circa-1980s photo album with a golden border on the cover, matching gold spiral binding. "I've put together a photo album of all the old pictures." Next, she slowly turned the pages, pausing to indulge in each solitary image. "This is my brother Mac on the farm." Turning another page, "this is my mother by the tractor." Turning another page, "this is my father in the barn." Was I bored or disinterested? No, far from it. The hour spent at the kitchen table held me in rapture or at least interest anyway. Here was a world that I knew nothing about, but it was my family, my people, where I came from. What struck me most, and what I remember to this day, some thirty-years after her untimely passing, was what she said to me next. "I'd like you to have this photo album because I know that you are the most interested in the old stories."

In truth, and I was only a young teen probably around fifteen years of age, that comment perplexed me. I was the most interested in the old stories? Really? Driving home along the backroad that evening, I glimpsed my mother, concentrating on the dark path in our 1982 General Motors station wagon. "Mom, is that true? Am I the most interested in these photos, in our family history?"

"Oh, I don't know about that. I think she just wanted to get rid of the photos."

What to make of the incident? I suppose it fits into my narrative thus far. My mother knew me better than anyone else in my world. I may have been able to fool my dad at times, but my mom always knew what I was thinking. Maybe the anecdote exposes that I never was that interested in family history after all.

On the other hand, though, my grandmother was older, perhaps wiser. I suppose on some level, she knew she was reaching the end of her time. Maybe, just maybe, it was some intuition that told her I was the one who'd be interested, who'd want to document and pass on the stories. I don't know, but I do know that I still have the glorious green photo album, and I always will.

In truth, there were a couple other brief dalliances into family research. During a 2010 trip to New York in celebration of Lana and my tenth anniversary, I had the chance to visit the immigration center on Ellis Island. I listened, transfixed, as the tour guide detailed the harrowing arrival of poor immigrants from various parts of the globe. I attempted to picture my grandparents arriving under these same adversarial conditions – although in truth, at that point, I don't think I was totally clear which ones may have been born in North America and which ones immigrated. At the end of the tour, there was an opportunity to look up family names; I can't remember if this resource was offered in paper or digital form, but I do remember the result. No names found.

Sure didn't seem like it then, but I'm convinced that the green photo album my Grandma Fryer gifted me foretold my future: I was destined to serve as our makeshift family historian. I just didn't know that my first assignment would be the mystery of my paternal grandfather's missing years.

# The Myth and the Memory

**Tuesday, September 17, 1896, 4:19 p.m.  King Charles I School, Woodfield, Bewdley Road, Kidderminster, Worcestershire, England.**

*Six-year-old Alfred is initially excited to be going to the King Charles I School, a voluntary church school.  He believes he looks clever in his grey collared shirt and navy trousers underneath his matching blazer.  His mother made sure to shine his boots, even though they are handed down from his brother, Charles.  Alfred looks forward to entering the world in which his elder brother experiences each day.  Also, the new building at Woodfield looks majestic and royal.  He recognizes most of the other working-class children from the Stourport streets.  His father has begrudgingly provided Alfred a notebook and two pencils, the fear of God within him that neither supply be damaged nor lost.*

*Many days Alfred tires of the lessons, wishing he could be with his father and uncle in the horse stables or at the agricultural market. He's begun to find the lessons on the boring side, namely the reading, writing and arithmetic. The trades lessons on woodwork and metalwork are a little more interesting. Mainly, Alfred wishes there were more opportunities to talk with his classmates. Even at this young age, he prefers the girls, but regrettably they're segregated into a separate classroom.*

*The teacher, Ms. Andrews is new to Kidderminster, recently moving from the academic town of Oxford. She is kind but can be stern, already threatening some of the older boys with the strap, lest their delinquent behavior continue.*

*This afternoon, like many, Alfred attempts patience as he yearns for his 5:00pm release, always looking to distract his brother by any means available.*

I suppose the Vancouver trip with my father fulfilled its purpose. I was able to visit the places that formed the narrative of my father's early life and play audience to his stories, some of which I'd never heard before. However, it was the story offered by Mrs. Blake that really stuck with me. In addition to feeling a new level of sympathy and understanding for my dad, I found a pointed curiosity about my grandfather was emerging. If I had to pinpoint one moment that motivated me to take a real interest in my grandfather and eventually focus on discovering his lost fifty-seven years, the visit to Mrs. Blake's house was it. Time to focus on our subject.

Alfred Victor Williams was his name. In truth, I was always at least a little interested in my paternal grandfather, a

*My grandfather, Alfred Victor Williams, in customary dress & hat.*

curiosity likely born from the unfortunate fact that he was the only grandparent who wasn't in my life. Growing up, I'd ask about my paternal grandfather, my "dad's dad." I was aware that he had died in late 1968, about four years prior to my birth. I didn't get the full picture, but I was given pieces, pieces that I found evoked my curiosity for as long as I could remember.

In terms of appearance, I was told he was a tall man with piercing blue eyes who always dressed in formal suit and when the elements dictated, trench coat and hat. His at-home leisure wear was a little more relaxed, apparently consisting of dark dress pants and a white button-up or on hot days, maybe just an undershirt. This was in sharp contrast to my father, who was most comfortable in worn GWGs and thin, tight Hanes t-shirts...black only and with a front pocket for his Old Port Cigars he once puffed on. I suppose my grandfather's attire matched well his career. He was a salesman, explaining the formal, trusted image his clothing seemed to project. What he sold ranged from dictionaries to jewelry to newspapers.

I was always told that my grandfather had my dad at a very old age. You may remember from the Introduction, fifty-eight years to be precise. The magnitude of this didn't make much of an impression on my young mind. As with most children, I suppose I grouped anyone over age twenty into a single, "old person" category.

Somehow, I became aware how he met my grandmother, Elizabeth Zelbel, whom I have and will continue to refer to as "Oma." Here's where we might be able to add a touch of romance to the story, maybe the only time, actually. "Your grandmother was working downtown at the Astoria Hotel. She was a chambermaid. It was there that she met your grandfather. They fell in love and soon married." I could picture it in my mind. My grandfather, a distinguished gentleman, newly arrived and looking ever so dapper in dark suit and hat, checks into a classy, big-city hotel looking to establish himself in business and set down roots. Soon, he spies my grandmother, beautiful and innocent, away from her family for the first time, some three-hundred miles from her parents' pastoral apple orchard in the pastoral-like interior of our province. The story goes that she was looking for a change in life, wanted something more than a farming wife, so when the opportunity arose for her to relocate to the city and take a job at a hotel that her Uncle Albert owned, she jumped at the chance. It seemed a classic, "small town girl moves to the city, falls in love, and lives happily-ever-after." At least that's how it was in my mind, which, as we'll discover later was partly accurate.

Of course, I'd ask my parents why my Grandpa Williams was dead, but my Oma was still alive. It was explained to me that my grandfather was a fair amount older than my Oma. I suppose I was satisfied enough by that explanation and pursued it no further.

I was also told that my Grandpa Williams was an alcoholic. More to the point, he was an abusive alcoholic. The thought of this scared me. Thankfully, my only exposure to alcoholism

*The Astoria Hotel (circa 1920s) was the site of the fateful meeting between my grandfather & Oma.*

and abuse came from poorly made TV movies or over-dramatic television episodes of my favorite sitcoms. Anyone else remember Tom Hanks' cameo role in *Family Ties*? Scenarios usually involved an out-of-control, overbearing male, quite often in business suit, raging and becoming violent, women and children the usual victims. Growing up, I wondered how my dad could speak of my grandfather with any type of fondness or love if this was the way my grandfather behaved with his loved ones. I suppose to the young mind, life can be a finite dichotomy, a clear case of things being, "black and white." As I loved my dad, the piece of information made me feel like I should hate my grandfather, based on the picture I had created in my mind.

There was also the story of my dad's brief career as an amateur boxer. Excited about a new program at the local community center, my dad enthusiastically signed up to try on the padded gloves. According to self-report, my dad was doing fine and enjoying the mentally challenging and physically grueling aspects of the sport. The excitement lasted all of a few days before my grandfather caught wind of this new activity. "No way," he insisted. "No son of mine is going to get his head bashed in." And with that, my dad retired. Interestingly, the subject of "boxing" would reemerge as I later delved into my research.

Oh, and there was another piece I was told about my grandfather. He was Irish. He was Irish and proud of it. "You're as Irish as the pigs in Dublin," he'd assure my father and aunt when they were young. To pick up from the earlier cultural confusion I described, I remember contemplating that I was, at least in part, Irish. Based on stereotypes that fill a young boy's mind, I pictured an antagonistic, belligerent red-headed man in a green suit and tight leggings with his fists cocked ready to strike. It made sense. I was always told that my dad was a fighter. Me? Not so much, although I did possess quite a temper when I was young.

I don't remember interrogating my aunt about her late father, but that doesn't mean she didn't provide any smaller pieces. During my semi-routine, childhood visits, she always had some interesting possessions around her house, including an eight-inch bound dictionary that supposedly was an item my grandfather had sold as a door-to-door salesman. She also had a few paintings inherited from him. One that specifically caught my eye was a four-foot horizontal color oil painting featuring the faces of five worn-out, seemingly Mexican or Spanish farmers from early in the century. I admired the bold hues and the ability of the artist to capture the excitement and opportunity in their faces. Another painting featured a demure young debutante in stocking feet sneaking up a staircase in the pale moonlight, her right index finger placed gently on the front of her lips, begging for quiet. "These are by a famous Vancouver artist and they're worth a lot of money," my aunt would explain. "They were left in your grandfather's home when he moved in and I've had them ever since his death. I've been offered a lot of money for them, but

I don't want to sell them yet." It was another magical story in the magical narrative that formed the tattered clues that presented the life of my grandfather to my young mind. From an early age, I was engrossed. My answers, however, would need to wait for another forty years.

And don't forget the inheritance. I was always told that close to the time of his death, my grandfather was researching an inheritance that he was entitled to receive. There was always the inheritance.

For most of my young life, that's all I knew. And I was fully satisfied with what I knew. As I grew a little older, though, I slowly began feeling dissatisfied with what I knew.

"So, dad, if your dad didn't meet Oma and have you until he was fifty-seven, what was he doing with his life before that?" I can't pinpoint the exact time I first offered my father that query, only to say it's something I wondered for a long time.

His response? "I don't know Ron. I really don't. He never talked about it, and you have to remember, I was only a young man when he died, twenty-years old. And a lot of that time, keep in mind, I wasn't with him. I was either living in foster homes or when I got older, away at logging camps."

Being so close to my dad, I really couldn't fathom the concept. How could he have no idea what his father had done all his life?

My mother, being the more practical one, offered a simple if not predictable assumption: "he probably had another family." I had to admit, the presumption seemed reasonable enough. Even by today's standards, marrying and having children, while not a requirement or even a prescription for a full life, is often an assumption that most adults fulfill. Added to this the early twentieth century's more prominent role expectations and one could reasonably assume that a man aged fifty-seven would likely have already been a husband and father and probably even a grandfather. So, you can see why my mother's assumption didn't cause too much kerfuffle. It was the addendum she added that provided the most enticing food for thought.

Her entire statement was actually, "he probably had another family in the United States." Well, I couldn't let that slide, asking my mother why she assumed his secret family may have existed in our neighboring country down south. She responded only that she had seen it written somewhere that he had arrived in Vancouver via the United States, a not-so-impossible assumption considering Vancouver's proximity to Seattle. United States, okay. That only made the mysterious story more enticing.

With the idea of discovering my grandfather's missing years becoming more and more fascinating, in my late thirties, I decided to get serious – a little more serious anyway. One evening, during an adult night school class I was teaching, I found myself sitting uncomfortably at an ancient, wooden chair coupled with an ancient wooden desk, waiting for my equally uncomfortable students to finish their compositions. Encouraged by recent television commercials, I was suddenly struck with the notion to open an *Ancestry.com* account. I suppose you could credit my ever-growing omnipresent curiosity, but in this case, it was likely pure boredom that provided the motivation. Even though they offered a "free" trial, I was predictably prompted to enter my credit card information with the sincere but schematic promise that it wouldn't be charged if I fortuitously remembered to cancel on or prior to the date identified on the screen.

"Type in the name you want to search," prompted the simple, straightforward opening message.

That's easy, "Alfred Victor Williams." I inhaled an anticipatory breath as the small hourglass did its thing. Finally, the screen jumped, then settled and I was faced with...a bunch of foreign documents. In truth, I'm unable to describe any search results with a satisfactory degree of accuracy. I can tell you, with utmost sincerity that I abandoned my efforts fairly quickly, having discovered nothing. Oh, and I made sure to cancel that evening. Automatic Subscription Renewal = 0; Ron Williams = 1.

Unprepared or unequipped to take part in any actual, if only Internet-based research, my efforts returned to the casual variety, which basically meant questioning my father and aunt more and more. Reflecting back, the saying, "blood from a stone," comes to mind. But there were some additions that slowly presented themselves.

During a Boxing Day visit over Chinese food, my aunt shared that my grandfather attended Oxford University, loved to do crosswords, had a brother named George and devoured dime store novels by Mickey Spillane. Minor details for certain, but they helped develop the picture that was ever so slowly coming into focus.

Now that I was well within adulthood, I started becoming more comfortable asking about adult things. My grandfather's unsuccessful marriage to Oma was an obvious topic of inquiry. I was already aware of the large age gap between my grandfather and my Oma. Now interested in specifics, I pegged their age difference to be twenty-seven years, meaning when my grandfather debuted at the Astoria Hotel soon to be a fifty-seven-year-old groom, my grandmother had just retired from her twenties. Later, as I delved further into my research, I noted that my grandfather was actually the exact same age as his new mother-in-law, both entering the world in 1889.

Piecing things together, I learned that the heart-wrenching separation of mother and child described earlier by Mrs. Blake was not to be the first or last time my Oma and grandfather parted. I am told that my Oma, along with my father, first left Alfred only a year or two into their marriage, returning to her parents' orchard located near Kelowna, British Columbia, then a small, farming community in the hot interior of the province.

It's unclear if Alfred knew that his wife was pregnant again; however, in January of 1950, it was in Kelowna, far from her husband in Vancouver, that my Oma would give birth to her second child, my Aunt Shirley. The arrival seemed to bring the couple back together again – for a time. Later in my research, I'd come across a "No-Debts Notice" in the October 17, 1953, edition of *The Vancouver News Herald*. The small one-inch ad announced, "I will not be responsible for any debts contracted or incurred in my name without my written authority." Thus, it seems their second chance may have lasted close to three years, before the sad farewell described aptly by Mrs. Blake in the previous chapter.

There was at least a third effort, affectionately described by my father: "Ron, I must have been around seven or eight when I returned home from school one day to my father's house on Hudson and was shocked to see my mother there. They were back together, and I couldn't have been any happier." That too would be short-lived. My father went on to describe my grandparents' final separation weeks later, involving a member of the Vancouver Police Department. It seems my Oma had left the day before but didn't feel safe in attempting any retrieval of her belongings. My father recalls with awkward fondness how the officer allowed him to examine his gun, silver and shiny, as the unlikely group sat at the kitchen table. Meanwhile, my Oma hurriedly grabbed any belongings she could fit in her suitcase, likely feeling equal parts terror, fear, sadness and desperation.

I can't imagine the heartbreak the officers must have experienced watching an oblivious, eight-year-old child warmly basking in attention from a police officer while his family crumbled amidst alcoholism and abuse. The fact my Oma and grandfather never legally divorced was an added curiosity but didn't provide much consternation.

While there would never be any official divorce document to provide eventual clues, at some point I learned that there was a separation agreement of a type, likely weighing in on spousal support and childcare. It's the one document my mother has been hesitant to show me, apparently owing to the detailed description of the fierce agony my Oma faced. "Oh, it's true," my dad would confirm of the implied violent spousal abuse. "Trust me. I saw it."

Was this a thread I should be pursuing towards uncovering the mystery? It's said that a leopard doesn't change its spots. Could divorce documents and court records lead to some discovery? Time would tell.

Of course, family break-up is often hardest on the kids, which can't be argued in this situation. For reasons I only fully understood much later, it was my Oma who walked away in this final instance, the kids being left with my grandfather, a mean drunk. An obvious issue was childcare. My grandfather worked long hours, often requiring overnight sales trips away from the city. The solution was foster care, or, in this case informal arrangements resembling foster care.

For large parts of their childhood, my dad and aunt were lodged out to various families, financial consideration offered. It seems some places were decent. It seems other places were not. This led at times to both my aunt and my dad simply running away, which accounted for the homelessness I alluded to prior.

Unpredictability seems to reign paramount in the life of an alcoholic and true to form, both my dad and aunt report that my grandfather could also be loving. Weekends were often family time and there were few occurrences when both my aunt and dad didn't spend time with my grandfather, usually at their Hudson Street home but not always. In an undated letter in anticipation of one such weekend visit, my Aunt Shirley writes, "I'm sorry I haven't written before now as this week has been very busy." After updating her father on the specifics of her busyness, she continues, "I hope you are feeling better than you usually are and can make it up Saturday. Did you find any drops for my pierced ears yet? I sure hope you did." She signs off "with all my love, Shirley," but hastily scribbles a final P.S. "Please bring cream soda pop Saturday instead of the other."

The more I heard, the more I asked. The more I asked, the more I learned. The more I learned, the more I wanted to learn. On more than one occasion my mother suggested there may be a letter and a few documents somewhere in a box or closet. However, for some reason no one ever took any action to present them.

Not too long after my mother's curious proclamation that Alfred likely had a family in the United States, she dropped another comment that I'd consider warranting "note-worthy" status. Timing being what it is, my mom had brief occasion to visit with Alfred a few times before his death in 1968. The courtship between my mother and father began at roughly the same time that Alfred was enduring his final days at Vancouver General Hospital. Although she was still very much the "new girl," my mom took initiative to duck in during visiting hours and keep Alfred company, my dad being away working at a logging camp. Apparently, the visits seemed pleasant enough, my mother having trouble reconciling the frail, polite old man in the hospital gown to the violent alcoholic homewrecker of past years. That is until one day when my mother's visit came to an abrupt end as Alfred reached to clamp both hands around her slight neck while he uttered the words, "you bitch!"

Obviously hallucinating to a time past, whom he thought my mother was and whom he might have been trying to strangle now became another mysterious part of my grandfather's lost fifty-seven years.

# A Maddening Quest Begins

**Friday, October 10, 1902, 3:05 p.m. Kidderminster Flats, Worcestershire, England.**

*Although only twelve, Alfred has come to love tagging along with his father and sometimes Uncle George while they travel the Worcester area looking to further their trade in horses. Their time is often spent visiting one farm or another, always endeavoring to secure purchases below market value.*

*In truth, practicing the horse trade is one of the only times Alfred can stand being around his father these days. However, it's his Uncle George whom Alfred is most enamored by. The squat man looking smart in dark suit and derby hat has a way with his words and is successful at sharply rebutting any potential seller bent on exaggerating a horse's worth. "Looks a little lame, not sure of foot," is a common observation. In one of his more favored techniques, Uncle George carefully places both hands, palm up, under the horse's side, only to proceed in a curious type of circular motion, before sharing with some alarm, "this horse is prone to colic...does it run in the bloodline?" Some sellers object vehemently, but most remain stoic, unmoved at the weak attempt of intimidation.*

*Alfred doesn't care much for the action behind the scenes, when, once back home, he's ordered to tend to the purchases in the small, dirty stable. The labor is difficult, trudging supplies back and forth over often muddy, uncertain ground. The horses, too, aren't particularly pleasant to deal with, Alfred not enamored with the animals like some of the others. It's the sales pitch, the negotiating, that most holds Alfred's attention. He feels he could grow to like that part enough, dressing sharp and playing a war of wits with seller and buyer, always with a flask of whisky for the down times.*

I t was around the fall of 2014 that I found myself at a type of crossroads. The long-standing interest I had fostered about the grandparent I had never met now reacted with both the impact I felt from the visit with Mrs. Blake and the newer information I had gleaned from my family. My curiosity was ripe to explode.

With everything in life, there comes a point when one needs to grow serious or abandon thought. This was the time to get serious. I began where most post-2010 projects tend to begin: the Internet. Of course, when it comes to family research, starting on the Internet likely means *Ancestry.com* or *Familysearch.com* or *MyHeritage.com*. Well, I chose *Ancestry.com*, if for nothing else, probably due to familiarity...I'd tried it before.

If you're at all like me, the process of logging into any new or existing account is most often fraught with obstacle and frustration. This time was no different. Entering my email address into the "sign up" page resulted in an authoritarian, partially mocking: "our records indicate there is already an account associated with this email address. To recover your username or password," and then I failed to read the rest. Re-type email address. Open new browser page. Wait for *Ancesty.com* email to appear. Go downstairs to grab iPhone. Enter two-level verification security code. Go to password page. Decline their suggested secure password. Enter my own usual password. Enter my own usual password again. Okay, you get the picture. After about five minutes and a few curse words, I was once again facing the same *Ancestry.com* start page I'd given up on just a few years earlier.

This time, though, this time would be different. A common theme in my research strategy was "start with what you know." By this time, my mother had produced those few documents she spoke about, and I was pleased to have a birth certificate to aid me in my search.

Before I'd even typed in so much as my grandfather's name, I'd discovered my first research discrepancy. The birth certificate my mother had bestowed upon me read, "1889, BIRTH in the Sub-district of Wribbenhall, Dorchester in the County of Worcestershire." Now, I'm not much of a geographer, but I was pretty certain – and Google confirmed – Worcestershire is in England, not Ireland. Mental note for later. I entered the information as provided on the birth certificate.

First and Middle Names: Alfred Victor
Last Name: Williams
Birth Year: 1889
Location: Wribbenhall, Dorchester, Worcester
Father: Alfred Williams
Mother: Emily Crane
"Search"

*The 1891 census report would be my first clue that I couldn't believe all that I'd heard.*

And true to the promise suggested in their catchy television ads, the results came pouring in. *1891 England Census, 1901 England Census, England and Wales Civil Registration Birth Index, 1911 England Census* and so on. Early indicators seemed pretty convincing, and I wondered whether I'd be able to discover my grandfather's missing years before lunch. The documents were all there. I guess I was excited but also skeptical. First, I clicked on the *1891 England Census.*

Name: Alfred Victor Williams
Gender: male
Age: 1
Relationship: son
Birth Year: about 1890
Father: Alfred Williams
Mother: Emily Williams
Birthplace: Wribbenhall, Dorchester, England
Civil Parish: Kidderminster

All the information seemed to match the birth certificate, including location, mother and father. Just below, there was another section titled "Household members."

Alfred Williams: 33
Emily Williams: 27
Charles Williams: 4

This was somewhat monumental, as it marked the first actual research I completed on my grandfather.

Just above, I noticed a blue oval "bubble" with the words "view image." Clicking on that button took me to the actual census document, scanned for my viewing and research pleasure. This page told me the Alfred Sr., was a "horse trader." This closely matched my grandfather's profession of "salesman," even if he chose not to peddle livestock. I could further see that while father and sons were born in "Wribbenhall," the woman of the house, my paternal great-grandmother, Emily Crane, was born in Chaddesley Corbett, confirmed by Google to be about eight miles to the east of their Kidderminster home. Those last two bits of information, employment and birthplace weren't especially transformative, but they did add a couple pieces to the puzzle, even if my metaphorical puzzle was approximately ten thousand pieces.

The next step was a "no-brainer," click on the *1901 England Census*.

Name: Alfred Victor Williams
Gender: male
Age: 11
Relationship: son
Birth Year: about 1890
Father: Alfred Williams
Mother: Emily Williams
Birthplace: Wribbenhall, Worcestershire, England
Civil Parish: Kidderminster

The fact that information was almost identical to the 1891 record both pleased me and confirmed the information. The "household members" section was enlightening though, not only was Emily now listed as sharing Alfred Sr.'s 1859 birth year, but there appeared a third child added to the list, Walter Dennis Williams, born in 1894. Again, I clicked on the "view image" bubble to see what I might further learn. This time Alfred Williams Sr. was listed as a "shop huckster" working on

| Sidney J. Do | Son | S | 10 | | | | | Do | Do |
| Sarah Price | Aunt | S | 49 | Dressmaker | own account at home | | Do | Do |
| Susan Tyers | Aunt | m | 52 | Carpet Setter | Worker | | Salop Bridgmorth |
| Edith Tyers | Cousin | S | 21 | Upon Window Carpet Weaver | Do | | Worcester Kidderminster |
| Alfred Williams | Head | m | 42 | Shop Huckster | own account at home | | Do | Middlenhall |
| Emily Do | Wife | m | 48 | | | | Do | Chaddesley Corbet |
| Charles W. Do | Son | S | 14 | Grocer's Assistant | Worker | | Do | Middlenhall |
| Alfred V. Do | Son | | 11 | | | | Do | Do |
| Walter S. Do | Son | | 7 | | | | Do | Do |
| Frederick W. Barlow | Head | m | 47 | Rug Weaver | Worker | | Do | Kidderminster |
| Olive Barlow | Wife | m | 47 | | | | Do | Do |
| William J. Do | Son | S | 25 | Insurance Agent | Do | | Do | Do |

*The 1901 census introduced me to Dennis. This would be the final official document showing all family members together.*

his "own account," the location offered as "at home." I mused how that would appear on a 2014 resume: horse trader followed by shop huckster. In all seriousness, the information again rung familiar, the definition of "huckster," being one who sold small goods oftentimes "door-to-door." I had been told that my grandfather was a "door-to-door" salesman at times. Like father, like son, I supposed. Other than that, no new information.

I seemed to have a good thing going, so I wasn't about to stop. The next logical step was the *1911 England Census*, where things got interesting. The entry shown was not for my grandfather, but for my great-grandfather, Alfred Sr. This time I jumped directly to "view image." I learned that Alfred Sr. was now a fifty-one-year-old widower, listed as working and living at the Nelson Hotel, owned by a brewery company, on Blackwell Street, still in Kidderminster. My great-grandfather's third occupation was, again, a familiar connection, not to my grandfather, but to me. No, I've never worked in a hotel bar, but my innate taste for English ales qualifies as a family connection in my book. The record also showed that my grandfather's younger brother, Walter Dennis, who seems to have gone by his middle name of "Dennis," was now a sixteen-year-old butcher's assistant. Flora Violet May, listed as a married woman serving as a business assistant, and Allen George May, Flora's young son, rounded out the household.

What was more interesting was what the record omitted. The absence of Charles could be explained easily. He'd have been twenty-five years old, certainly old enough, given the time period, to be on his own as an adult. However, the omission of Emily Williams, my grandfather's mother, was notable, suggesting she may have been deceased by then. Of paramount interest to my research was, of course, the omission of my grandfather. He would have been twenty-one years old, again, old enough to be out of the house. Was he already overseas? Perhaps feeling fresh wounds from the death of his mother? I looked further in the search results for the 1911 *England Census* and was able to locate Charles in nearby Staffordshire, working for the railway and boarding in a rooming house. I was unable to find any potential match for my grandfather living elsewhere in England.

Now into early afternoon, I chose to accompany my brisk success with a frosty IPA. This time, I chose Fat Tug, from Driftwood Brewing on nearby Vancouver Island. It remains one of my all-time favorites.

Back to the computer results, I found, *UK, Railway Employment Records, 1833-1956*, with a listing for my grandfather. This one proved particularly interesting. My grandfather, identified by his correct birthdate of November 23, 1889, was listed as an employee of Great Western Railway in Kidderminster, his exact position either a "hand porter" or "land porter," not sure of which is correct. The document listed his starting date as March 1904 when he would have been fourteen years old, his last day of employment being June 8, 1906, putting him at sixteen years of age.

A likely, though unsubstantiated, timeline began to form in my mind: upon the untimely death of the woman of the house, Alfred's home life had grown tenuous, leading to him quitting his job and purchasing passage to begin fresh in the new world. I recalled hearing my father explain Alfred had a tempestuous relationship with his father. Of course, I'd have to fill in some blanks before seriously considering my working hypothesis.

My mind raced with possibility, settled with an early sense of satisfaction.  In only a couple hours, I'd been able to make some progress in accounting for the first sixteen years of my grandfather's mysterious life.  At this impressive rate, I was dazzled with the notion that the next sixteen years would come equally as quickly, followed by the sixteen years after that, until before I knew it, I arrived at 1947 when he seemed to unceremoniously resurface on the face of the earth.  That wasn't to happen.

I had high hopes that the census reports that had been so helpful would continue to enlighten and guide.  I couldn't access any 1921, 1931 or 1941 census report for England on *Ancestry.com.*

Of course, what did that matter if I hypothesized that my grandfather was already in North America by that point anyway?  I suppose it didn't; however, I didn't have any more luck in following the census reports in North America either.

Canada seemed to have adopted England's practice of taking census reports during the first year of every decade: 1901, 1911, 1921, etc.  If Alfred had in fact immigrated to Canadian, as opposed to American, soil in 1906 and stayed for any decent amount of time, he should have appeared on one or more of these reports, right?

Not so fast.  Under the "card catalog" menu, I typed "Canadian Census 1911."  Pleased to see the document was available, I again entered the pertinent information.

First and Middle Names: Alfred Victor
Last Name: Williams
Birth Year: 1889
Location: Wribbenhall, Dorchester, Worcester
Father: Alfred Williams
Mother: Emily Crane
"Search."

Predictably, my search was met with a plethora of possible matches, over one thousand and two hundred to be more precise. The results were organized on twenty-four separate pages. Thanks to the good people at *Ancestry.com*, I was able to scroll through cursory information on each listing without having to actually "click" on each entry. This allowed me to quickly discount some of the obvious non-matches, while clicking and reading the ones suggesting potential. Lots of "Alfred Williams." Lots of them born in England. A few born in 1889. None matching my grandfather.

After a few clicks of the back arrow and some strikes of the keyboard, I found myself staring at results mined from the *1921 Census of Canada*. Again, there were several hundred potential matches. Again, there seemed no accurate ones. I had officially struck out on the Canadian census reports. Not that zero for two should be much to be upset about!

Frustrating? Well, they say there's no such thing as a failed attempt, so I blindly reasoned that I'd eliminated one non-helpful area of research and I bravely moved on. In fact, his non-status on the Canadian census reports only made me more excited to check census reports for the United States. After all, hadn't my own mother suggested his presence in the country?

As we know, the United States likes to do things their own way, so it reasoned to follow that they took census reports on what might be considered the final year of each decade: 1910, 1920, 1930, etc. Having established that Alfred seemed to have departed England prior to 1911 and that there was no sign of him in Canada near that time, I began with the obvious, the *1910 United States Federal Census*.

After entering the specifics in the search form – an act I would eventually exercise no fewer than a thousand times over the ensuing years – an impressive list of potential matches once again appeared. And after going through my usual vetting exercise to eliminate obvious "non-matches," I was struck with an entry that at the very least elicited some cause for hope.

Name: Alfred Williams
Age in 1910: 23
Birthdate:1887
Birthplace: England
Immigration Ycar: 1909
Father's birthplace: England
Mother's birthplace: England
Occupation: Salesman
Industry: Silver Smith

Yes, the birth year was a couple years off of my grandfather's 1889 arrival into the world, but I reasoned that if he had sought employment or respectable lodging, he may have added a couple of years to suggest experience or maturity. The rest of the entry definitely caused me to raise an eyebrow. All the birthplaces were a match. The immigration year could have made sense. As for occupation, my own father often said Alfred sold jewelry. With the understanding that I may discover conflicting information in future, I added the census to the family tree I'd begun to create.

Next up was the *1920 United States Federal Census*. Nothing of interest. Then, it was the *1930 United States Federal Census*. Nothing of interest. Finally, the *1940 United States Federal Census*. Nothing.

Once again, I engaged in regular, if not routine, self-talk, attempting to convince myself that with each non-fruitful research query, I was eliminating sources and, in the process, moving closer towards that one super-clue that would blow the roof of the mystery and help me uncover everything. It wouldn't be any census reports that would fulfill that hope, at least not at this point.

Reader, you may get the impression that all this occurred during one stationary sitting, perhaps the duration being two or three cold IPA's and a spin-through of only a few of my cherished jazz albums. Well, that's not the case. The above steps likely comprised a period of a week or so, at times committing a couple of hours in one sitting, and at other times sneaking only a minute or five. In fact, the notion was beginning to grow that perhaps I wasn't making best use of my research time, as I feared I was replicating already completed research at various stages, simply because I forgot what I had looked at in certain situations.

Amidst these early and often unsteady steps, I had occasion to run the information past my parents regularly and my Aunt Shirley with a little less regularity. She showed mild surprise that there was no brother named George. She showed greater surprise that her father wasn't born in Ireland. I found myself attempting to reason a compromise. "Well, maybe somewhere along the line one of his ancestors had come from Ireland...maybe they identified as Irish." I knew both Alfred's parents had identified their birthplaces as England on the census reports. My suggestion was at best a long-shot, totally uncorroborated by any documents, but it was possible. I guess.

Then there was the whole business about Oxford. I couldn't rule it out. Maybe that explains why he wasn't in the family home in 1911. Also, it seemed plausible that census recorders could have missed a university student, that is, if they even bothered to record them.

But wasn't Oxford a school of privilege for those who are privileged? That's the way it always seemed in movies and television programs. The census reports showed a family whose sole breadwinner was horse trader, shop huckster and bartender. Nothing wrong with any of the aforementioned, but none seemed the type of occupation that would pay Oxford tuition for one to three offspring. Without looking it up, I surmised any federal student-aid programs, if they existed in 1906, likely wouldn't amount to much. Alfred had worked for a couple years in the railway, but that also didn't suggest Oxford money.

For the first time, but not the last time, I experienced some doubts about the details my grandfather did offer. As well, if he did prevaricate – in these instances to his children – it seemed likely that he could have stretched the truth in any other potential sources of information. Did I mention the role overindulgence in alcohol may have played? In short, if he was prone to lying, how could I take any existing clues seriously? Truly, this was shaping up to be quite a mess.

Of course, one could say, I was getting ahead of myself. There were still a number of scenarios in which a far younger or older, maybe half-sibling, named "George" may have existed, possibly even born of an earlier marriage to an Irish partner. Also, there had to be other ways to get to Oxford, wasn't there? I seem to recall the protagonist of meager beginnings in F. Scott Fitzgerald's *The Great Gatsby* attending Oxford for a short time as part of a military program for veterans. One could argue, however, that Jay Gatsby was of dubious integrity also. Oh well.

Another aspect of *Ancestry.com* I began exploring was "Public Member Trees." What a wonderful aspect of the site, in which other members have already done all the work and constructed detailed family trees, complete with supporting documentation and additional notes. In theory, this tool had the potential to answer all my questions instantaneously. If some benevolent citizen had already included my grandfather in an existing tree, it could very well spell out his specifics throughout the entire lost fifty-seven years I was hoping to discover. I enthusiastically explored the member trees and even found a couple that offered pause for inspection. In the end, however, none were helpful. While my grandfather's story proved to be strangely elusive in the real world, it was also shaping up to be strangely elusive in the cyberworld.

Then there was the case of military records. Alfred was twenty-four when World War I began in 1914. He was twenty-nine when it mercifully ended. Whether residing in England, the United States of America, or Canada, he would have been prime age to not only serve but to fall under guidelines for conscription. To be sure, plenty of military records emerged. *UK, World War I Service Medal and Award Rolls 1914-1920*; *US World War I Draft Registration Cards 1917-1918*; and *Canada World War I CEF Attestation Papers 1914-1918*. All contained entries for "Alfred Williams," but each failed to list any substantive corroborating details.

Now, there were extenuating circumstances that allowed for a healthy male of prime military age to avoid serving their country, including unique family obligations or unfortunate health conditions. It makes sense that my grandfather may have fallen into a category of exclusion. It also made sense that he may have eluded conscription through more devious means. While I couldn't be sure of either, the absence of any military record served only to deepen the increasingly formidable mystery.

After a couple weeks, I was satisfied I'd given *Ancestry.com* a decent test drive. The thing about the website, though, is that every so often, maybe due to luck or maybe because the searcher inputted information in a slightly different way, the search tools seem to conjure the unexpected, something that didn't appear before. This would be my first such experience. While stealing a few minutes before driving Tommy to hockey, I came across a listing for "Alf Williams," in *Canada Passenger Lists, 1865-1935*. The information presented on screen seemed promising

Name: Alf Williams
Gender: Male
Arrival Age: 17
Birth Year: abt. 1889
Departure Port: Liverpool, England
Arrival Date: 13 Apr 1906
Arrival Port: Halifax, Nova Scotia, Canada and Saint John, New Brunswick, Canada

*Appearing as "Alf," this entry in a ship ledger shows my grandfather running to an overseas land in 1906.*

Nothing was there that I didn't like. I noted that the arrival date matched-up with his March resignation from the Great Western Railway in Kidderminster. Clicking on the "view image" bubble, I was taken to the actual document where I noted "Alf" was marked as a "Railway Laborer," and that the country and "countie" of origin was "Worcester, England." With so many details matching, I was convinced it was him. Oh, and one more notable detail was found under "Place of ultimate destination."

Toronto.

# A Most Unusual Declaration

**Thursday, January 4, 1906, 10:01 p.m. Lord Nelson Hotel, #16 Blackwell Street, Kidderminster, Worcestershire, England.**

*The tension at home is building. The family's residence is far more cramped in the suite above the Lord Nelson Inn, but running the pub is good enough opportunity to justify the relocation. Perhaps sharing the same Christian name has resulted in a natural rivalry, but the two Alfreds continue to be at odds. Although only sixteen, Alfred Victor routinely shares his desire to leave the house. Adding to it, he doesn't think he's cut-out for the traditional family business of horse trading. He has the "gift of the gab" for it, but the work and labor of raising horses fails to appeal to him. His family doesn't know how seriously he is thinking of leaving England for the "New World." He'll need all the money he can muster from his job at the railway station.*

*At the station, he has fit in well, his co-workers jokingly referring to him as "Major," due to his propensity for giving orders to others rather than taking them for himself. The position, too, has allowed him experience with his older brother, Charles, away from the home and social constructs of their parents. Alfred admires the steady, level-headed approach of his elder sibling. Although at times, Alfred is mildly disgusted at Charles' failure to stand up for himself when met with an adverse order or co-worker. In any event, while Alfred periodically defended his brother with fists in the past, he'd do no such thing now that they were adults in the world of employment.*

So, there it was. The facts were clear. In 1906 at only age sixteen, my grandfather, "Alf" he called himself, quit his job at the railway and fled England to begin life anew in Toronto. My goal was to discover what my grandfather had been doing with his life prior to 1948. I figured I'd covered a fair amount of ground, having now confidently traced his life up to 1906 and possibly again in 1910. "Only around forty more years to go," Lana laughed.

Of course, I couldn't be totally, absolutely sure this "Alf Williams" was my "Alfred Williams." However, with matches for birthdate, birthplace, employment resignation, and the likelihood that he had left England for North America before 1911, I allowed myself to be convinced it was him. Additionally, I had at least one more document that confirmed he was in Toronto.

At the beginning of the last chapter, I shared that my mother had given me a few documents she had tucked away in a home office drawer for the past forty years or so. In truth, I had been pouring over each since I received them, mining any clues I could. The birth certificate that served as catalyst for my initial modest success was the first document. In truth, I also received a letter, a photograph, and a legal affidavit.

The letter, sampled in the introduction, written December 6, 1942 and post-marked, "Toronto, Ontario" was from Alfred's older brother, Charles Whittingham Williams. Judging by the details, it seems that my grandfather had only recently reconnected with Charles through letter and what I had in possession was Charles' virgin response. I've already shared the profound opening lines, "I think I got one of the pleasantest shocks of my life, when I was handed your letter yesterday, as I had long given you up for dead." Reading this, it was clear that in addition to my grandfather keeping his life secret from my father and aunt, he had also kept his life secret from his family in England. Interesting.

Charles continues, "I thought perhaps you had been killed in the last war." Seeing as World War I ended in 1918, this helped me narrow down the last date my grandfather had made any contact with his family. I was pleased to mine a geographical clue, as Charles noted, "your last letters, which I still possess, were posted from the U.S.A." This told me that sometime between 1906 and 1918, Alfred had left Canada to make his home in the United States. In his employ as railway engineer, Charles shares, "I have taken thousands of Canadian troops across the country, but of course it was not much use trying to get information, as I had so little to go on."

At this point, through my construction of a family tree on *Ancestry.com*, I was becoming familiar with some of the names in my grandfather's family. Charles' letter made the names a little more human. Of the youngest Williams brother, Dennis, Charles writes, "I've been in touch with Dennis until a few years ago. He is living somewhere near London, and I adopted one of his daughters and I have had her since she was eighteen months old." I found it interesting that Charles had recently lost touch with his youngest brother. Was this the

*My grandfather's older brother, Charles Williams, whose letters would provide the first clues to my grandfather's mysterious life.*

family dynamic? Was this a sign of the times? Maybe it wasn't that strange that Alfred kept his life separate from family members.

Charles shares that he has a boy, "Bernard," and that their father "has been dead several years," adding that "he was seventy-six years of age." Through a quick mathematical calculation, I marveled that Alfred had been estranged from his family for all of his adult life, but even at his old age, he missed re-connecting with his father by a mere eight years. He updates Alfred that their "Uncle George is keeping an outdoor beer house and grocer shop at Stourport and is doing a great trade in horses." These were the same professions that my grandfather's own dad had recorded on census reports. "Aunt Annie is still living in the old house in Bewdley." From my family tree, I recognized this as my grandfather's aunt, Sarah "Ann" Williams.

This marked the first I had heard of Bewdley, and it made me realize that to optimize the little information I had, some geography might be in order. Moving from the general to specific, I learned that Worcestershire is a county in the West Midlands of England. If you're looking at a map, it's roughly in the center of the country. Historically, it was first settled some 700,000 years ago, but grew during the "Bronze Age," if that means anything to you. It doesn't to me. I hesitate to offer many details for fear that I'll most certainly expose more than a little ignorance, but it seems that the county has a rich history, prominent during the Norman Conquests and the English Civil War. In the late nineteenth and early twentieth century, my grandfather and his immediate family occupied Kidderminster, a historic town that seemed a bustling center of industry and commerce. Some four miles from Kidderminster, sat Bewdley, originally known as "Wribbenhall," as marked on my grandfather's birth certificate. I'd later track that the Williams clan likely relocated from the small, sleepy, Bewdley located on the west side of the River Severn to the larger Kidderminster on the east side of the river by the time the census was taken in 1901.

Back to the letter, Charles reports "the old Nelson Hotel was knocked down for road improvements." I'd recognize this local as both residence and place of employ for my great-grandfather as recorded in the *1911 England Census*. Charles was confident Alfred would identity with the place, likely home to Alfred before his 1906 departure. Near the end, Charles remarks he "saw Archie Fletcher last week, and he wanted to know if I had heard from Major." Was that Alfred's nickname? Major? I'd later search the name "Archie Fletcher" only to discover that he, Charles and Alfred had all worked at the railway at the same time. Childhood friends?

Another point of interest was in the question, "do you still see any members of the Turley family?" This prompted me to enter Turley into the mighty *Ancestry.com* search engine. I discovered that Alfred's mother, Emily, had a sister, Agnes who married a George Turley. A few clicks and I discovered that their eldest son, William Turley, had immigrated to Canada by 1905, settling in Toronto soon after. Immediately, I considered that Alfred was venturing to Toronto to reside at the home of his first cousin, William Turley, an assumption for certain, but I felt it was a pretty good one, soon to be confirmed. And as I had no reason to discount the *1910*

*My grandfather looking professional in what we erroneously believed was the posh Vancouver Hotel.*

*United States Federal Census* showing a New York residence, I posited that he may have remained with the Turley family for up to four years.

In the final lines, Charles writes, "well, Alfred, I expect you are like me, now settled down and finished with roaming, so we must not again lose touch with each other," before signing off in grand, formal style, "with best wishes from myself and family, I remain your affectionate brother, Charlie."

A goldmine of information for sure, but I wished I could have seen the initial letter Charles was responding to or Alfred's subsequent response for that matter. My grandfather's end of this written correspondence had survived over sixty years. Could it be possible that Alfred's end of the contact existed in a trunk somewhere over the Atlantic Ocean, kept safe by a child or grandchild of Charles? I'd just have to wait and see.

Another item my mother brought over wasn't quite as rich in clues. My dad identified it as my grandfather standing in the lobby of the posh Hotel Vancouver, a then very-much upscale venue in the city. The photograph looked to have been developed using a "sepia" filter, but more likely that was just the way photos were in the mid-1900s. The image presents a serious-looking, older gentleman, wearing a wool overcoat covering a shirt and tie, possibly a suit underneath. Alfred, very somber and serious as he casually gazes from the camera lens, has a "trilby" style hat perched atop his head, grey hair showing only subtly at the side. Upon closer inspection, I realize the image is shot not with the backdrop of any swanky lobby but rather in front of a screen, no doubt in a photo studio.

I wondered why Alfred would have the need for a personal photo session. Was it customary to give out to friends and family? Special occasions, maybe? I suppose it could have been some type of requirement for his sales jobs. I really wasn't sure. If nothing else, the image confirmed the vision I had in my mind of the well-dressed, formally attired gentleman my dad described.

If the photograph didn't offer much in the way of clues, the opposite could be claimed for the next item my mother delivered.

Dated November 11, 1942
IN THE MATTER OF
ALFRED VICTOR WILLIAMS
Statutory Declaration
OF
WILLIAM E. TURLEY

To share that the title piqued my interest would be an understatement of immense proportions. It was a legal document prepared by Francis G. Peddie, a Toronto lawyer. In the document, William Turley, some seven years my grandfather's senior, offered seven separate declarations, likely at the request of my grandfather's representation and to be provided to an official of some sort.

Declaration #1: "That Alfred Victor Williams is my first cousin."

Declaration #2: "I knew him in his early life when his father, Alfred Williams and my mother's sister, Emily Crane Williams resided at Cookley House, Parish of Wolverly, County of Worcestershire, England from 1895-1898." Back to Google and I was able to locate "Cookley House" some three miles north of Kidderminster.

Declaration #3: "To the best of my knowledge the said Alfred Victor Williams was born either in the Village of Wribbenhall near the town of Bewdley, or in the town of Bewdley itself...on the 23 of November 1890." I noted the year of birth was one off and made note that Wribbenhall could be referred to as a village within Bewdley, not just an antiquated name for Bewdley itself.

Declaration #4: "Subsequently the said Alfred Williams resided in the town of Kidderminster, Worcestershire, where his father operated the Lord Nelson Inn on Blackwell Street." I was familiar with this address from the *1911 England Census* listing Alfred's father and younger brother.

Declaration #5: "In the year 1906 the said Alfred Victor Williams came to Canada and lived with me on Portland Street, Toronto. Shortly thereafter, I believe, he took up residence in the United States of America owing to the fact that I returned to England with my family, where I remained for some considerable time." My hypothesis was confirmed that Alfred had chased the Turley family oversees. This point also suggested that my grandfather didn't stay in Canada for long and may have relocated to the U.S., specifically New York, by 1910.

6. The said Alfred Victor Williams has recently returned to Toronto, Canada, and he is, I am convinced, my first cousin.

7. Since his entry into the United States he informs me he has been going under the name of Roy Hammond.

AND I make this solemn Declaration conscientiously believing it to be true, and knowing that it is of the same force and effect as if made under oath, and by virtue of "The Canada Evidence Act."

*The unexpected bombshell that both confused the story and provided the essential clue.*

Declaration #6: "The said Alfred Victor Williams has recently returned to Toronto, Canada, and he is, I am convinced, my first cousin." I found the wording amusing if not interesting. "I am convinced" sounds more like "I can't be one-hundred percent certain," to me. Jesus, was the man I believe to be my grandfather an imposter? With that monumental notion turning in my scrambled mind, the next assertion certainly had me heading to the wine rack.

Declaration #7: "Since his entry into the United States he informs me that he has been going under the name of Roy Hammond."

"Going under the name of Roy Hammond." Thus far, I'd been searching for "Alfred Williams," "Fred Williams," "Al Williams," "Alf Williams," and now I had to accept the necessity to include "Roy Hammond" in my online explorations. That didn't even include the potential nickname, "Major." Seemed more than a little challenging. The news did clear up how my father's middle name of "Roy" was selected.

According to "Declaration #6," Alfred was in the process of re-entering the country. As best I could tell, this affidavit was something either required or deemed helpful to attain some type of citizenry status. While the information floored me, I couldn't help but question the soundness of any legal advice that included the voluntary confirmation of identity fraud. At any rate, Alfred seemingly remained in Canada for the rest of his years, so I accepted that Mr. Francis G. Peddie was capable of sound advice.

Of course, this is assuming the legal affidavit was something my grandfather was undertaking on his own behalf and not something ordered by the courts against his wishes. I can confirm that a receipt discovered years later confirmed this assumption. Eventually, I would discover a financial statement from Mr. Peddie in which he charges for "attendance with you and Mr. Turley when we prepared affidavit as to your identity to be taken by William Turley." An additional charge is noted for "telephone conversation with Mr. Malcolm on receipt of his reply from Ottawa, where he advises me that you should go down and make out the necessary papers with William Turley." Finally, there is a charge for "drawing affidavit, attending on execution thereof, and handing same over to you." Certainly seems that Peddie was working on my grandfather's behalf and not for the courts in any action against. Incidentally, the total bill amounted to a whopping twenty-dollars, or about three-hundred and seventy-five bucks in today's world. Something of a bargain, I'd say.

Also, why? Why was my grandfather going under an assumed name? My first notion was that he had no choice. He felt he had to flee Canada and seek refuge in another country under an assumed name. Potential, but unsubstantiated, reasons for fleeing could include pending criminal charges, a distasteful marriage or maybe just money owed. It couldn't have been much, I guess, otherwise why would he return to Canada years later and reclaim his true identity? With relief, I accepted that this likely ruled out any potential murder charge. In reality, he could have assumed the name "Roy Hammond" for any number of reasons. Maybe he learned there was money owing to a man of that name. Maybe there was a job opportunity. Maybe he initially entered the United States illegally and had the good fortune to find a

Dated    November 11th    19 42.

IN THE MATTER OF

ALFRED VICTOR WILLIAMS

**Statutory Declaration**

OF

WILLIAM E. TURLEY

Dye & Durham, 3-11 Yonge Street Arcade, Toronto, Can.
Law and Commercial Stationers

*The early clue that introduced me to the elusive William Turley.*

random piece of identification. Eventually I'll share with you what I discovered years later...that the *nom de plume*, "Roy Hammond" may not have been entirely random.

And for that matter, why did my grandfather require a legal affidavit to enter the country anyways? Common practice for new immigrants? Initially, I wasn't privy to the receipt for services, but I think I guessed correctly anyway. I imagined my grandfather went to these lengths out of necessity because he possessed no proper identification with the name, "Alfred Victor Williams." It's possible what he deemed unimportant in the early 1900s had become more important by 1942.

In addition to providing the origin of my father's middle name, "Roy," the document also cleared up how my mother knew he had been in the United States. I wondered why this information hadn't been shared all along. Why wasn't this a part of the mythology that I had grown up with? Why wasn't "Roy Hammond" mentioned when it was clear my curiosity was growing? The more I read about genealogy, the more I

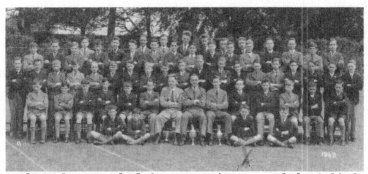

*A class photo marked six years prior to my father's birth.*
*Did my grandfather have a long-lost son?*

learned that noteworthy omissions, rather than being a rarity, are something to be expected. There are details that may be vitally important or interesting to a diligent genealogist that others may deem trivial. Also, people can simply forget details until a situation arises where they are pressed for recall. Lastly, documents can be filed away and forgotten about, which was the case with this affidavit. My parents likely paid a great deal of attention to the document when it was first discovered upon my grandfather's death in 1968, but it hadn't been examined in some time, close to fifty years to be exact.

Genealogy sources further suggest that a formal interview is scheduled with relevant family members with preparation including brainstorming a list of questions, as well as gathering documents and pictures that may act as a catalyst for information and memories. Also, scheduling a time for a follow-up session for information that comes to mind after the initial interview is a useful tip. While I was to spend time on formal interviews with my mother and father at a much later date, I initially put it off, reasoning that I had interviewed them sporadically throughout. Just one example of my foolishness along the way.

At this point, there was an abundance of new information to add into my *Ancestry.com* tree. My grandfather's profile now included that he left Canada for the U.S. between 1906 and 1910, used the name "Roy Hammond" for a period in his life, and that he returned to Ontario, Canada in 1942. Additionally, I was able to add information for the Turley family that I hoped would prove useful in later research.

Also, worth mentioning is the very date of the affidavit, "November 11, 1942." Later, I would connect that the 1942 letter from Alfred's brother Charles was dated, "December 6, 1942." I deduced that Alfred must have written the original letter, reconnecting with Charles, at some point in November. Thus, Alfred's reconnection with his family coincided exactly with his return to Canada. Possibilities ran amuck in my mind. What event could account for both? Running away from an existing, secret "Hammond" family he had hoped to remain secret could be one solution. Being released from prison seems equally plausible. Lana and the boys agreed that the details were beginning to prove interesting.

With the affidavit now resting peacefully in my file folder, I turned to the final document my mother shared with me: a school picture. As with the previous documents, my mother and father had kept this photo under proverbial "lock and key" only to be examined sporadically – if at all – since initial collection in 1968. Marked "1942" in bottom right corner, the image shows four rows of stern-looking, arms-crossed, males ranging in age from approximately six to forty-something. The younger boys appear adorable with their ties and blazers, coordinated with their "short pants," while the older males appear dapper in full suit attire. Taken on a lined, sports field with impressive foliage serving as the backdrop, three shiny trophies are impressively displayed front center, likely celebrating some scholastic or athletic achievement.

Given that any child born of my grandfather prior to the 1948 arrival of my father was undiscovered at this point, a 1942 class picture of young men resulted in an immediate curiosity. My mind simply wouldn't allow me to consider any possibility other than the potentially bombastic: this had to be an earlier child of my grandfather's. By this time, I had learned that my grandfather abandoned the United States in

1942 for some type of retreat to Canada. Was this photo evidence of the "family left behind" theory that my mother had initially introduced?

It's easy to accept that he would have cherished any last photo of a son he'd had to leave under unknown circumstances. By 1942, my grandfather was a fifty-two-year-old man, who certainly could have been raising a boy anywhere from kindergarten age through to senior class. In truth, any thoughts of age were immediately obliterated by the large "X" marked in ballpoint directly underneath a young boy in the first row. Gingerly turning over the photo, my eyes were immediately drawn to the middle of the space where a smaller "x" denoted an identifying caption.

"My son, Donald Roy Williams."

# A Visit to Aunt Shirley's

**_Wednesday, April 4, 1906, 5:18 a.m. Kidderminster Railway Station, Station Approach, Comberton Hill, Kidderminster, Worcestershire, England._**

*It's still dark as teenage Alfred makes his way down Comberton Hill to the Kidderminster Railway Station, a familiar building that until yesterday served as his place of employment. Although there is a morning spring chill in the air, the ten-minute walk is a welcome relief to his troubled mind. Sleep proved elusive the previous night, both for himself and likely the rest of the family. In the end, he hadn't the fortitude, or desire, to say all the things he'd dreamed against his father. Maybe it was a subconscious attempt to spare his mother the upset, or maybe he still fears the paternal figure who's caused such measure of horror in his young life.*

*At only sixteen, leaving his mother is painful. As well, he's sad to be leaving before really getting a chance to know Dennis, not even twelve years old. He will also miss his older brother, Charles, whom although different than, he has grown somewhat close to in recent months. The constant battles with his father, however, will not be missed. Once he arrives for the 6:00am train, he will begin his one-hundred-and-ten-mile journey to Liverpool, a journey which will take just under two hours. In his hand, he clutches a single piece of paper, containing an address "Cousin William, 140 Portland Street, Toronto, Ontario," as well as details of his lodging. Alfred is looking forward to seeing Liverpool, perhaps enjoying a beer or whiskey in one of the local establishments at the Albert Docks.*

L ife continued at its usual, ferocious pace. As the calendar turned to 2015, I found myself forty-three years of age, still happily enjoined to Lana. The boys now ranged in age from nine to fourteen. Suffice to say, I continued to have little free time to focus on this increasingly interesting mystery, which remained very much only a part-time hobby. Whenever I was fortunate to steal a precious slice of time, the first indulgent moments were often spent examining and reexamining the ever intriguing 9x12 black and white class photo.

After some time, I was now partly convinced that my grandfather may have been parent to another "Donald Roy Williams," one whose delivery superseded my father of the same name, likely born sometime in the 1930s. Yes, I did consider it peculiar that my grandfather would name two sons the same name. As well, I pondered the surname, "Williams" for a child born in the 1930s, as I'd accepted that my grandfather was using the name "Hammond" during much of

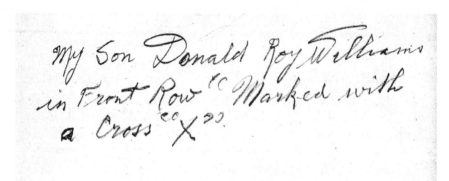

**The note in my grandfather's very hand suggested there could be more than one Donald Roy Williams.**

the first three decades of the twentieth century. While these factors rested uneasily in the narrative I was constructing, based on the facts so far, I reasoned that there were bound to be irregularities in any current or future discoveries I was to make in the life of this strange man.

Future discoveries were prominent in my mind as I prepared for my next move. I'd continued to be in touch with my Aunt Shirley – through phone or email – whenever I'd made any interesting finds. Impressed with my early findings, she had promised to dig out an old box that had some of my grandfather's possessions, again, fortuitously collected at the time of his 1968 passing. Pre-scheduling an August day when I was relieved of my summer school teaching duties, I found an opportunity to meet my aunt in person with the plan to indulge in our mutual interest. During the surprisingly rainy, thirty-minute drive to the nearby city of New Westminster, my mind was occupied with a mix of excitement to share the totality of what I'd discovered as well as anticipation of what I would further learn. I understood that the long-neglected box contained letters, documents and other mementos that could help solve the mystery of my grandfather's secret years, which I could now specify to the years between his 1906 arrival in Canada to his 1942 return.

The setting was a three-story heritage house in what is nicknamed "the royal city." Likely eighty or more years old –

*Seemingly content during a family outing, I wonder what secrets my grandfather is considering.*

a rarity in this part of the country – the house was home to my aunt's business, a preschool and daycare that she owned. The kids and staff occupied, we set up in the second-floor kitchen, poured cups of hot, black coffee and got to work amidst the pounding rain outside the single-pane window.

From a box that looked every bit as old and worn as I'd expected a box from 1968 to be, she began pulling items much as a magician may extricate from a shiny, black top hat.

My aunt started with a small collection of six to eight photographs. The pics featured my grandfather, my Oma, and a young child identified as my father, posing inside and around an imposing dark, 1940s coupe. Whether I was told the photo session took place in nearby Stanley Park or I made up that detail escapes me now, but the shots are clearly taken in the parking lot of a large park, mature, imposing trees and grassy, fielded areas serving as the picturesque backdrop. My grandfather and Oma take turns posing with the baby. The fact that there are no photos of the trio together could be the simple result of a lack of desire to impose on any random bystander. My mind tells me it's more than that.

True to form, Alfred is attired in formal, dark suit. While his collar may be loose, the customary trilby hat is perched upon his head, hiding what looks to be the familiar grey

*Dressed in full business attire and ready to make some sales. Taken on Granville St., Vancouver.*

whisps appearing at places. Most of the pictures display a straight-lipped stoic expression, which could be indicative of the times. A subtle smile seems to invade his expression in one shot.

My father looks to be only a few months old in the photos, which makes me ponder the state of my grandparents' relationship during this day. Likely only acquainted for a year and a half or so, I suspected the cracks had already been shown in their fragile union. Here though, I could see a real effort, authentic and genuine, if not sustainable. Again, I reflect upon my dad bending to kiss the grave marker during our visit to the cemetery.

Next, I was presented with a photo of my grandfather strolling down Granville Street in what was likely 1950s Vancouver. It was clear that my aunt was rediscovering these photos for the first time in years, likely decades, and she was equally invested in the details as I was. Of course, she had the

*My Aunt Shirley and my father looking serious. These
photos were cherished by my grandfather.*

advantage of age and was able to offer information that would
have eluded my own eyes.

She explained that this was a street-shot, most likely taken
by famed Granville Street photographer Foncie Pullice. A
later Internet search would tell me that Foncie operated
between the years 1935-1979, a successful forty-five-year
enterprise. He'd snap a photo, sometimes candid, of a passing
pedestrian and then quickly present a numbered slip. The
subject could visit Foncie's studio the next morning and for a
small fee acquire the one-day old photo, a convenient practice
in the days when many didn't own their own cameras. Again,
my grandfather is decked in a dark suit, draped with a formal,
tan overcoat. Likely a business day, he sports a diagonally
striped tie down the front of his shirt, but only two-thirds of
the way, which, I gather was the style in those days. As for
clues, this really didn't offer any. I noted that he carried his
left hand in his coat pocket, a habit first described by my
father.

The next small collection of photos shows my dad and Aunt
Shirley, still young children, in various locals around the city.
Based on dress, the photos seem to come from three separate

67

*A grandfather & his children celebrating Christmas. The photo shows both pride & joy as well as the absence of my Oma.*

photo shoots if not dates. One commonality is the impressive, formal dress adorned by my dad and aunt in each instance, not at all indicative of the hand-me-downs my father reported them often wearing. While the children's facial expressions display a reserved smile, again indicative of the times, I can't help but note happiness also. Pride of parenthood is a constant in the photos, the care and attention to both dress and setting not too dissimilar to the many pictures of my own happy family, albeit with the absence of a mother.

A Christmas tree serves as the backdrop for the next photo, emerging as a single shot not connected to any set. My father and aunt, still a few years from entering teenagehood, kneel in the forefront flanked by a slightly older boy to the left and a medium-sized canine on the right. Directly above in the middle row, two "grandma-types" with a third, slightly younger woman playfully balancing a jug of wine in her right hand. The third and final tier includes my grandfather, customary suit but with no formal hat, along with a possible, father and son combo, likely around fifty and seventy respectively. While the men and women balance at three each, I wonder there may have been a seventh adult behind the lens, but I can't rule out a timer either.

A dichotomy forms in my mind with two contrasting impressions. On one hand I see a father and two children, the absence of complete or extended family which, as we say, is what the holidays are all about. On the other hand, I see a single father taking efforts to provide his children a memorable Christmas with the seasonal goodwill of friends opening their door. My father seems to be having fun!

My aunt refills the coffee, and we sit back a minute to reflect. She can't pinpoint the location of the Christmas photo. "There were a lot of happy times," my aunt shares, "but it was tough also...your father and me. We didn't have an easy go of it." The photos now partly organized but laying loose on the wood table, I instinctively reflect upon the green photo album described in chapter two. How much easier this exercise would have been had my grandfather followed a similar suit, a well-organized guidebook of the past, complete with chronologically placed photos and explanatory captions. There would be no such advantage here.

Next up, a letter. "Mr. Alfred V. Williams, a customer of this branch, and an employee of *The Vancouver News Herald*, is planning a visit to Seattle, Washington for a period of ten days to two weeks." Composed by a Mr. D.C. Harris, Pro Manager of the Bank of Montreal, Homer and Hastings Street Branch, Vancouver, British Columbia, the typed letter is addressed to "U.S. Immigration Authorities, Vancouver, B.C." The letter does not state the purpose of the visit, but includes that Alfred, "will be returning to his permanent home in Vancouver, British Columbia."

More than providing information, the letter raises several questions. Did this mean that my grandfather had lived in Seattle? Was he returning to his long-time home for a visit? Seeing as he had lived in Ontario in his early life and returned to Ontario in 1942, I subconsciously accepted that he had lived his life in the east before finally venturing to Vancouver in

*Vancouver Realty*
All forms of Insurance

MORTGAGES ARRANGED
BUSINESSES FINANCED

Vancouver, B. C. __August 14__   194_7_

Mr. Alfred Victor Williams

| Terms | STATEMENT |
|---|---|

Re purchase of lots 26 and 27, of block 33,
District Lot 187, Group 1, Plan 1282

Received from Mr. Alfred Victor Williams three
thousand six hundred dollars ($3,600.00) pay
ment in full for the above property, and
seventy-four dollars and sixty-three cents
payment in full for documentation and legal
fees on the purchase.

The above property is free of all encumbrances
to date.

Dorothy Bellinger
Paid Aug 14/47

*Was the perplexing Seattle trip necessary to secure funds*
*for the cash purchase of a home?*

1947. Now I was seriously considering that Seattle may be the
key to the mystery. Could this be where a potential "secret
family" resided? Too bad the class photo from the last chapter
didn't include an identifying sign.

Almost immediately I took note of the date on the letter,
July 21, 1947. Seeing as my father was born on March 3, 1948,
I calculated that this trip would have likely occurred at a time
when my Oma was already pregnant. Did my Oma
accompany him over the border? Was my grandfather taking
care of possible "loose ends" before preparing to settle into a
new family structure? Similar to the Turley affidavit, was it
normal for someone to require a letter, from a bank manager
no less, to cross a border? I'd never heard of that.

It was another curious clue, with the Seattle connection
piquing my curiosity.

Not unlike any old box sitting dormant for almost fifty
years, we found a lot of, well, random items, I suppose. I
certainly couldn't bring myself to call it "junk." There was a
membership card for the "Senior's Club," at Cineplex Odeon
Theatres, a claim ticket from Pacific Airlines, an identification

card for another senior's pass, this time for the West Coast Soccer League, and four or five more items which seemed to lack any real informative value.

There was a receipt for cash purchase of 4141 Yale Street, the first house my father lived in, once standing very near the home of Mrs. Blake who played a prominent role in chapter one with her story of my Oma's departure. Dated August 14, 1947, the receipt noted, "received from Mr. Alfred Victor Williams three thousand six hundred dollars ($3,600.00) payment in full." My father had suggested an upbringing punctuated by a lack of disposable income, so I found it impressive that my grandfather was able to pay cash for a home. As with the lawyer bill described previously, I was curious to determine the equivalent value in today's funds. A quick search identified the value as just shy of $50,000.00, a small fraction of what the house would actually cost in 2023, but an impressive sum, nonetheless. I noted that the August date was a mere three weeks from the start of my grandfather's Seattle trip. Is that why he had ventured across border? Did he sell a previously occupied real estate holding? That would explain the uncertain time period he allotted to the trip. It was just a thought.

We temporarily put aside a sizeable collection of personal letters, accepting that our time was somewhat limited, and I'd likely prefer to indulge in the letters in a more leisurely environment on my own time. I gently placed the stack in my tote bag, full of anticipation for later discoveries.

Back to the box, one document of particular interest was a brittle, two-sided, legal-sized page titled, "Old Age Security Pension Application Form." The essence of my grandfather came alive as I set eyes on his handwriting. While this would have been true of the photographs and other documents also, I felt a spark of connection as I held the paper in my hand, knowing that my grandfather had done the very same at some point well in the past.

Underneath the heading, I look over the details and vitals my grandfather provided. One line reads, "if born outside Canada, give place and date of entry into Canada." In his unmistakable combination of block letters mixed with flowing, cursive script, my grandfather responds, with "1906, Saint John." If good genealogical practice includes verifying facts and details, I can feel confident in the immigration document I uncovered prior. For the second time, I pause and consider him venturing to a new world at only the age of sixteen.

Additionally, even though I was aware that my Oma and grandfather never officially divorced, the name, "Elizabeth Williams," written by my grandfather beside the requisite line does cause me to pause. A look at the backside of the form shows it was likely filled out in 1959, some time since their final separation. Whether he remained a little hopeful or was simply filling out the form accurately is up for debate, I suppose.

Now turning over the thin, brown-tinged, legal-sized paper to the backside, the true value of this document comes into focus. My grandfather records the names of two references, "J.J. Poirier" and "Geo Barnes." These names pique my interest. Friends? Coworkers? Despite the unsubstantial evidence offered in the Christmas photo, my father reported no recollection of any robust social circle. In fact, it seems most of my grandfather's spare time was spent with the aforementioned Mickey Spillane novels, accompanied by a whisky and ginger he would have acquired via a short stroll to the Fraser Arms Liquor Store, a sixteen-minute walk up Granville Street.

I look up both names in the *1959 Vancouver and New Westminster City Directory*. While details are confirmed, there is no additional information given. Of course, contacting present day "Poirier" and "Barnes" relatives would be too onerous a task given the unlikeliness of any useful information.

9. Addresses where you have resided in the twenty years immediately preceding the date of this application. This is to include residence **outside** Canada as well as **within** Canada. Give complete detail. Changes in street address within the same city or town do not need to be given. If more space is needed, use an ordinary sheet of paper and pin it to this form.

| FROM | | TO | | City, Town, Village or Post Office | County or District and Province or Territory | Country |
|---|---|---|---|---|---|---|
| Month | Year | Month | Year | | | |
| 1. Nov | 1942 | Oct | 1944 | Toronto | Ontario | |
| 2. Oct | 1944 | July | 1947 | Edmonton | Alberta | |
| 3. July | 1747 | Aug | 1957 | Vancouver | BC | |
| 4. | | | | | | |

*Otherwise so accurate in detail, why did my grandfather purposely omit his whereabouts between 1939-1942?*

The next section asks the subject to "please list below all periods of residence in Canada." Again, I'm pleased to witness some confirmation of the story I have slowly put together thus far. My grandfather confirms that he resided in "Toronto, Ontario," from "1906-1911." The "1911" date causes me to ponder. If true, this would preclude my grandfather from appearing in New York in the *1910 United States Federal Census*. I reason that an error by a single year does not preclude possibility. Also, in his affidavit, William Turley remarks, that Alfred lived with him in Canada in 1906, but that "shortly thereafter...he took up residence in the United States of America." Not so sure that four or five years constitutes "shortly thereafter," but close enough, I suppose.

Additionally, in Charles' 1942 letter, he admits he had "given [Alfred] up for dead" thinking he "had been killed in the last war," referring to World War I. With World War I ending in 1918, this piece told me that Alfred had moved on the United States before then, anyway.

Still with the theme of world conflict on my mind, I immediately wonder if that could be a reason why Alfred left Canada. I realize shortly though, that my dates are off. World War I begins in 1914, with Canada not instituting conscription until 1917. I rule this out as a reason Alfred originally left Canada for the United States in 1910 or 1911. I had reasoned that he may have left England in 1906 for an adventure or a better life, but the best I could do – at this point – for his entry into the United States would be...a change?  Any more likely hypothesis would require further evidence.

Also, noteworthy was the next section, "Addresses where you have resided in the twenty years immediately preceding the date of this application." Instructions continue that, "this is to include residence outside Canada as well as within Canada."  One further comment warns the applicant to "give complete detail."  My grandfather lists the following:

November 1942 – October 1944, Toronto, Ontario
October 1944 – July 1947, Edmonton, Alberta
July 1947 – August 1959, Vancouver, BC

Immediately, I noted that the "November 1942" entry matched with both the Turley declaration and my grandfather reconnecting with Charles, both events previously documented.  The entry point into Vancouver, "July 1947," matched family lore that my grandfather had newly arrived in the city at the time of his initial meeting with my Oma.  A notion hatching in my mind, I shuffle papers to uncover the letter from the bank manager.  Locating the sheet, I noted that the letter outlining my grandfather's Seattle trip was dated July 21, 1947.  Okay, so Alfred arrived in Vancouver, opened a bank account, secured employment, met my Oma and then almost immediately needed to make a trip to Seattle.  Not sure what conclusions I could draw, but it definitely caused pause for thought.

Then, of course, there was the middle entry, "October 1944 to July 1947, Edmonton, Alberta."  I looked up to my aunt, searching for her reaction.  "I didn't know that!  Wow."  I didn't quite feel the same sense of surprise and wonder. That's not to say I didn't find it interesting.  Certainly, it was a fact I wasn't aware of prior.  The dates immediately became a large part of his life story I was constructing, but it didn't necessarily provide any detail on the prime missing years which I had narrowed to 1910 to 1942.  Oh well.

In truth, what I found most interesting was what was not included in the application. Accepting that the document was filled out in 1959, my grandfather should have listed places of residence going back to 1939. If you remember, the instructions clearly state, "addresses where you have resided in the twenty years immediately preceding the date of this application," followed by "give complete detail," a requirement that doesn't exactly leave much open for interpretation.

My only conclusion could be that my grandfather had purposely omitted his whereabouts from 1939 to his return to Canada in 1942. Truthfully, I'm not sure the word "omitted" is appropriate. While it's true that, with the exception of those three years, my grandfather filled out the form in its entirety, I had to remind myself that he never actually mailed it in! Whether this was a first draft that he practiced or whether he had reason not to apply for any financial support is anyone's guess. What isn't debatable is the fact that he purposely left this information out.

Again, I pined at the missed opportunity. How informative it would have been to be sure of his occupancy during those years. Any indication of residence could have been the thread that unraveled the entire story. The omission also solidified my mind's two leading, possibly wild, theories: running from a family he didn't want discovered or occupying a space in some state or federal prison.

The discovery didn't stop there though. In keeping with the burgeoning practice of filling out forms and not actually sending them anywhere was a completed "T.1-Special 1944" income tax form. I was especially interested as the document was filled out during his time in Edmonton, a fact recently discovered. In addition to providing his Edmonton address, the form listed his two most recent places of employment. I learned that he had worked at the Christie Street Hospital in Toronto until his departure from the province in October 1944. From there, he reported finding almost immediate employ at the Alberta Provincial Mental Hospital in Oliver, Alberta. I noted that these career choices seemed to have little in common with the usual "salesman" vocations reported by my father.

Remembering that a few months later he would pay $3600 cash for his house on Yale Street, I took note that he reported a 1944 total income of $1294.65. The fact that a house close to Vancouver would cost only three years' salary of what seemed to be an entry-level job aside, I was somewhat impressed that he had managed to have that amount available in savings. I suppose it was likely that he either owned some property prior – in Seattle as I contemplated – or he had managed to save from previous earnings.

Oh, I should mention one last point of interest. In the line asking, "name and address of your wife or husband," my grandfather responds with a singular identifier.

"Clara."

# Letters of Long Ago

**Thursday, April 5, 1906, 7:57 a.m. Royal Albert Dock, Liverpool, Lancashire, England.**

*Alfred's night in Liverpool was enlightening if anything. With a single room at the Adelphi he felt independent, if not rich. Downstairs at Crompton's, his beef and potatoes were as good as anything he ever had at home, and he felt like a man ordering two glasses of ale. He splurged a little but felt he'd deserved it after being so disciplined over the past few months. Being the youngest in the establishment, he lacked the confidence to join any conversations. However, his eavesdropping allowed him to learn that a large group would be boarding the Victorian with him this morning. The air was jovial with others, like him, optimistic about beginning life anew. If they were as nervous as Alfred, however, they didn't show it.*

*Now, waiting in line under the banner reading "third class," Alfred feels truly alone. He can't help note the bleak situation as characterized by his lack of luggage. While many of those around him have enlisted travel companions to assist with their sizeable trunks, Alfred easily swings his comparatively light canvas bag over his right shoulder. It is then that the full magnitude of his decision heavily rests on his conflicted mind. His first cousin, William Turley is very generous to offer room and board at only five shillings a week. Alfred admires William for his wit and intelligence, as well as his impressive boxing skills. However, almost ten years his junior, Alfred is also more than a little intimidated by his cousin, but hopes that he'll show some interest, maybe act as a role-model or father figure of sorts.*

*As he enters the room marked, "health," for his final checkup, Alfred wonders if it will be the last time he'll ever touch British soil.*

T he visit to Aunt Shirley's could be viewed as nothing but a success. In addition to a potential wife, the exact dates of his migration held the potential to also be extremely useful. I hoped that it would help me narrow down potential search fields and also rule out other options. The dates also helped me to form a more exact timeline, albeit with the years 1910 to 1942 still constituting a glaring omission:

1889 – Alfred born in Bewdley, Worcestershire, Eng.
1906 – Alfred (16) resides with Turleys in Toronto, Ont.
1910 – Alfred (20) becomes Roy Hammond in U.S.
1942 – Alfred (52) returns to Turleys in Toronto, Ont.
1944 – Alfred (54) married to "Clara" in Edmonton, Alta.
1947 – Alfred (57) married to my Oma in Vancouver, B.C.
1968 – Alfred (78) passes away in Vancouver, B.C.

While this information was helpful, I wondered at the fact that he never submitted the form. Did he discover he was not eligible for old age security benefits and put the paper aside? Perhaps he had visited a government office with questions and a clerk filled the form out for him on the spot? Maybe it was conscience or the fear of discovery that prevented him from submitting a form in which he entered false information? The possibilities didn't offer much in the way of confidence.

Truthfully, it was that last point that made the most sense to me. Clara. Was there actually a Clara? It was my opinion that my grandfather had chosen not to submit the form. Wasn't it a possibility that he entered the name of a fictitious wife with the confidence that a female dependent could result in a more favorable pension allowance? I'm no expert, but it seemed at least plausible.

Further to that, the dates themselves didn't offer much to the root point of the mystery. From the outset, I had been aware that my grandfather immigrated from England as a young man and that he surfaced in Vancouver in 1947 as a relatively old man. It was the years in between that I was focused on discovering. Any information my grandfather recorded here conveniently left out the years I so passionately sought. With the discoveries I had made, the missing years still comprised the majority of his existence, from age sixteen to fifty-two, the prime of a man's life. The fact that he took measures to offer exact details and dates at some points in the form, but curiously or purposely omitted his residence from 1939 to 1942 further confirmed that there wouldn't likely be any quick answers. In life and now in death, it seems my grandfather was committed to keeping his years unknown.

For his part, my father was pleased at my efforts. While he found the small discoveries tantalizing and curious, I believe he was more satiated by the simple fact that I was taking an interest in my grandfather at all. Of course, Lana was alongside constantly, not only encouraging me and checking on my progress but both acting as a sounding board and providing worthy suggestions. If she ever grew tired of my frequent frustrations and rare victories, she certainly never showed.

With that, it was time to jump back on *Ancestry.com* with this new information. I was focused on the possibility that he may have brought Clara from the United States with him. If true, this was a detail that had the potential to help me locate him in that country. Again, I mused that one solitary clue could lead me down the exciting rabbit hole of discovery. They say timing is everything, and this was not to be the time. Further searches turned up nothing. No marriage certificate. No immigration papers or border crossings. No Clara.

What I did have in my hand, however, was the stack of new letters I'd placed in my tote bag. Nineteen new letters to be exact, born of the same weathered box of my aunt's that contained all the above clues. The afternoon was slowly turning to early evening and my aunt had daycare responsibilities to fulfill. Still grey and drizzling, I returned to my Jetta and pointed in the direction of home. Whether I cued any music for the commute is a forgotten detail, my thoughts racing with possibility as I imagined the potential of information revealed in the letters. I had successfully gleaned a decent amount of information from the single letter I had possessed to this point.

Thus, my excitement that several more could very much help fill in curious details of the missing years. With each pause graciously offered by a red stoplight, I used my unoccupied right hand to fumble with an envelope or loose-leaf page, unable to exercise the patience of waiting until I returned home. I considered pulling into a coffee shop and going through the missives with haste and privacy, but I knew I had been away too long, and dinner would be on the minds of Lana and the boys.

It was Lana who would be the first to vet the correspondence while I prepared our meal. It isn't through necessity that I most often take on the kitchen duties. Cooking is one of my passions. Dinner over, I carefully spooned the remaining spaghetti carbonara into the white bowl as Lana offered small but interesting details. Finally, as the cloudy summer evening turned unusually dark, I poured from the open bottle of Merlot and joined my fully engaged wife at the kitchen table. In truth, this was the setting I looked forward to, much preferred over the front seat of my Jetta or a cold, unfamiliar chain coffee shop.

With nineteen letters and a potential goldmine of details, I felt a little overwhelmed. I decided to order my study based on people rather than dates. I was familiar with Charles from his 1942 letter, so he seemed a good enough subject to proceed. Charles' next letter was dated February 7, 1943, only a few months after the November 1942 letter I previously described. It's worth noting that both letters are addressed to "351 Ashdale Avenue, Toronto, Ontario, Canada." I am not sure if I was able to establish at this point, or if confirmation came later, that this was the address of William Turley, meaning that, as in 1906, Alfred was a guest of the Turley family.

Charles begins, "dear Alfred, I received your letter and photo safely two days ago. I don't think I should have recognized you had we met in the street, which is hardly surprising, considering how long it is since we parted." My mind jumped to the rather formal photo of my grandfather that I described previously. Where I originally thought the photo may have been for employment purposes, I now considered that he may have had the photo done to satisfy the curiosity of his England family. The fact that he donned formal attire and commissioned a professional photographer suggested that he hoped to make a favorable impression on his working-class relatives, show them that he had "made good."

Charles continues, "I hope this war will soon be over, so save your money and come and pay us a visit, as I don't think I shall ever have enough to visit you in Canada." I would rue

81

continuously that I didn't possess any of my grandfather's return letters, but this line seems to corroborate what I surmised from the photo, that he presented himself as a success to some degree.

From the further information offered, I do believe that this is the second letter Charles had sent. An official capacity seems to be served as Charles offers, "I have enclosed the date of your birth etc. and if you would like a proper birth certificate, I dare say I could get you one." True to his word, at the bottom of the page, Charles pens, "Alfred Victor Williams, born November 23, 1889 in Wribbenhall, Bewdley, Worcestershire." I had to chuckle that my grandfather seemed unsure of his birth year, recalling William Turley reporting "1890" in his affidavit, a date I surmised came from my grandfather's mouth. At least he had the day and month correct. It wasn't a stretch to assume he may have needed a birth certificate to complete his immigration status.

As well as the issue of birth, the letter provides a more detailed, but sill basic summation of close family members. Charles writes dad "died about six years ago," confirming a 1937 date I had already found on *Ancestry.com* and shares "you would not know Alfred, but Mother died in September 1910. She was awfully worried about you and talked about you right up to the last." Any specific date could be useful, so I pondered this last line. In the first letter, Charles shared that he still possessed the last letters that Alfred wrote from the United States. This suggested that Alfred was in the United States prior to late 1910, which would add confidence to the New York entry in the *1910 United States Federal Census*. In this case, Alfred's record of entering the United States in 1911 would have been a touch inaccurate. I had to consider another option, however. It's possible that Alfred continued to write home during his early days in the United States but that he was either unwilling or unable to accept any return letters, likely not providing any return address. If this second option was the case, what did it mean? Was he transient with no

*Alfred's mother, Emily (Crane) Williams, who never stopped worrying. What did she know about his hasty departure at age 16?*

return address to give? Again, I considered he may have been incarcerated, but wouldn't any correspondence from corrections be marked on the envelope? From what I gathered, I didn't consider that Alfred may have simply been disinterested in family. Current evidence was proving the contrary.

Additionally, I determined that any letters Alfred had written home must have ceased prior to 1918 as Charles incorrectly guessed that Alfred may have perished in the first world war. Well, if I had the correct dates, that meant Alfred's family was unable to contact him between 1910 and 1942, which, incidentally, corresponded with the years I was currently missing. This was another piece of the puzzle, but I wasn't entirely sure what I could glean from the information. Perhaps it would be of clear value at some later point of research.

Continuing with family members, Charles offers "I don't' expect you would remember much about Dennis, he was only a kid when you left home." Born in June 1894, Dennis

Williams would have been around eleven when Alfred left home. The fact that Alfred was putting in what were likely long days at the railway confirms that he may have known little of his younger sibling. "He joined the regular army when he was sixteen years old, before the last war, and was in France as soon as the war started," Charles reports, continuing that Dennis, "got married and started some kind of business in London, but would not make it pay, and when I heard from him next in 1922, he was absolutely down and out."

It was at this point, that I first considered how the brutal nature of the time played into my grandfather's story. Here was Dennis, cast oversees into a brutal war when he was still a young man, only to return home with the challenge of earning a living under also brutal conditions in a London city that likely offered little hope for a potentially damaged veteran from a family of horse traders. Life was difficult, meaning that family correspondence may have simply taken a back seat.

In addition to "when I heard from him next in 1922," Charles explains that he "kept in touch with [Dennis] and visited him regularly until about six years ago." These details suggest that periods of family estrangement may not have been all that uncommon – at least in the Williams family. I considered that Alfred's estrangement may have not been too suspicious after all, but then I reasoned that a thirty-plus year gap was a little more serious than a six-year estrangement.

The situation further exposed itself when Charles continued that he and Dennis "had a row, which was mostly the fault of [Dennis's] wife." The story continues that in the early 1920s, Dennis and his wife, Dorothy Halsey, were unable to care for their eighteen-month-old daughter, the appropriately if not obviously named, Dorothy Denise. This explains Charles' report in his previous letter that he and his wife had adopted one of Dennis's daughters. According to Charles, family relations were good, and all were happy until, "the girl had grown up and was able to earn a living," at which time Dennis's wife "wanted her [daughter] back." According to the letter, Dorothy Denise protested which resulted in the row between brothers. Made sense to me, but I would learn more details in the letters still unstudied.

Mirroring the information offered about Dennis, Charles outlines his own efforts in World War I, sharing he "joined the army...in 1914 and went to Egypt, Mesopotamia, India and Russia." While this didn't surprise, it did cause me further wonder regarding Alfred's apparent lack of military records.

Charles nears the end, requesting, "please remember me to Mr. and Mrs. Turley," referring to his Uncle George and Aunt Agnes, parents to William Turley. Lastly, Charles cautiously urges, "now that we have found each other, we must keep in touch, and I would like to see you again if it is possible."

Writing this, I make the troubling recognition that I have spent an exurbanite amount of time on just one of the nineteen letters I recently acquired. While I hope a future edit can cutdown the concerning word count, I comfort myself that this first basic letter was of special importance and crucial in establishing context.

In Charles' next letter, dated June 23, 1943, he begins "I take the opportunity at last to write to you again and send you the birth certificate which I have kept you so long waiting for." He continues that "Aunt Annie" had to go to Kidderminster for a copy. Again, Charles mentions the current war affecting the world. In his job as train engineer, Charles shares that he "was talking to some Canadian Airmen" from Toronto, but they "did not know the Turley family." At the close of the letter Charles projects, "when the war is over, we will visit the old spots together again, and I will look around for a nice widow for you." This amusing promise shows me that Alfred has shared his bachelor status as of 1942. I have to accept this makes the likelihood that Clara followed my grandfather from his United States' life before 1942 improbable. At the same time, I wish I was privy to Alfred's account of his marital status. Did he report a divorce? Was he a widower? Or maybe he shared that he had never been married. I suppose if my

**Alfred's younger brother, Dennis, apparently just like his father. He accused his oldest brother of kidnapping.**

grandfather did leave behind a family, Charles was kept in the dark also.

A September 1943 letter from Charles' wife, Eva, piques my interest. She begins by apologizing for neglecting Alfred lately, an ironic footnote considering the decades Alfred seemed to have evaded correspondence. She explains that domestic life can be hectic and offer little time for personal indulgences such as letters, rationalizing that Alfred, "being a bachelor may not know anything about these sorts of things" and suggests that she doesn't "expect for a moment" Alfred is interested. Pausing, I consider it appears as if Alfred has reported never being in any long-term domestic situation. Eva reports that they have recently visited Aunt Annie and Uncle George, both on Alfred's paternal side. Then the letter grows interesting.

*There is one little bit of advice if you don't mind taking it.
Don't say anything against your dad to them as they are
your dad's sister and brother. I know I have had one or
two skirmishes with them, because, you see, I happen to
be very fond of your mother's sister and she told me a lot.
Of course, she wouldn't have anything to do with them
and Dennis was all his father. Don't think I am
interfering, but I am just letting you know how the land
lies. They are all very nice to me.*

The passage took a few minutes and a few sips of my Merlot
to unpack in my cluttered mind. To begin, I needed to
pinpoint the identity of Alfred's "mother's sister." Alfred's
mother, Emily, had only one full sister, Agnes Crane, who
would eventually marry George Turley and become mother to
William Turley. Other than Eva offering that Agnes has "told
me a lot," I am left to fill in the details myself. Of course, the
information must have been negative about Alfred's father,
my great-grandfather. Additionally, I felt that Agnes must
have objected to the treatment Emily or perhaps their
children received at the home of Alfred Williams Sr. Poor
treatment, of course, could include a myriad of possibilities
from simply being cold and distant to horrific mental and
physical abuse. Following my train of thought, the caution
that my grandfather, not "say anything against [his] dad"
strongly suggests that Alfred sided with his mother and was in
conflict with his father. Sharing this detail with my own father
piques his memory and he reports hearing his dad share a
predilection for his mother over his father.

I wonder that this could be the reason Alfred left home so
young, constant conflict with his father over his abusive
behavior. Moving to the bottom of the letter, Eva confides she
"would like to be able to visit the interesting places you talk
about in your letters," signaling out "Niagara Falls." I rued the
fact that the only specific geographical clue was Niagara Falls,
hardly a surprise seeing as Alfred was in Ontario and possibly
New York. If Alfred had visited so many interesting places,

*My grandfather's father, Alfred Williams Sr., whom my grandfather was warned not to disparage.*

why couldn't Eva have mentioned any of them? The Grand Canyon, Florida beaches, or the Cascade Mountains all would have served as monumental clues. Nonetheless, the picture my grandfather painted in this letter was becoming increasingly clear: a footloose bachelor indulgently roaming the continent and enjoying life.

In April 1944 Charles and Eva enclose separate letters in a single envelope. After thanking Alfred for sending tea, a cake, and some chocolates, Charles cautions, "Uncle George has viewed your letter and was quite pleased with it, except the part about having gypsy blood in the family." Again, this confirmed that Alfred was reporting extensive travels. Charles relays Uncle George's assertion that the Williams have "aristocratic ancestors," explaining that the family can be traced back to "William the Conqueror" and come from the "Castle at Shrewsbury" where the family is "supposed to have originated."

I take notice of Charles' superlative, "supposed," and wonder at his own thoughts. By this time, Charles had established himself as a credible figure in my grandfather's life. He had served military time, supported a niece, and maintained an honest living. Earlier in same letter, Charles remarks "I should like you to meet" Uncle George, referring to him as a "queer figure." While the royal connection seemed intriguing, I had to wonder at its authenticity. Another future task for *Ancestry.com*.

In truth, I was more interested in my grandfather's use of the term, "gypsy blood." He must have been referring to a penchant for travel, never remaining in any one, single place for long. Charles questions whether Alfred would ever "settle down in this country...after travelling so much." In the matching letter, Eva remarks she doesn't "blame [him] for having a good time. We have only one life to live, it is up to us all to make the most of it." Eva finishes with the admission that she and Charles "lead quite uneventful lives but are quite happy." I find it interesting that Eva asserts she "doesn't blame him," before defending her own simple, domestic existence. Did Alfred report guilt at his supposed lifestyle or did he boast of it? Again, I can only guess at the experiences and adventures my grandfather reported.

Reader, you may wonder at my use of the term "reported" as being overly skeptical. I may be guilty, but, even at this early stage of research, I had already gathered enough to make up my own mind that my grandfather could be something less than completely honest. Whether justified or not, what other reason could there be for living under an alias?

A February 1945 letter from Eva, who seems to have taken over head writing responsibilities from her husband, is largely unfruitful, with the exception of the corresponding envelope. The destination veers from the familiar "Ashdale Avenue" address to "10130-155., Sub. Post Office 23, Edmonton, Alberta, Canada." A quick shuffle to the floor of my office and I confirm that address matches my grandfather's entry on the mysteriously unmailed 1944 Alberta income tax form. Also, of note is the opening salutation, "Dear Fred." What catches my attention is not simply the fact that my grandfather has seemingly changed his preferred Christian name to "Fred," but that the address and the letter itself omits any mention of "Clara." On the 1944 form, Alfred not only lists his wife as Clara, but leaves unmarked the line asking him to "state marital change, if any, during 1944." While possibilities are almost endless, Alfred seems to be reporting that he and Clara were together before 1944. Thus, the omission of a corresponding salutation, not to mention any inclusion of Clara in the very polite text of the letter, makes me question her very existence. My mind again moves to the possibility that he was simply considering sending in an income tax form with a fictitious partner in a bid to keep more of his hard-earned money.

The fact that there exists a twenty-year gap before Eva's next letter, dated 1966, doesn't suggest a whole lot. Through *Ancestry.com*, I had learned that Charles died in 1952, making the final long-distance reunion between brothers a solid decade. I remind myself that, while I have commandeered an impressive collection of letters, I have no way of knowing if they represent a comprehensive set or if others were discarded. In 1966 Eva writes what seems to be a response to my grandfather. The response focuses on Alfred's younger brother, Dennis. Eva is, once again, apologetic at not being able to help Alfred locate him. My research has already shown me that Dennis passed in 1958, meaning that he was alive when Alfred originally enquired in the early 1940s, but is no longer of this world by 1966.

My interest in the letter moves to the bottom page, where Eva queries, "you don't say anything about your family, and I can't remember ever hearing anything about them. Anyway, I hope you are not alone." It is true that the collection of family letters I have amassed cease – for the most part – before the birth of my father in 1948. While not particularly

*Uncle George, who reminded my grandfather the Williams were "castle breed."*

useful to my mystery, it does seem that Alfred again loses contact with his England family at some later point, likely owing to the fact that his mother, father, brothers and other family members were no longer alive to maintain any such correspondence.

At this point, I ask you to rewind to 1943, so we can begin reviewing letters from my grandfather's Uncle George, the very relative described as a "queer figure" by Alfred's trustworthy brother, Charles. Uncle George is actually George Thomas Williams, younger brother of Alfred's father and a type of partner in Alfred's father's one-time horse-trading business.

Uncle George's first letter, undated, begins "you will be surprised to hear from your long-lost Uncle George." George shares that he is "keeping a grocers shop and an off-license beer house at Stourport." He proudly continues that he "still does a bit of horse dealing," before admitting he is "getting too old for that now." I fascinate at the inclusion of horse trading, matching what I'd learned in an earlier census report. I marveled at the personal, intimate voice added to the facts I had discovered in the census reports.

Family seems foremost on George's mind as he continues, urging that Alfred write to two of his aunts, Aunt Annie in Bewdley and Aunt Lizzie who has immigrated to Australia. Now George enquires whether Alfred be "married or single," and that Alfred write him to "let us know all about yourself and what you are doing." I find a satisfying degree of amusement in the final line where George shares, "I shall expect to hear from you soon."

In what seems to be the second letter, both lacking a written date at salutation and featuring a long-faded post mark I am unable to decipher, George's words ring what is now a familiar tune, writing "you have seen a bit of life and you will see more travelling about," but holds Alfred accountable that he "never mentions in his letters what trade [he is] at and if single or married." I take note that, even though Alfred is now in his mid-fifties, he must have reported his intention to continue travelling about. Travelled a lot. *Check.* Secretive personal life. *Check.*

The letter did offer the origins of a family legend I alluded to in an earlier chapter...the inheritance. George explains, "your Aunty Annie is going to write to you. She lives in Bewdley by herself." George announces, "she thinks of leaving, Charley, Alfred and Dennis £100 each at her death." Years later, I am able to discover Aunt Annie's will, where I learn the following:

> *Subject to the payment of my debts...I GIVE and DEVISE the residue of my estate...equally between the following persons namely, my Sister Lizzie Christie, my Niece Lizzie Gwendolen Wade...the said Charles Williams, and my Nieces Annie and Fanny*

I accept this as the "lost inheritance" my grandfather believed he was entitled to, as per Uncle George's letter. As to what happened to sway Aunty Annie between the time of her correspondence with her brother, George, and her ultimate death seven years later will never be known. What is known, is that my grandfather's relatives were to split a not totally unimpressive sum of about fifteen thousand American dollars in today's exchange.

By what seems to be the third correspondence, Uncle George has remembered his grade school lesson to include the date in the opening of a letter. Marking the note, May 7, 1944, George sets right down to business, sharing, "I daresay you quite forgot what I was like after so many years." Repeating Alfred's claim to have "travelled about the world," George reports he "laughed" where Alfred mentioned "gypsy blood," setting the record straight. "No far from that. You belong to castle bred family. Your grandfather belonged to a Shropshire family at Shrewsbury Moreton Corbet Castle now in ruins, but the Corbets live in Sundorne Castle, Shrewsbury." As some type of evidence, George offers "I have enclosed a cutting of your mother's brother, a Mr. Crane, [who] kept a large horse business in Stourport."

I find two weathered, roughly one by one-and-a-half-inch newspaper clippings in my Aunt Shirley's brown box. However, both related to the Corbet family with no mention of Alfred's mother's maiden name, Crane.

Also familiar, Uncle George promises he will "do [his] best to find Dennis." It does seem curious that Alfred is so bent on locating a brother whom he intentionally stayed away from for over thirty years. I suppose, however, now that Alfred is in touch, it makes sense to want to contact a sibling. Again, I find myself asking why Alfred imposed this thirty-year radio silence. It just seems to contradict this innate desire he holds to connect with family. Of course, if he did have reason to keep his anonymity, well, that would qualify as an explanation.

*Dorothy Denise Williams, somewhat forgotten by siblings but forever remembered here.*

In Uncle George's January 1946 letter, again the envelope is addressed to Alfred's home in Edmonton, but prior to dissecting the body, I take note of the opening salutation: "My dear Fred and Clara." With this I'm satisfied that the mysterious "Clara" can be confirmed as a real person. Sure, my grandfather may have been capable of stretching the truth – lying – on an unmailed government form, but I could see no reason why he would willfully hoodwink family members in this capacity. George writes, "I have received your lovely parcel, and I don't know how to thank you both for your kindness." Here, I picture a husband and wife happily immersed in domestic routine, time and resources to maintain a household as well as take care of the extras, like gifts for extended family. Could that accurately describe Alfred's situation in Edmonton?

Recognizing that Clara is not acknowledged in any previous 1944 or 1945 letters from George, Charles, or Eva, leads me to believe that Clara is new on the scene. This, coupled with the fact that Alfred is in Vancouver by mid-1947 to begin a brief courtship with my grandmother, would show that Clara isn't around very long either. These details can easily fit into what might now be considered a pattern. I have already described the brief, unsuccessful marriage between my grandparents. I make the assumption that abuse may have hastened the expiry date of his union with Clara also.

A stolen glance at the clock shows evening has slipped nicely into night, the streets now dark and the house quiet. I contemplate retiring for the night, but instead find myself pouring another glass of Merlot and lighting a candle. Curiosity has embraced my being and I know I cannot retire to bed until I've at least taken a cursory scan of the remaining seven letters.

I select a February 1966 letter from the aforementioned Dorothy Denise Williams, eldest daughter of Dennis Williams, who was raised by Charles Williams. A look at my *Ancestry.com* family tree and I learn she would have been forty-five years of age at the time. The letter is postmarked from Barbados and the text explains that she and her husband have called the island home for quite some time. I wonder at her view of the situation, being raised by an uncle only to be called back to her birth parents once she became a potential breadwinner. Of course, by 1966, these events would have been nothing but distant memories to Alfred's eldest niece.

"Dear Uncle Alfred, this is a most difficult letter for me to write as I don't quite know where to begin," Dorothy Denise offers, tentatively. She explains, "I regret to say that I haven't seen my father or mother for nearly thirty years." I take note at the estrangement, linking it not only to Alfred's prolonged disappearance from family, but also, the divide between Charles and Dennis. I contemplate whether it is a product of the times, or maybe just the way of the Williams family. Life was tough. People didn't always stay connected. Quickly though, I consider surrounding details, including Charles pleading that he and Alfred don't fall out of touch again and even Dorothy Denise's regret she expresses at her unfortunate situation.

Corroborating Charles' earlier account of events, Dorothy Denise describes the situation concerning herself, her father and her uncle. "At the age of fifteen I returned to my parents [Dennis and Dorothy] for eight months, but I'm afraid I was unhappy – through no fault of theirs may I add." She continues, "I ran away from London back to Wolverhampton and my father sent two detectives to Charles' house accusing him of kidnapping me." Okay, that certainly explains what Charles referred to as a "row" between brothers and would account for a prolonged falling-out in most families.

Understandably, Dorothy Denise reports that "Charles and Eva were most upset at the attitude [her] father had taken," adding that Charles and Eva had given her "an excellent house and environment" and had also helped Dennis and Dorothy out with their additional children, three sons and two daughters. The tone turns from explanatory to regretful, as Dorothy continues, "I on my part have felt a little bitter thinking that my parents had no love for me, otherwise why did they give me away?" Finally, she divulges "I admit I feel a little guilty and perhaps I should have tried to locate my family. But then the war broke out, and I got married." Dorothy Denise shares that "years later Uncle George tried unsuccessfully to find them. There was no trace of them whatsoever and we presumed the whole family may have been killed by a flying bomb." Her words made true George's promise in an earlier letter to my grandfather to attempt to locate Dennis.

Near the close, Dorothy Denise echoes another common notion, assuring, "if you do decide to visit England, perhaps you would care to visit us here in Barbados on your way through." In the earlier letters I examined, it was unclear whether it was Alfred or the others who promoted an overseas visit. Here, Dorothy Denise's phrasing, "if you do decide" shows that Alfred must have shared his contemplation, his goal likely being to find Dennis. My own father reports that no such visit would ever materialize.

In a bemusing postscript, Dorothy Denise shares that she and her husband, "called in Vancouver for a few hours in July 1958" before catching a connecting flight to their home in Barbados. This detour would have placed them no more than a fifteen-minute drive from my grandfather's home. A quick look at the family tree confirms it as the very year Dennis Williams died. I wonder at this fateful occurrence that never quite happened.

Probably the most intriguing letter, dated December 1967, came from Lola LeDuke of 1202 East Pine Street, Seattle, Washington. The fact that my grandfather knew someone in Seattle lent some fuel to my earlier theory that his unusual visit to the emerald city may have been to settle personal or financial affairs prior to marrying my Oma and purchasing a home. An online look at the Seattle phone book brought up a few "Alfred Williams" and "Roy Hammonds." Several of these offered names of wives or even professions but none of the listings offered any corroborating clue that convinced me it could be my grandfather. If I had been fortunate to discover any entry that listed an Alfred Williams or Roy Hammond living with a "Lola" or some variation thereof at 1202 East Pine Street, I would have been convinced immediately. Sadly, nothing like that would appear.

Immediately, I take notice of the greeting, "Dear Al." Taking stock, we now have letters addressed to "Alfred," "Fred," and now "Al." Add to that, the name on the 1906 immigration document, "Alf," and I consider if individual variations of his name could provide context. It's possible, he went by "Alf" in his younger years, only to return to Alfred when he reconnected with family in 1942. Soon after, it seems the letters were addressed to "Fred," and now we have Lola who addresses him as "Al." I could only guess that the authors of each letter would address him as he signed his own letters. If I could glean anything from this, maybe it would help to use specific variations of his name when using the Internet to search for different documents from different eras. Of course, this ignores any use of "Roy Hammond," his apparent United States' alias. Moreover, the very fact that Lola addresses him as "Al" and not "Roy" suggests that Lola knew him only in Canada, but I had to also consider the converse, that maybe he did use "Al," at times in the United States, Lola being privy to his secret identity.

This was the only letter I had from someone outside of the direct family, a stranger, at least to myself. If I could somehow discern the specific nature of their relationship, perhaps I could steal a clue about my grandfather's whereabouts. There were several possibilities: friend, coworker, neighbor. I couldn't rule out ex-partner or even daughter either.

The letter itself offers some potential clues. Lola writes that she hasn't "been up to Mona's since Labor Day weekend." Offering specifics of the trip, she relays that she and her husband, Bill, "went on a picnic" then "drove to Burnaby and stayed at Mona's overnight." Burnaby, if you'll recall, is neighboring city to Vancouver and the location of my grandfather's Yale Street home that he purchased in 1947. Later, she shares that she and Bill "are going to take their vacation on Vancouver Island." The familiarity in which Lola mentions Burnaby and Vancouver Island, and the fact that Alfred and Lola have a mutual acquaintance in "Mona" suggests that Lola lived in Burnaby or Vancouver for a time. The letter is dated 1967, so there is plenty of opportunity for Alfred to have known Lola in Burnaby or Vancouver prior to her and her husband Bill moving to Seattle.

In the next paragraph, Lola asks Alfred, "how are all your old lady friends." I recall my father sharing that Alfred, in drunken influence, would sometimes brag about all his past female relationships and how he was successful with the fairer sex. My father, of course, wasn't interested in such boasts. I wondered that Alfred displayed similar behavior with Lola. Also possible, is that in her time acquainted with my grandfather, Lola witnessed first-hand his female companions. In addition, I pondered the descriptor, "old." Is

Lola asking about past girlfriends, or rather, is she playfully suggesting that Alfred, now a seventy-seven-year-old man, is still active on the dating scene? My dad replies in negative when I ask if Alfred ever dated after separating from my Oma. Lola, it seems, was teasing at some level, I suppose.

The letter, while not very long, offers some additional causes for consideration. Lola asks, "how is Donnie have you seen him lately and Shirley, where is she?" The fact that she refers to my father as "Donnie" somehow suggests that she was first acquainted with him when he was a young boy. My father, of course, has no memory of ever meeting Lola, but my Aunt Shirley vaguely recounts an introduction at one point to a "friend from Seattle."

I consider Lola's age at time of her writing. She shares that her husband's, "son stayed with us for a month in October," and that "he drives a truck Handcrest and Light House of the Blind." I gather that neither Lola nor Alfred is close to Bill's son who must be of adult age. It's possible that Lola has recently married Bill, who must be in his forties or older suggesting that Lola, too, must at least be middle age. Near the close, Lola states, "I still remember that picture. Don't forget to will it to me." With this, I accept that Lola must be a degree younger than my grandfather's seventy-seven years. I reason that Lola is likely in her forties or fifties, old enough to be newly married to a man with a grown son, but young enough to distance her from my grandfather's age at the time.

Putting down the letter and grabbing my not quite empty glass of Merlot, I begin to favor the theory that Lola was likely a neighbor or coworker, someone in my grandfather's Vancouver world long enough to know details of his personal life. I guessed that at some point in the preceding twenty years of the 1967 letter, she moved to Seattle to marry a man named Bill LeDuke. This, of course, is what my skeptical mind affirms. I also couldn't see any reason that I could absolutely rule out that my grandfather and Lola's relationship was something more or that my grandfather and Lola enjoyed mutual time in Seattle. I even accepted that Lola may have been a close confidant who knew of his dual identity all along. This was beginning to sound like a move script.

In any event, I didn't see any further immediate evidence to be gleaned from Lola's letter and my mind was in a confused state, part tired, part overwhelmed, and maybe part inebriated, so I washed out my wine glass and ventured to bed, knowing I'd be up early to read the very words written by Alfred Victor Williams, himself.

# Alfred Victor Williams Speaks

**Tuesday, April 10, 1906, 1:06 p.m.  45°N40°W, Atlantic Ocean.**

*By this, his fifth day on the Victorian, Alfred is slowly finding a degree of comfort with this life change. He's decided to call himself, "Alf," believing it seems more mature, adult. For certain, he's already being exposed to the globe, with his fellow third-class travelers, mostly single men, coming from all parts of the world, including Sweden, Denmark and Australia. Of course there are many fellow Englishmen aboard the ship also. While there's no one else from Worcestershire, he's grown familiar with a few.  His roommates include Sam Sayers, at nineteen, a few years Alf's senior. Sam is a farmer from Sussex hoping to make his life in Canada, where he has heard farm acreage is available to any young man willing to work. The remaining two roommates in his four-bed space are George Cole, a 39-year-old farmer from Bedford, and John Wharram, a 26-year-old bricklayer from York, both pleasant enough but keeping their distance.*

*Last night's meal of soup, roasted pork, carrots, pudding and biscuits was excellent, and he enjoyed being waited on by the staff. Outside of meals, he remained largely in his room for the first few days but had spent time in the "General Room" the day prior and plans to visit again. He enjoys hearing his fellow travelers entertain on the piano, even if their amateur skills contrast with the first-class experience above.*

*Alf knows to try and enjoy the eight-day voyage though he looks upon his arrival in Canada with excitement and anticipation. His life is truly about to begin.*

H ow early I did rise the next morning is lost upon me. The boys being a little older, I was no longer sentenced to morning rounds of juice boxes, cartoon management, and constant supervision duties. Although, I do miss those days at times. Being that I was on summer holiday, it was likely sometime in the eight o'clock hour that I awoke, coffee being first on my mind.

Once settled at my desk, it was back to the letters. You may have discerned that the last chapter's contents fell short of the nineteen letters of which I claimed possession. In truth, I did scan all nineteen the day previous. However, I saved inspection of the potentially most intriguing letters until this second day.

I was staring down at four letters written in my grandfather's very own hand. I couldn't help but lament the date of the letters, spanning 1967 to 1968 and the fact that all were addressed to my dad. That's not to say the letters were void of value. At time of writing, I've possessed them for close to ten years and I continue to reread regularly, cherishing the intrusion in my own father's world as a young man and also delighted to hear the actual words of my grandfather.

I must remind, however, that while deeply personal for myself, this book is focused on uncovering my grandfather's missing years, which, at this point, spanned around 1910 to 1942. From this standpoint, my grandfather's words failed to present any proverbial "smoking gun," but they provide some insight into his character and a few interesting scraps which could prove useful in future.

The first letter dated February 21, 1967 is addressed to Donald Roy Williams, and features not one, but two, familiar addresses. Originally, the envelope is marked, "Donald Roy Williams, c/o McMillan Bloedel Lumber, Juskalta, Queen Charlotte Islands, B.C." I identify this as a logging camp my father worked in as a young man, calculating that he would have been nineteen years old at time of writing. The address, however, is crossed off, and written between margins is the destination, "3357 W. 4th, Vancouver, B.C.," my Oma's residence during this period. Almost fifty years later, my dad can only suggest that he was not in the logging camp at the time, and they were forwarding his mail to his permanent address, which he had given as his mother's apartment, though it never served as his primary residence for any extended period. This makes sense, as the additional address does not seem to be in my grandfather's unique script comprised of a combination of light, flowing cursive with intrusive block lettering.

Aside from the offering of some pocketbooks at the end of the letter, the entire page and a half is dedicated to a recent accident my grandfather suffered.

*I went outside to the shed to get fuel for the heater, and when I was coming back with a full pail of oil, the steps were so wet and slippery that when I had just reached the top step, I slipped and fell. I reached for the handrail, and I missed my footing. I fell to the bottom and my left forehead hit the concrete walk. I don't know how long I lay in all that rain, but when I came to, I was in a pool of blood.*

I picture a man whose body and awareness are beginning to fail him, his seventy-seven years already far surpassing his brothers, Charles and Dennis, as well as his mother and father.

Alfred continues his recounting.

*The cut was over my left eye right through the left eyebrow. Well, I didn't have it stitched because I thought it would leave a scar. I used some plastic tape and drew the scar together. I am still carrying an awful black eye. I do think I have been walking around and sleeping most of the time. I must have been in a coma. Since I fell, I found a letter yesterday in my old coat pocket. It was unopened and it was dated Feb 9, 1967. That must have been the day I fell.*

I pause to sympathize at the regrettable lack of aftercare Alfred is forced to self-administer. Possibly not uncommon, even today, amongst seniors, the absence of anyone to properly take care of an old man brings sadness.

The second letter, also addressed to my father residing at one of his logging camps is marked March 23, 1968, just over a year from the first. I can only imagine that there were correspondences and visits in between, but these are the letters I have. Again, my grandfather's health is featured prominently.

*I am sorry to have to write you such an unpleasant letter, but circumstances sometimes alter cases. I was in the Vancouver General Hospital as a patient a few days ago. But I kept begging them to let me go home, so they said it was up to me, so I went home. The last three days I have spent in bed. I was forced to get up today as I had no food in the house. Don, please don't let this worry you. It is just a case of a nervous disorder.*

It's unknown if the one-year gap between letters featured any other concerning medical instances; however, the pattern of a man whose body and mind are faltering becomes more concrete.

Next, my grandfather switches topics, making an extended plea for my father to come home. Alfred expresses doubt about my father's chosen vocation, stating, "your job is uncertain. First, too much snow, then shut down through a labor dispute. Then a fire hazard." He explains, "Don, the only real thing in life is happiness. I have invited you...to come to Vancouver and stay at my place, no rent to pay." I'm pleased to see my grandfather showing my father – whose upbringing was often fraught with difficulty and even neglect – such degree of love and concern. A part of me wonders if the offer is somewhat less altruistic, Alfred simply needing someone close by to offer care. Either way, I'm confident my grandfather yearns for his son's presence. Comforting, but offering little in the way of my mystery.

Next, my grandfather shares that he hasn't heard "anything so far of those pension checks...that went astray," and that he is "very lucky to have a friend like Mrs. Everett at the Marpole Hardware to lend [him] money, with no security." He continues that the loan is going to hurt him "badly at the end of next week." My sympathies continue to present as I picture not only poor physical and mental health, but also a concerning lack of financial security. While the missing cheques seem to account for a share of his woes, it still exposes a man living "paycheck to paycheck" as many of us are familiar. Later, my grandfather announces that Albert Widmer, a husband to one of my Oma's five sisters, whom Alfred seems to continue to be close to despite separating from the family almost twenty years' prior, "is talking about moving to Vancouver," in which case my grandfather would sell his house and "invest in an apartment block with" Albert.

Is it at all realistic to consider a seventy-eight-year-old man in poor physical and financial state to undertake a major investment project with the bulk of financial reward likely to materialize after his death?  While he may have been considering a legacy to my father and aunt, it seems more the product of a confused, aging mind.

While the real estate venture would never materialize, I consider if my grandfather may have done similar in his younger years, again remembering the strange trip to Seattle in which he seemed to return with the funding to purchase a house.  I can't ignore, however, the fact that any investment laden real estate holdings he may have been involved in did not include the final twenty years of his life.

My grandfather signs off this letter with a plea that my dad produce a certain key to a certain safety deposit box that my grandfather seems quite interested in possessing.  I consider what items and clues may have been in that box, as well as the timing of such request, suggesting my grandfather was becoming more aware of his mortality.

The third letter, post marked April 5, 1968 is sent roughly two weeks after the previous letter and it begins with a more serious tone.

> *I have written two consecutive letters to you.  I have asked you to tell me about a certain safe deposit box for which I think you have a key.  Don, I won't ask for you again to give me any information that you don't want to.  I only asked you to help me to be fair to you, since I have been in the hospital recently and I think it is only good judgement on my part to prepare a will in your favor in case I am not given too much warning.  After all, I am getting older every day.  Don, I don't know how to finish this letter.  You seem so indifferent lately, like you hate me.  Don, I only ask you to be honest with me and tell me if I have done anything to offend you.  Don, I am still your father and I love you and I always will.*

The text exposes a clear level of desperation. Alfred cannot know precisely that he has just shy of eight months to live, but he knows it's not long.

Introducing another common topic, Alfred shares, "Don, I have got a surprise for you. The Red Cross Society have located my younger brother, and they are trying to establish my identity, because there was an estate left and I have had difficulty in establishing my relationship with my brother who was too young to remember me." I read this with some irony, aware that Alfred's younger brother, Dennis, had passed some ten years prior and that the totality of the inheritance, the only one as far as I knew, had not included either Alfred or Dennis Williams as beneficiaries.

Alfred ends by hoping my father has "decency and respect to answer this letter," before a final note that he has "began saving money" with the "fatal date coming."

The final letter I possess, post-marked, April 22, 1968 or roughly two and a half weeks from the one prior, is void of acrimony, suggesting that my father may have in fact written a response. This opening, however, is no more positive than the previous, starting, "I don't' feel much like writing. I have had the blues for the past month I don't seem to be able to shake it." I note the continued decline in spirits.

The text soon switches to a positive note as Alfred reports, "Lola was up here about a week ago from Seattle." I mark that another visit to Vancouver so soon after her 1967 visit only seven months prior suggests it's likely that Lola is connected to Vancouver, rather than Alfred having close ties to Seattle. Is it possible that Alfred's 1947 visit was simply a call to Lola, perhaps even romantic in nature prior to him marrying my Oma?

Later, Alfred asks, "Don, how would you like to take a few days off at the end of this week? I will have some money then. If you think Toronto is too far, how about just going to Osoyoos." The mention of "Toronto" requires no explanation, exposing my grandfather's desire to return to visit his home most recently of twenty-five years ago. "Osoyoos," too, makes sense, serving as the home to Albert Widmer, the aforementioned brother-in-law. Later in the evening, my father would listen to my recital of these very lines, but it would fail to evoke any memories and he confirms any such trip failed to materialize.

My grandfather's suggestion turns part plea, as he continues, he would "consider [the trip] as an Xmas gift...or a birthday present," before asking once more to "think this trip to Osoyoos up," as he knows "we will enjoy it."

It comforts me to see a type of hope in my grandfather's mind, although the disappointment he may have suffered is unknown given this is the final letter I am privy to. My grandfather signs off in his consistent, usual matter, "I Remain – your Loving Father."

It would be fewer than six months later when my grandfather would find himself in hospital bed, biding time until his last, "fatal day."

# Enraptured in a Photograph

**Friday, April 13, 1906, 7:42 a.m. Saint John Harbor, Saint John, New Brunswick, Canada.**

*Retiring to his chamber the night prior, Alf accepted he'd wake the next morning on Canadian soil or close to at least. Some men vowed to stay awake for the monumental occasion the ship docked in Saint John Harbor. Alf is more practical than that and reasoned he would be wise to bank as many hours of sleep as possible.*

*Now morning, Alf once again finds himself beginning another stage of his journey. His bag packed, Alf bids farewell to George and John, where there is a brief shared excitement, even if he never really had the chance to know them. Along with Sam, whom he's grown fairly close to over the past week, Alf finds a spot in line with the other third-class travelers and makes his way to the Waterhouse Shed on Ramp #4. There, he shuffles to the second floor and enters the Department of Immigration and Colonization. The inviting staff is a welcome sight and a sign of things to come, Alf hopes. He continues to foster some trepidation about the risk he has taken. It is, however, a feeling mostly quelled by the excitement of things to come. The young women manning the desks appear fresh, a contrast to the weary, tired state Alf finds himself appearing this morning. Once through the initiation desk, Alf sits at a cubicle, ready to meet with the colonization agents from Canada Customs. Comfortable, with letter from his cousin in hand, Alf patiently follows procedure, answering questions about his family, his trade, and his immediate plans. In truth, it's the medical examination he's most concerned with, lice being the primary obstacle to immediate Canadian freedom.*

*One hour later, having successfully completed his lice check for the second time in the past eight days, Alf feels a welcomed sense of relief as he offers the contents of his bag for immigration officials before being given clearance to begin his new life. Waiting for Sam, the next stop is the CN Railway station also located in the Waterhouse Shed. There, he and his companion, both headed to Toronto, Ontario, purchase their rail passage. Again, Alf marvels both at how far he's come but also how far he has to go in making this new life for himself.*

I reveled in the personal details offered in the letters. Specifically, the words composed by my grandfather lent both a distinct personality and an intimate voice to my mystery. At the same time, I lamented the lack of any overt clues, again wondering if I'd ever bear witness to any of

Alfred's other letters which have the potential to expose far more than I had learned thus far. I took some perverse comfort in the fact that he likely didn't show his cards to any of the others either.

I also accepted that I'd likely exhausted any readily available clues, including first-hand information and recollections from my dad and aunt, as well as letters and possessions collected at my grandfather's time of death. At this point, we had all learned some new information about my grandfather and I was comfortable I had emerged as something of the family expert, a self-imposed title that reflected the data I had gathered void of any personal relationship previously experienced by my father and aunt.

Still, my grandfather's years from 1910 to 1942 – age twenty to fifty-two – remained unknown.

As the calendar turned to September 2015, I took stock of my findings, creating a sort of comprehensive timeline that included both dates and extended information where possible. I couldn't be entirely sure of all the information but decided to allow some temporary trust to many of the details provided by my grandfather. This troubled me some as I found it a little unsettling to be basing my research direction on the words provided by a man who purported to live a secret identity for the bulk of his life, but I saw little alternative and figured I could attempt to verify all information point by point in future. Here is what I had:

1889 – Alfred born in Bewdley, Worcestershire, Eng.
1906 – Alfred (16) resides with Turleys in Toronto, Ont.
1910 – Alfred (20) becomes "Roy Hammond" living in U.S.
1942 – Alfred (52) returns to Turleys in Toronto, Ont.
1944 – Alfred (54) married to "Clara" in Edmonton, Alta.
1947 – Alfred (57) moves to Vancouver, B.C.
1968 – Alfred (78) passes away in Vancouver, B.C.

While the timeline may appear substantive, the years between 1910 to 1942 remain woefully unaccounted. At the risk of over-stating the obvious, this unknown period could easily be considered the prime of a man's life. It's during these years that a male could be expected to take a wife, raise children, establish a career, attract life-long friends and possibly even become a grandfather. Now, I couldn't rule out the possibility that my grandfather had done all those things. I couldn't include any details into his timeline either.

I remind myself again of the old adage, "each failed attempt is one step closer to a solution." Sadly, I couldn't say I had ruled out many possible solutions to the mystery. My suspicions included that he had raised a family and abandoned them, which would not directly explain why he estranged himself from his U.K. family; he had been incarcerated for an extended time, which would explain why he estranged himself from his U.K. family; or the less glamorous, but increasingly plausible theory that he was simply leading an uneventful life, family estrangement an unfortunate byproduct of both the times and the Williams family dynamic.

The foremost clues, or curiosities, I was pursuing included the elusive "Clara," who failed to appear in any online directories or documents; the quick and timely jaunt to Seattle, possibly in preparation for a real estate purchase and crack at domesticity; and the very formal school photo showing an unfamiliar face marked with the familiar tag, "Donald Roy Williams." I must also include the unusual alias, "Roy Hammond" as a leading point of interest.

I found that the scope of the mystery was altering in a subtle way. I tried to remain focused and remind myself that I had only a single goal: I wanted to account for my grandfather between the years 1910 to 1942. Now, I was unsure if that was enough. I wanted to know who exactly "Clara" was, even if she only appeared in my grandfather's life for a short period. I wanted to understand the Seattle trip and how it seemingly led to the purchase of his home. I wanted to account for the mysterious picture marked "My Son, Donald

Roy Williams," which was not my own father. And, yes, I desperately wanted to discover why Alfred Victor Williams became Roy Hammond.

Any answers I discovered from this point forward were going to have to originate through outside research, which mainly meant the Internet. So far, I have attempted to share my steps and discoveries in a controlled, organized process, in which I slowly, but systematically added facts and details. In truth, my work on this project was anything but controlled and organized. In the evenings, I'd grab a Fat Tug IPA and sneak upstairs to steal one or two hours perusing various online sources, searching any name or location that caught my whimsy. During lunch breaks at work, I'd find myself going down the rabbit hole concerning a third cousin whom I felt was interesting for some reason. The cell phone, too, provided me a number of random opportunities to lookup names whenever I was waiting in a doctor's office, watching one of the boys' lacrosse practices, or sometimes even while out for a meal with Lana.

Further to that, I wasted a heck of a lot of time. Genealogy books suggest a notebook or even software program to record names, dates, and relationships. It seemed that I favored single sheets of letter-sized office paper, which, more often than not, failed to properly land in the organized file folders I had prepared in an unused drawer at the bottom of our filing cabinet. This poor system of record-keeping could result in frustration at times, as I'd spend up to an hour looking for a name or date that I knew I had discovered prior.

Also, I was cognizant that my project lacked a clear direction of attack. One day, I'd reason that a deep dive into the Williams family prior to 1889 was necessary. For example, I'd discovered the possibility that one of Alfred's aunts, Mary Ann Williams, had immigrated to New York in the late 1800s. Was it not possible that if Alfred was in New York in 1910 that he may have sought temporary refuge in her home while setting up in a new city? I would need to go back

113

and learn all I could about her time in England before she ventured overseas. In another case, I was able to follow Alfred's maternal grandmother, Matilda Perry, to Boston in the early 1900s, not too far from New York. Would the two not have enjoyed an overseas reunion? That prompted me to spend hours researching information about Matilda that could possibly expose information about my grandfather.

While the situations described above could be interesting, there was a nagging voice in the back of my head reminding me that my mystery now spanned from 1910 to 1942 and that efforts to learn information prior, or after, those dates were fruitless and unlikely to yield any discovery. What resulted was an overall cloud consisting of an ever-present amused frustration. Overall, I couldn't deny, however, that I was enjoying my work on the project – most of the time, anyway. In this sort of constant roundabout of study, I had managed to make some progress, even if it was slow.

I've mentioned *Ancestry.com* several times thus far, and my membership to the website was truly instrumental in most that I'd discovered. At this point, I'd built a decent Williams family tree consisting of approximately two-hundred and fifty names. Additionally, I found a website called *FreeBMD.com* to be quite useful. The "BMD" stood for birth, marriage, death, and contained documents for all of England from the 1800s to late 1900s. Also, there was *Familysearch.com* maintained by the Jesus Christ Church of Latter-Day Saints. I had also built a family tree on their site and found the webpage quite useful, printing off several documents related to the Williams.

I can compare my experiences using these various sites to digging through a basement storage room for an old coat. One day you may throw your hands up in frustration, unable to locate the item that you were certain you packed in the green bin. A week later, you check the same green bin only to discover the three-quarter length, wool peacoat you're certain was not in there six days ago. My Internet research was like

*My father claims that romance alone could not account for my grandparents marrying in a foreign country.*

that. One day I'd search an item and come up empty; the next week, I'd enter what I believed was the same search data, only to find a match.

It was on one such day, that I discovered a marriage certificate for my grandfather and Oma. The "Certificate of Marriage" written in impressive, bold, black calligraphy featuring an image of a ring encircling some type of flower was on bronze-colored, letter-sized paper, bordered by a complicated pattern of what seem to be stems from a flower.

*This is to certify that the undersigned, a Justice of the Peace by authority of a license bearing date the 21st day of July A.D. 1947 and issued by the County Auditor of the County of King, did on the 22nd day of July A.D. 1947...join in eternal lawful wedlock Alfred V. Williams of Vancouver, State of B.C. and Elizabeth Zelbel of Vancouver, State of B.C.*

Looking over the certificate, I calculated July 22 to be approximately seven months and two weeks prior to my father's birth. The fact that my Oma was pregnant is hardly a surprise both in 1947 and today. Of more interest was the subtitle, also displayed in bold, black lettering: "State of Washington, County of King." Seattle. Immediately, I scrambled to locate the unusual letter Alfred had procured from his bank manager. Scanning the text, my inkling is confirmed, the letter bearing the date, July 21, 1947. It seems Alfred had begun the morning at the Bank of Montreal, Homer and Hastings Branch in Vancouver, only to complete the three-hour car ride to Seattle in time to procure a marriage license in anticipation of the next day where he married my Oma. The specific text of the letter stated Alfred "is planning a visit to Seattle, Washington for a period of ten days to two weeks, at the expiry of which time he will be returning to his permanent home in Vancouver, B.C."

My immediate thought was that Alfred must have already been married in Canada after all, the obvious candidate being Clara, identified as spouse in both old age security application and personal letter circa 1944 to 1946. However, the fact that my dad had already completed unsuccessful, formal, government-agency marriage searches in both Alberta and Ontario during those time periods suggested the union between Alfred and Clara was most likely "common-law." I entertained the possibility that Alfred had been married in Canada prior to the 1940s, possibly in Toronto prior to 1910, which – if unhappy – could account for his fleeing to the United States and adopting an assumed name.

Another possibility was less nefarious. If, as suggested through his connection to Lola, Alfred had called Seattle "home" in previous years, is it not possible that he simply desired to be married in a familiar place surrounded by the loving support of life-long friends? An opportunity to show off his new, younger bride, so to speak? If Seattle was, in fact, his U.S. home, he had lived away for at least the previous five years, but that time doesn't seem too extreme for a reunion. The period of "ten days to two weeks" seemed to constitute a type of honeymoon, an opportunity to celebrate. I even imagined for a brief second that he may have had kids in

Seattle he wished to bear witness to the union. I quickly determined that was too fantastical. The phrase, "mixing business with pleasure" comes to mind as I again consider that he may have sold property or tied up other loose ends that would have allowed him to purchase his Yale Street house for $3600 just over three weeks later.

There were problems with my neat, idealistic theory. If he was known as "Roy Hammond" in the U.S., how would he explain the name change to Alfred Victor Williams? Also, when asked if a two-week, romantic getaway combination honeymoon was in my grandfather's nature, my father's response was immediate and to-the-point: "No."

Sharing their nuptials in the U.S. also suggested that my grandfather may not have been married in that country previously, which was somewhat surprising, given that he was supposed to have lived there from age twenty to fifty-two. Also, it seemed to rule out that Clara may have been from the U.S., a direction I had continued to search, in hopes that it could lead to Alfred's American whereabouts. I needed to accept, however, that marrying under the name, "Roy Hammond," would have made my grandfather's 1947 marriage under his actual name nonproblematic. Also, who's to say Clara didn't know him as both "Roy" and "Alfred?" The possibilities where just too vast to draw any conclusion.

Next, I briefly celebrated the discovery of a long-form death certificate. The 1968 "Province of British Columbia, Registration of Death," contained interesting vital information. To begin, it put his time in Canada to be twenty-three years, the last twenty-two being in Vancouver. This would have placed his return to Toronto to be in 1945, three years after his actual 1942 arrival. Also, Alfred had indicated his Vancouver arrival to be 1947, whereas the death certificate indicated 1943. Both the date and location of birth matched what I'd discovered. As well, his mother and father's names were consistent with what I had. One notable difference was Alfred's mother's birthplace listed as "Ireland," which was at odds with information indicated in the England census reports I'd found, as well as data gleaned from *FreeBMD.com*. I did take note though, as it matched the family lore I reported at the start of the book. Lastly, his listed occupation of "salesman: jewelry" bore familiarity. Thankfully, prior to contemplating this both confirming and contradictory information for too long, I took note of the "signature on informant," D.R. Williams. My twenty-year-old dad had simply provided the information he thought to be true. He did a pretty good job.

The document also contained some interesting medical information which was provided by a doctor, of course, rather than my father. I learned that Alfred's death was as a direct result of senility from which he'd suffered for one year. I thought of his 1967 and 1968 letters illustrating a man whose mental health seemed to be consistently deteriorating. An antecedent cause of death was repeated cerebral thrombosis attacks, from which he'd suffered the past two years, likely causing the vicious fall he suffered on his doorstep as outlined in a letter to my father. A third condition, listed as "contributing to death" was arteriosclerosis, heart disease from which he'd suffered for "years." I accepted this information with interest, although, to my laypersons understanding, it seemed a catchphrase for "old age."

I was contacted around this time by my Aunt Shirley who had found my grandfather's wallet, or rather a wallet of sorts. It was a wine-colored, flimsy, plastic card holder embossed in gold letters reading, "with the compliments of 'PEMBERTONS' MU 2-311." Whether it was to be judged as a cheap giveaway novelty item or a classy accessory is beyond my scope. Its contents though, were of note. I studied Alfred's 1960 driver's license. My father was confused that he was required to wear corrective lenses when driving, as he couldn't place his father with a pair of glasses at any point. Also, there was a Social Insurance Number card, bearing his unique number as well as his now familiar signature. There was a

**PROVINCE OF BRITISH COLUMBIA**
DEPARTMENT OF HEALTH SERVICES AND HOSPITAL INSURANCE
DIVISION OF VITAL STATISTICS
**REGISTRATION OF DEATH**

Reg. No. (Office use only)

68-09-014789

1. PLACE OF DEATH
Name of city, village, town, district municipality or place ... VANCOUVER, B.C.
(If outside city or municipal limits add "Rural")
Street or road ... VANCOUVER GENERAL HOSPITAL
(If death occurred in a hospital or institution, give the name instead of street and number) House No.

2. LENGTH OF STAY
(In years, months and days)
In Municipality where death occurred: 22 years
In Province: 22 years
In Canada (if immigrant): 23 years.

3. PRINT FULL NAME OF DECEASED ... WILLIAMS, Alfred Victor.
(Surname) (All given or Christian names in full)

4. PERMANENT RESIDENCE OF DECEASED
Name of city, village, town, district municipality or place ... VANCOUVER, B.C.
(If outside city or municipal limits add "Rural")
Street or road ... HUDSON STREET House No. 8168.

5. SEX: MALE
6. CITIZENSHIP (See marginal note): CANADIAN
7. RACIAL ORIGIN (See marginal note): WHITE
8. Single, Married, Widowed or Divorced (Write the word): MARRIED.
9. BIRTHPLACE (City or Place and Province or Country) England
County of Dorchester

10. Date of Birth: NOVEMBER 23rd 1889
(Month by name) (Date) (Year)
11. AGE (Last Birthday): 78 years.
YEARS / MONTHS / DAYS / HOURS / MIN.

OCCUPATION
12. (a) Trade, profession or kind of work as logger, fisherman, office clerk, etc. ... SALESMAN.
(b) Kind of industry or business, as logging, fishing, bank, etc. ... JEWELLERY.
(If labourer specify kind of work above) (If Housewife in own home answer "At Home")
13. Date deceased last worked at this occupation: 1962
14. Total years spent in this occupation: 22 years.

15. If married, widowed or divorced give name of husband or maiden name of wife of deceased ... ZEBEL ELIZABETH.

16. Name of father ... WILLIAMS, ALFRED
(Surname) (All given or Christian names)
17. Maiden name of mother ... CRANE EMILY
(Surname) (All given or Christian names)
18. Birthplace — Father: ENGLAND. Mother: IRELAND.

*My grandfather's 1968 death certificate solves the Ireland mystery, until I learn the identity of the informant.*

"Senior Citizens Association of British Columbia" card that reminded of regular meetings on the first and third Tuesday of each month. Next were various employment cards for the *Vancouver Sun, The Vancouver News Herald,* and National Albums Incorporated. The two newspapers were familiar to me. I was much more interested in the latter employee I.D. card.

The "Beverly Hills" location indicated on my grandfather's National Albums Incorporated business card created some excitement before I reasoned it was simply the address of a home office, likely designed to impress. My grandfather was listed as an "authorized representative," but the date, partially undecipherable, seemed to read nineteen-sixty-something, so both my father and aunt were able to rule out a California trip. My curiosity was now piqued, however, and I looked up this National Albums Incorporated.

What I found was a 1961 "Federal Register" produced by "The National Archives of the United States." The twenty-four-page report outlined various United States business practices that warranted concern. Under "Part 13 – Prohibited Business Practices," it charged National Albums Incorporated with "misrepresenting oneself and goods," accusing representatives of calling "upon mothers of newborn children" and "making such false representations as that persons solicited were specially selected [and] were to receive free a photograph album worth $49.95 and up and that the value of the album and photographs provided by the certificate was approximately $165.85." Reading further, it seems that salesmen were approaching random new mothers, explaining their baby would be perfect for an album of newborns the company was producing. If the mothers agreed to visit their private studio and pay for a photo session, they would be provided a copy of the finished album, free of charge. The misrepresentation would either be the failure to produce said album or the overall quality being so poor as not to justify the price of the photo session. At what time or to what degree my grandfather was aware of the unethical aspect of the trade is uncertain.

Discounting credit and debit cards, which were not used in the 1960s, the contents of Alfred's wallet were not so different from what I hold in my own black, leather wallet today: two or three pieces of basic identification, a driver's license and a social insurance card. In addition to those staples, I proudly carry four separate grade school photos of my boys, each sporting a blue polo and wearing proud smiles, hair freshly styled. Even in this case, Alfred's wallet may contain similar.

It's a black and white, three-inch by two-inch, photo, featuring a thick white border limiting the size of the actual image. There are several creases, not quite folds, that interrupt the clarity of the subjects. In the background we see the bright sun peeking through full length curtains featuring watercolors of ornate rose bulbs and long stems. Along the right border sits a lamp, the black cord dangling behind a table. From the design of the curtain, as well as the fact that it's an electric lamp, and the style of the subjects' hair and dress, I've been told the photograph is likely 1940s. Facing the camera with bright smiles, arms around each other's backs, the two girls, sisters possibly, look to be about three and five respectively.

Are these Alfred's children?

# PART II – VOICES IN TIME
## (2015-2022)

# Connecting with Linda Turley

**Saturday, April 14, 1906, 11:14 a.m.    Union Station (Bay Street & York Steet), Toronto, Ontario, Canada.**

*It's been a busy week and a half for Alfred, who is now feeling much older than his sixteen years. It was only nine days ago that he left his parents' home in Kidderminster, but he feels he's aged a year. His journey is finally over, as he stands in Union Station, bound by Bay and York Streets in downtown Toronto. Briefly resting his bag at his tired feet, he scans the crowd for his cousin.*

*A little shorter than Alfred, William shouts out to his younger cousin before greeting with an enthusiastic hug. William takes a minute to admire Alfred's suit, even if it is worn and fatigued from his international journey. Allowing Alfred to carry his own bag, William directs Alfred to the nearby streetcar, before entering the final stage of his long journey. Once in the car, the two settle into conversation, or rather, Alfred listens to William boast of his immediate successes in this new country, making sure to imply he's found the time and opportunity to make a few clandestine female acquaintances also.*

*Alfred is not the first border, as William and his wife Louisa have taken in several young boxers hoping to fight their way to success in this new world. Expectation does sit uneasily on Alfred's mind, however. His cousin has not asked if Alfred intends to box, but Alfred hasn't shared his tentativeness either. He hopes the topic simply won't come up.*

*In any case, he's arrived in Canada and is ready for his new life.*

W ith the bright smiles of the young girls clear in my mind, I allow myself to indulge the wild possibilities of their identities. The girls could very well be Alfred's children. Why else would a man carry a photo in his wallet for what could have been twenty years or more. There were now clues that Alfred may have had three children prior to my father, the younger, "Donald Roy Williams," making it a trio. On the other hand, in our original look into Aunt Shirley's box, we had also found photos of relatives from England – Charles, Dennis, Uncle George – that would have accompanied their letters. I remember too, Charles commenting on a photo that Alfred sent of himself. The two girls could very well be nieces or grandnieces of a relative in the U.K. A look at my family tree doesn't present any obvious options.

The wallet was a nice surprise, but barring any additional discoveries, I was confident that I'd exhausted all possessions

*For what other reason would my grandfather carry this photo in his wallet?*

and letters. I would continue with Internet searches, getting good use from Ancestry and Family Search memberships and regularly taking advantage of other online resources. More often than not, however, my research time was proving unfruitful, small discoveries appearing with less frequency, minimizing my confidence in discovering the missing years presently narrowed from 1910 to 1942.

As 2015 marched on, I decided to change my focus. I was determined to track down some of the characters who had presented themselves in this intriguing drama. Given the advanced age that my grandfather became parent to my dad and his corresponding 1968 death, I had the disadvantage that aside from my father and aunt, there really was no one left who would have known my grandfather. Any peers closely acquainted with him were long dead. That doesn't mean I would attempt to commission burial extraction for my Great

Uncle Charles or the unknown Lola LeDuke. Rather, I would use what I had in an effort to contact their children or, more likely, grandchildren.

Some of the individuals involved, mainly those in the U.K., would be relatively close family members. It's possible that I'd be able to find second or third cousins. Doing the math, I considered that connecting with a first cousin to my father, a child of either Charles Williams or Dennis Williams, was also not inconceivable. Would they be able to assist with my mystery? Possibly not. Yet, I also considered that I had come to possess nineteen letters and a collection of other possessions my grandfather had left almost fifty years prior. I had to entertain that there may be one like me out there in that big land overseas. It was possible that someone else cherished, or at least possessed, letters and other trinkets from their late grandparents. Is it so far-fetched that Charles or Uncle George's offspring would have passed down some boxes? Is it impossible to consider that my grandfather's letters outlining his travels and adventures could be included in any such collection? Additionally, if I was able to successfully make contact with any family in England it would satisfy on a personal level, a reconnection of sorts. Maybe there would be more to my little project than simply nosing in my grandfather's personal business.

The value of tracking down other characters may not have been so obvious. It's possible that children or grandchildren of Lola LeDuke or Clara may actually qualify as very close family if my grandfather did procreate with either. Alternatively, if not related through blood, these people connected with my grandfather somehow. Maybe learning about their lives would point me in directions I would otherwise have not considered. For example, while I suspected my grandfather met Lola in Vancouver, it was still possible they had connected in some other location years prior. Wouldn't that be a clue!

Through one of the forgotten genealogical titles I had checked out from the Maple Ridge Public Library, I was carrying the idea that it's best to start with those closest. I determined the curious William Turley would be as good an option as any. According to what I knew, he may have been closer to my grandfather than anyone. With their respective mothers, Emily and Agnes Crane, being sisters, Alfred and William were first cousins, William about seven years the older. Their relationship began in Worcester, England prior to the turn of the twentieth century, continuing to a cohabitation in Canada in the early 1900s, before a 1940s reunion, in which Alfred turned to William for assistance. As well, from his 1942 affidavit, it seems that William had some knowledge of Alfred's time in the U.S. and his mysterious alias as well.

From my work on *Ancestry.com*, I had learned a little about William Turley. While I've chosen to present that information more or less chronologically for your convenience, my own learning was much less organized. William immigrated to North America in 1905, at twenty-three, already married to his Worcestershire bride, Louisa Maria Sanders, and raising a son, Frederick William Turley. Three daughters would arrive in quick succession: Winnifred Agnes, born in 1907, would survive scarcely a year. She was followed by Gladys May Turley in 1908 and Elsie Edna Turley in 1911. The family would not be fully complete until the arrival of William Alderson Turley in 1918.

I remember William's declaration. "In the year 1906 the said Alfred Victor Williams came to Canada and lived with me on Portland Street, Toronto." A look in the Toronto phone book corroborates William, placing him at 140 Portland St, Etobicoke, Ontario. While there is no listing for Alfred, Alf, Al or Fred Williams in 1906 or 1907, I do find a 1908 entry for "Williams, Fred, wks Toronto Fire Brick Co, h Melrose." While there is no street number given on Melrose, Google Maps informs me that the street is no more than a six-minute

**The one and only William Turley, first cousin and possibly much more to my grandfather.**

walk to the Turley house on Portland Street. The name, vicinity, as well as the occupation suit my grandfather so I'm confident of the match. I rejoice in the small victory that even though my study of William has just begun, it has already helped me confidently place my grandfather in 1908.

With Alfred only eighteen in 1908 and now on his own, it seems to support William's account that shortly after Alfred's 1906 arrival, William "returned to England with [his] family, where [he] remained for some considerable time." This is at odds with the fact that William's daughters, Winnifred, Gladys, and Elsie were born in Canada, 1907, 1908, and 1911 respectively. What could account for the discrepancy? I do find a 1910 immigration document in which the Turley family, father, mother and three children return to Toronto from England, so a visit between 1908 and 1910 likely occurred. This lends credence to William's account; although I am not sure that two years constitutes "some considerable time." As there is no listing for a Fred Williams in the 1909 and 1910 Toronto phone directories, I reason that my grandfather may have ventured south by the time the Turleys had returned to Toronto. Of course, this matches the 1910 census report putting an Alfred Williams in New York.

I learn that in 1911, William brought over his parents, George Turley and Agnes (Crane) Turley. The couple, Alfred's uncle and aunt, would remain in Toronto until their deaths in 1943 and 1946 respectively. Their Toronto home, at 351 Ashdale Avenue, would be the address that Alfred boards when he eventually returns to Toronto in 1942.

In 1914, William jumps between Toronto and the nearby city of Montreal to begin a sports journalism career, cut short by his enlistment in September of that year. His time oversees is also cut short, with William returning to Toronto in December 1915 due to an eye injury. Through newspaper articles, I learn that William's commitment to battle did not stop there. A February 7, 1916, article explains that a local Toronto boxing club arranged a benefit for William, as he had served as head instructor there for some time. During the benefit, "the news came that the parliament buildings at Ottawa had been blown up by the Germans." Hearing the news, "Srget. Turley tore off his [protective] smoked glasses and declared with emphasis that if the powers above would restore his sight he would go back tomorrow and fight the 'unspeakable Hun.'" The article further quotes him exclaiming, "I have done my little bit...I have a brother in the trenches now, and yesterday my dear old Dad put on the king's uniform." His speech effective, the story adds that "thirty-three lads climbed right out of their seats and enlisted then and there."

A later check suggests that the damage was due to a fire – began innocently enough – in the reading room. However, I guess the erroneous account of a German bombing certainly makes for a better tale.

I am both bemused and even bewildered at the conflicting nature of the next article I uncover. The September 16,1919 article in the *North Bay Nugget* is titled, "William Turley Gets Hot Reception at Veterans Meeting." At this time, William is serving as Provincial Secretary of the Great War Veterans Association (G.W.V.A.). Apparently, during a meeting, Turley is "branded as a traitor to the returned men, hooted, jeered, mocked and taunted, and finally driven by a mob of several hundred men and girls." The article continues that "Turley left the platform, being pursued until he made his escape by boarding a streetcar." Naturally, I wonder what William could have done to amass such extreme vitriol. I'm unable to find any more articles on the subject, making note that, if nothing else, William Turley must have been quite the character.

My interest is piqued when I discover a strange trip that William made on December 24, 1916. Given that it was Christmas Eve, and William must have been tasked with some preparation for his young family, one would think only a trip of dear import would be undertaken. Thus, my surprise at discovering that on the morning December 24, 1916, William Turley, by all accounts travelling alone, crosses the nearby Canada/ Unites States border, his intended destination, LeRoy, New York. Given the fact that Christmas is the next day, and LeRoy is a mere seventy miles from Toronto, I assume that it's a day trip only, possibly even no more than a few hours.

A quick search tells me that LeRoy is a small town located in the northwest of the state of New York in Genese County. Largely nondescript, their claim to fame is the invention of the ever-popular Jell-O gelatin desert that we all grew up on.

It's entirely possibly the trip is nothing more than a quick business transaction. William's profession at that point unknown, he could merely have been making a sort of pickup or delivery. However, I have my "Alfred Victor Williams" glasses on and must consider the trip could be much more, the obvious being a quick holiday greeting to his former housemate and cousin.

Exactly the type of lead I was hoping for, I furiously search *Ancestry.com*, studying records of phone books, border crossings, employment records, anything that could place an "Alfred Victor Williams," or "Roy Hammond," in little LeRoy,

New York. Uncertain when my grandfather may have adopted the "Roy Hammond" moniker I begin with his given name.

Aware that phone book documentation, and really all documentation, is only as accurate as the hourly-paid overworked representative transcribing the information, I immediately find several listings that seem close enough matches for an Alfred Williams near LeRoy. One by one, comprising short periods of five to fifteen minutes, I am able to eliminate prospective candidates by virtue of tracking their existences, usually finding a death certificate reading a date in the 1940s, or 1950s, or 1960s. After some time, cross-referencing names, addresses and dates, I find one particular "Alfred A. Williams" of nearby Rochester, New York, who holds some temporary promise. In this case, it is only after a few more hours of research that I am able to rule out, finally locating him in the state of New York beyond 1942. A moment of bitter frustration ensues. A search for Roy Hammond, living in LeRoy, New York during the years around 1916 brings up far fewer prospective matches and yields no positive results.

In 1921, William is cohabiting with his wife, four children, mother and father at 667 Carlow Avenue in Toronto. Despite his unfortunate and dramatic escape from a regular meeting two years prior, he is still dutifully serving as secretary of the G.W.V.A.

By 1923, he begins to stretch his legs a little. I find a January 1923 border document that has William crossing from Port Huron, Michigan. Travelling with Gladys, fourteen, and William, four, he lists his final destination as a visit to his elder son, Fred, almost nineteen years of age and residing in Denver, Colorado, likely with William's sister, Minnie. It is in Colorado that William files for divorce from Louisa.

Some five years later, I track William, a now forty-five-year-old newspaper editor marking Chicago, Illinois his home, renouncing British citizenship, expressing his written desire to "become a citizen of the United States of America and to permanently reside therein: So Help Me God." Not totally sure what role God plays in William's life, I learn that the man jumped back and forth between the U.S. and Canada for the next few years, before returning to Toronto for his final act in the early 1940s, just in time to welcome his first cousin, Alfred Victor Williams, back to the land of the north.

My working theory being that Alfred and William may have connected in the United States, I immediately make it my focus to run searches for Colorado and Chicago. Their connection could have been personal or business. I had documented two occasions, 1906 and 1942, in which Alfred had entered a new country, Canada, and retreated to the Turley family for shelter. It only made sense that he may have done the same when traveling to a new area in the U.S. Reflecting on the 1942 affidavit, my theory doesn't quite fit William's statement that "this man, I am convinced, is my first cousin, whom I knew early in life." If William and Alfred did connect in the U.S. in the years preceding 1942, the phrases, "I am convinced," and "knew early in life," wouldn't apply. My sixth sense told me I couldn't rule out that both Alfred and William were capable of some level of trickery, deception, or just being rascals, so I deemed further Internet searches necessary.

My experience was similar to the results from LeRoy, New York. Back on *Ancestry.com*, I entered both names, "Alfred Victor Williams" and "Roy Hammond" at separate times. Initially faced with thousands of matches, none particularly appealing, I used their "filter" options to narrow my search to Colorado between the years 1921 and 1925, and Illinois, between the years 1923 and 1932. I felt the five-year window in each place provided ample opportunity to connect with William Turley and establish a presence in a phone book, employment record, or even the 1920 or 1930 U.S census reports. Still faced with an overwhelming number of results, again none of particular interest, I went back to the filter option and specified "England" for birth.

With these harsh filtering options, I am left with one corresponding "Alfred Williams." I discover Mr. Williams in 1926 living in a home for Disabled Volunteer Soldiers in Danville, Illinois. He is five foot eight and a half, married and working as a painter. He's also African American. I have even less fortune looking for "Roy Hammond" under the same conditions.

I find a rather brief obituary in the January 1, 1954 issue of the *Ottawa Journal*. "William Turley, bantam boxing champion of Canada in 1907-08." The absence of his parents and children, not to mention his military contribution and various careers is noteworthy.

At this time, another instance of what was becoming a pleasant, semi-usual phenomena occurred. Again, I reflected that no matter how much time I spent on *Ancestry.com* and websites researching a family name, I'd manage to strike-gold at the most unlikely times. Again, it may be attributed to inconsistent search-fields or a general lack of care for details, but despite looking up the name "William Turley" what seemed like dozens of times over the past few months, for whatever reason, on one particular cloudy November afternoon, I came across what I hoped could be a grand discovery: another Ancestry member had constructed a family tree listing the name, "William Turley."

Now, during my relatively short time conducting research of this type, I had learned that finding a family tree didn't necessarily result in any useful discoveries or connections. Often, the person I was interested in was one of over a thousand entries. If the owner of the tree did bother to respond to my enquiry, it was just as likely to be a polite, albeit useless comment, such as John Smith "was my great-aunt's second husband. He died in 1906. Unfortunately, I don't know anything about him. Sorry." It's fair to say, my enthusiasm was tempered.

The so named, "Turley Family Tree" I'd discovered, held some reason for optimism. To begin, the title listed the surname, "Turley," suggesting it was William Turley's immediate family members who were the focus, not some distant third cousin or great, great nephew. Additionally, there existed only around two-hundred and fifty people in the tree, which increased the odds someone might know something of William. Lastly, I appreciated the fact William appeared closer to the bottom of the tree, suggesting that any living relative would not be too far removed.

Bruce Wilson from Brooklin, Ontario identified himself as "60+" reporting that he was "active" on the site and "willing to help" others with their research. On November 18, 2015 I contacted Mr. Wilson with the following:

*I was delighted to see your work on the Turley family tree. William Turley (1882-1954) was my grandfather's (Alfred Victor Williams, 1889-1968) first cousin. My grandfather's mother was Emily Crane, sister to Agnes Crane, William Turley's mother. In fact, my grandfather lived with William Turley in 1906 on Portland Street, Toronto, Ont. I also have some legal documents signed by William Turley in 1942, verifying the identity of my grandfather. Currently, I am researching my grandfather's very mysterious life. I am wondering if you have any information that you could share regarding William Turley's time in Ontario. Thank you very much.*

It was two days later on November 20 that I received Mr. Wilson's reply. "I completed the tree for a friend, Linda Kenney, who is a neighbor. I just spoke to her, and she is willing to share information as William Turley was her grandfather." The message included an email address for Ms. Kenney. With that, on Monday, November 21, I put the correspondence into action:

*Dear Ms. Kenney: I was delighted to see Bruce Wilson's "Turley Family Tree" on the Ancestry website, and I appreciate you allowing me to contact you. My mother, father, and I have been researching my family and specifically my grandfather for some time. Our family tree is on Ancestry.com under the title of "Williams Family Tree" if you are interested.*

*Your grandfather (William Turley) and my grandfather (Alfred Victor Williams) were first cousins. William Turley's mother was Agnes Crane; Alfred Victor Williams' mother was Emily Crane (sisters). I think that makes us 3rd cousins, but...I could be mistaken!*

*I have some information suggesting that our grandfathers were pretty close: (a) they were around the same age and both from the Kidderminster area, (b) according to a legal document I have attached they lived together on Portland Street, Toronto, Ont. in 1906, (c) according to family letters, in 1942 Alfred lists his address as 351 Ashdale Avenue, Toronto, Ont., which I have seen William Turley list as his address.*

*Alfred left Ontario for good in 1945, eventually settling in British Columbia where he began a family late in life. Before 1942 he led a very mysterious life, so his connection with your grandfather, William Turley - who seems like a very special man - has been very interesting to us!*

*I am a 44-year-old teacher and father of four living in British Columbia. My mother (65) and father (68) live close by and are also very interested in the family. I look forward to hearing from you. Thank you very much. Sincerely, Ron Williams*

There exists a three-hour time difference between my home on the west coast and Ms. Kenney's home in the east. Thus, when I awoke the next morning, I was delighted to see that there was already a response waiting. Rising early, I shuffled down the stairs and made my way to the kitchen where I turned on one dim light. Having set the timer the evening before, I poured a cup of black coffee, found a spot at the kitchen counter and pored over the message.

*I am William's granddaughter. My father, Frederick William Turley, was his eldest son. William had four children, my father, Elsie Bradbury, (who married an east coast man and lived on Cape Breton Island), Gladys Michell (a very accomplished artist of children's books, who married and lived in Chicago) and William Jr. who was killed overseas in 1945. I am seventy years "young" and have four older brothers, three of whom are still alive. The oldest, Ronald William Turley, aged eighty-six, moved to Laurel, Maryland. The second, Frederick Arthur, aged eight-four, lives in Halifax, Nova Scotia. The third, Albert Roy, aged eighty-two, lives in Melbourne, Australia. Sadly, my youngest brother passed away three years ago.*

While I had suspected that Ms. Kenney was a grandchild, this confirmation gives me chills. To have actually made contact with someone, on the other side of the country, who has a connection to both my family and my mystery seemed surreal and intoxicating. I make note to look up the name, "Gladys Mitchell." Excited, my eyes naturally rush further down the letter where I spot the words "William Turley," and "Kidderminster."

*Now about William Turley. He was an extraordinary man. You are right about Kidderminster. He was a golden gloves boxer who brought his boxing career with him when he immigrated to Toronto. In the early 1900's he had many bouts at the Massey Hall, which still stands in Toronto today. My brothers recall vividly many young boxers coming over from England that my grandfather would sponsor. Jokingly, my brothers would name them "canvasback" because many of them were soundly beaten. He married Louisa Maria but after having four children, divorced, taking the two youngest, Gladys and*

*William, with him to Chicago for a time. My father and Elsie remained in Toronto with their mother. I know that he was a notary public and had his office on Ashdale Avenue, which was his home. After returning from World War I, he helped to start the Canadian Legion and Poppy Day. He was very well known in Toronto for his legion activities.*

Again, I was pleased to be able to match several of the facts I'd uncovered myself. Ms. Kenney's words made true what I had learned about William's migration from England to Canada to the United States to Canada again. Also, the message confirmed that he had divorced. I was pleased to see the same "Ashdale Avenue" mentioned, matching it to the letters sent to my grandfather in the 1940s. Also, I'm impressed that a family member of mine was instrumental in starting, "Poppy Day," looking forward to sharing the proud fact with family and strangers each early November. Although, both realism and a quick Internet search tells me that William was likely not the sole driver behind the successful one-hundred-year tradition. Of course, I do find humor in the military legacy points that Linda adds, remembering the article where William is chased from a meeting. In addition to facts, Linda shares some details that help me learn about the man on a personal level, which I hope could offer some direction in my search.

*William was a reporter during World War I and became a reporter for The Toronto Telegram. William was a dapper gentleman. He never went out without his suit, high buttoned shirt, spats (maybe ask your parents about them), or his cane. He was a very fetching sight. He had two special lady friends and kept them both thinking they were the only one. He died in 1953 at Sunnybrook Hospital, the veteran's hospital in Toronto, of colon cancer.*

I immediately note two connections to my grandfather. First, both William and my grandfather favored formal attire at all times, especially when in public. Second, if I am to believe the stories my grandfather told to my father, both were very much interested and successful when it came to the opposite sex. I contemplate the idea that William was an influence on my grandfather, maybe even something of a big brother. Is this why Alfred ventured overseas at such a young age? Was he following in the steps of his older, influential cousin? Perhaps, young Alfred even did have boxing aspirations. If he had a negative experience, this could account for the disapproving actions he would take years later when my own father took up the sport.

Unaware my morning coffee was growing cold and fully enraptured in the text, I couldn't help but predict that the preamble was wearing thin, and I was moving to the part where Ms. Kenney would add details about my grandfather. I was at least partly correct.

*I am sorry, but I cannot help you with the relationship your grandfather and my grandfather had. Knowing how he helped people, I am sure he was a very helpful cousin. I will consult with my brothers to see if they can add any information. Because I was born in 1946, they have more memories of Grandpa than I do. If I can recall anything more after talking to my brothers, I will gladly pass it along. I am so happy you contacted me. Let's keep the lines open. Sincerely, Linda (Turley) Kenney*

Well, I cannot say I was totally surprised, but I was disappointed. In some romantic vision, I had dreamed Ms. Kenney would express unbridled bewilderment that she had finally made a connection between someone living and the mass of letters and family legends regarding her grandfather's legendary first cousin, the infamous Alfred Victor Williams.

I cannot deny that I was pleased to have made contact with a close member of the Turley family. Conversely, I cannot deny that I was disappointed Ms. Kenney had no information to share. There was a sliver of hope in her promise to consult her older brothers. A look at the family tree informed that her male siblings were born in 1930, 1934, and 1939 respectively. Those birthdates pleased me. If the Turleys were a close family living in near proximity, there was a decent chance her brothers would recall something. After all, her eldest brother would have been between the ages of twelve to fifteen in the time that my grandfather resurfaced in Ontario. Addresses on letters suggested that Alfred lived with the Turleys for an extended time. It didn't seem too far-fetched that a person would recall family visits at age fifteen that included an older cousin who lived with their grandfather. I responded politely to Ms. Kenney, assuring that I, too, was pleased to have made the connection, but also exposing my sincere hope that she would query her brothers.

Well, Ms. Kenney came through but not in the way that I'd hoped. In her second message, sent November 26th, she begins, "my brothers were no help with your grandfather's name. The home on Ashdale Avenue was originally the home of George Turley and Agnes Turley which was left to William." She lamented that I "seem to have so much more info than [they] do, except my brother in the east coast, Fred, just received a box of our grandfather William's mementos, which my brother is going to go through with his son who will be visiting November 28. Hopefully, there will be some more info contained within." It was both a letdown but also a further reason for optimism.

Whatever was in the box, I would never know. Ms. Kenney sent me an email explaining there were no documents or information about my grandfather. I was disappointed, but also pleased that I'd made a connection.

As 2015 rolled to a close, I reflected upon the Kenney/Turley correspondence of the prior six weeks. I hadn't made any real progress in narrowing down my mystery. However, that didn't mean the exercise was a complete bust. It's always satisfying to make contact with a distant family member, which I had just done, on the other side of the country. I could now reasonably eliminate a Turley connection holding the answers I was seeking. On the positive side, the correspondence certainly helped build a picture of the type of man William had been: an involved character with restless legs. Was my grandfather the same way? Perhaps, I'd never find exact facts and details outlining my grandfather's life. Perhaps, the best I'd do is learning about those around him which would eventually define the man my grandfather was.

I tried to console myself with that thought. However, the mystery continued to burn. I also couldn't shake the feeling that William's strange upstate New York trip was noteworthy. It would certainly confirm the *1910 United States Federal Census* record with a prospective Alfred Williams residing in New York. Also, in her letters, Alfred's brother's wife, Eva, had mentioned Niagara Falls. It's possible my grandfather was in New York for the entirety of his missing years, and I should limit my focus there. Despite the evidence, I wasn't quite ready to limit my efforts in that fashion or to that extreme.

With William checked off the list, I focused my attentions to the supposed next closest person to my grandfather, his brother, Charles.

# Bernard Williams is Located

**Monday, September 14, 1908, 6:18 p.m. Melrose Street, Toronto, Ontario, Canada.**

*Alfred's time with his cousin has come to an end. It was difficult enough the year prior with the birth and early death of William and Louisa's daughter, Winnifred, at only six months. Now with Louisa about to give birth again, and the Turley family's uncertainty in Canada, Alfred feels he needs his own space. His new home is on Melrose Street about a six-minute walk from his cousin. For the first time in Alfred's eighteen years, he'll have some quiet. True, it's only a room that he's renting, but with no family members he'll be left to himself plenty.*

*Lately, he has been needing the rest. With his time at the Kidderminster Railway, he's not a stranger to hard work. This job at the Toronto Fire Brick Company, however, is taking a real toll on his body. Although Alfred has been spending time enjoying Toronto's nightlife and the many young woman in the city, he still finds time to write home, even if he does so solely for his mother, who seems to be in ever increasing poor health.*

*He'll stay in the house on Melrose Street for the time-being. Same with the job at the brick company. But he knows that's not why he left his home and country, just to settle in one place. Alfred wants to see the continent, if not the world. There's also the problem, which has begun to keep him awake at night. He begins contemplating his next move.*

T he calendar turned to 2016 and I continued to be as busy as possible working on the project. Busy as possible, still, did not mean every day. Pleased to have made the Turley family connection, but less than overwhelmed at what information it exposed about my grandfather, I turned my attention to the family of Charles Williams. As far as I knew, Alfred had been in contact with Charles, and his wife, Eva, more than anyone else. In truth, it was Charles whom I had coveted first; however, I had not been successful in finding any living relatives who may be in possession of either information or clues.

Charles Whittington Williams was born in 1886. In 1911, he was a twenty-five-year-old railway engine fireman stationed and boarding in Wolverhampton, Staffordshire, about fifteen miles north of his Kidderminster home. According to his letters and confirmed by online records, at thirty-one years of age he joined the Allies in World War I. It was only after the war, in 1921 that Charles married Eva Gladys Stiles. From letters, I was aware that Charles and Eva informally adopted their niece, Dorothy Denise Williams, at some point. In her February 1945 letter to my grandfather, Eva writes that their son "Bernard is nearly fourteen and getting [to be] quite a big chap." Bernard Williams' 1931 birth would have made him eighty-six years old, if still alive, at this point. Similar to the case with William Turley, I accepted it was more likely that I may be able to contact a grandchild of Charles and Eva, although eighty-six years of age certainly did not rule out the possibility that Bernard was still with us.

In moments of somber daydream, I would imagine connecting with Bernard who would express wonder that he could finally connect relatives to the collection of saved letters my grandfather had written to his father. I imagined the details and stories in the letters, as well as photographs and perhaps other trinkets from my grandfather's life. My mother suggested that if we were able to make contact, there may exist childhood photos of my grandfather. The possibilities were rich and enticing; however, my rational mind cautioned not to allow my hopes to run too high.

Finding Bernard wasn't an easy task, however. Being born in 1931, England census reports were not available. As well, I had difficulty narrowing down which Bernard Williams I was looking to find. It was still early in the year when my mother shared some news. She found that Charles and Eva's son's full name was Bernard James Stiles Williams. Writing this some seven years after the discovery, neither my mother nor I can recall precisely how this discovery was made, other than it must have been an online source. Immediately, I was sure of its accuracy due to the "Stiles" middle name matching his mother's maiden name.

Armed with a full name and back on *Ancestry.com*, I learned that Bernard was born May 8, 1931. Also, he had married Ann Clements in Staffordshire on March 6, 1962. I contemplated whether either or both would still be with us. I hoped to find out. Moving to a Google search, I learned that Bernard had published a series of books, with titles like, *Microforms in Education*, and *Miniaturized Communications: A Review of Microforms*. I discovered listings for these books on *Amazon.com, Goodreads.com* and

Google Books; however, there were no images of the book or descriptions of the text. Ordering a copy was out of the question as there were none available from any of the sources. The most regrettable fact was the absence of any author biography that may have given me some clues or contact information.

Despite the initial promise, what followed was a few months of barren research. I'll remind the reader that my efforts often lacked a consistent level of focus or strategy. With what little time I had to devote to my search, I would often spend the minutes or hours on whatever name happened to inspire me at the moment, which sometimes meant a further search for Bernard, but just as often resulted in double checking "William Turley," "Lola LeDuke," and most often "Alfred Victor Williams."

One summer evening, Lana and the kids occupied with other pursuits, I entered "Bernard James Stiles Williams," into a Google search, as I am certain I had done several times before. On this evening, however, the stars or search words decided to align themselves. I found an online copy of the March 2016 newsletter for "The Club for Professional Engineers and Scientists in and around Hertfordshire." Digesting the name, I was a little confused at the acronym the club had chosen, "HELC." With mixed emotions, I scanned the newsletter until I spotted Bernard's name.

Bernard J S Williams – 8 May 1931 to 6 March 2016

My heart sank as the unfortunate date was absorbed in my mind. March 6, 2016. My synapses were firing on all cylinders as I attempted to sort which doors were swung open and which would be permanently closed. I had to accept that Bernard was deceased, that I would not be able to connect with a first cousin of my father. The realization that Bernard was alive and possibly well during the first year of my research was frustrating. I'd had a good chance to make contact with this man. Now it would remain nothing more than a missed

***Bernard Williams: his final act was reuniting the Williams family across an ocean.***

opportunity. At the same time, I welcomed delight at the realization that I had discovered a connection with family in England. However, Bernard's death would mean that any contact would be another generation removed. Any memories or information Bernard may have held were lost forever. Any family letters he may have saved from the mid-1900s were all the more likely to be gone.

The newsletter featured three separate written tributes to my deceased first cousin, once removed. I learned that Bernard was a librarian by profession and had spent a large part of his career at the University of Hertfordshire. In addition to writing his own books, Bernard was active in editing and publishing, including both founding and contributing to several trade newsletters. Given his chosen profession and expertise, I couldn't help muse that he was precisely the type to hold on to documents and letters in some organized fashion. While the tributes were professional in nature and void of any personal or family information, it was clear that Bernard was a man well respected and well-loved amongst his peers.

My immediate action was to contact the editor of the newsletter, a Mr. John Deans, with the following email:

> *My name is Ron Williams, I live in Vancouver, Canada. I noticed that in the March 2016 HELC Newsletter, you reported that Bernard JS Williams had passed away. Bernard was my first cousin-once removed (my father's cousin). I understand that he married Ann Clements in 1962; after that he had a career at the University of Hertfordshire, and he published several books. Can you provide any more information on Bernard? I am especially interested in any children he may have had, or any other family I may be able to contact. Thank you, Ron Williams*

It took only a day for Mr. Deans to respond. Similar to the written tributes, Mr. Dean's response was void of personal information. He did, however, share that he had forwarded my email to Bernard's family. That information didn't overly excite me, as I was enjoying more immediate success pursuing another angle.

With the exact date of Bernard's regrettable expiry, I was able to find his actual obituary online. As well as listing family members, the obituary provided the name of the funeral home responsible for arrangements. My message to Austin's Funeral Directors was not much different from the message sent to Mr. Deans.

After an excited call to Lana, the next call went out to my parents. I shared that I had discovered Bernard had just passed, but that he had likely lived in or near Hertford a small city in Hertfordshire. Like myself, my parents were hopeful that the two emails would yield some positive results. I reminded them that it was nearing night in England and that we might have to wait until at least the next day for any response. Innate caution also warned me that there was no guarantee that either missive would elicit any response, at any time. We'd need to be patient.

My dad didn't necessarily share the same thoughts. Whether it was his overwhelming excitement or simply his attitude of getting things done swiftly and directly, he was determined to take immediate action to give life to this potential connection. In this case, immediate action meant picking up the phone.

A long-time master of the phone book, my father had recently been tutored by my mother in adopting more up-to-date online tools. In this case, he was able find the Hertford phone book and identify only a small handful of listings with some degree of similarity to the name Ann Williams. After a few wrong numbers, it seemed my father's long-distance arrow hit the bull's eye. Ascertaining that he had connected with Ann, recently widowed partner of Bernard Williams, my father introduced himself and explained the relation. Ann's response was as acute as it is now humorous: "I lived with Bernard for over thirty years, and he never once mentioned a cousin in Canada!" My father was a little chagrined, but I admit I was fully amused at the smooth savvy of this recently widowed octogenarian.

Waking around 6:00 a.m. on the following morning, my sleepy eyes attempted to focus on the following message:

*Dear Ron: Your email to Austins has just been forwarded to me, and I gather you are related to my dad, Bernard. Dad died in March after a slow decline with Alzheimer's over many years. He was a wonderful man, the greatest father that I could ever have wished for. I am interested to know how you are related to dad. As a first cousin once removed, I think that means that you are the son of a cousin of his - presumably on his father's side. I never met his father as he died when dad was still a young man. Dad was fascinated by family history and spent many hours researching - though I have to admit he had greater success on my mother's side than his own. He also wrote*

149

*a very interesting autobiography which gives a real insight into his life - first of all in Wolverhampton and then later in the south. I believe we must be second cousins. I look forward to hearing from you. Kind regards, Nicki Branagan*

Certainly, my discovery and connection with Linda Kenney – William Turley's granddaughter – was special but hearing from Nicki seemed more monumental. Chalk it up to generations, I suppose. Linda is a first cousin, twice removed to my father, whereas Nicki is a first cousin, once removed. The difference in terminology may not seem much but it felt different making connection with someone whose grandfather was sibling to Alfred Victor.

A second reason this connection likely felt stronger, more monumental, was basic geography. Linda was in Ontario, Canada, same country, even if her home was two thousand five hundred miles from my own. The connection with Nicki was a connection to family in England, family we had lost touch with for decades...almost a century really. The thought of connecting with members of the Williams family in England felt like re-opening a long-closed door.

The third and most profound reason I viewed this connection as exciting was the possibility previously mentioned above. I'll remind you that Bernard was a scholar, a librarian to be precise. He was someone who had dedicated his professional life to the organization and preservation of important texts and documents. If his mother and father, Charles and Eva Williams, had held on to any of my grandfather's letters, I could be fairly confident that Bernard would have not only kept them but valued and organized them. As well, with Bernard's sad death so current, there was a good chance that the family may not have cleared his possessions. Even if that unfortunate purge had occurred, it was possible that Nicki and other relatives could have perused the letters before discarding them, which could allow them to

*The lovely Branagans: an anonymous email that connected a family. (From left to right) Kate, Nicki, Martin, & Lucy.*

share some much-sought information on my part. Oh, to dream.

In the ensuing days, Nicki and my family learned about one another in a continuous stream of emails. My dad was able to contact Ann again, both enjoying a modest laugh at their earlier communication. We learned that Nicki lives in Welwyn Garden City, a small town in Hertfordshire, with a beautiful family that includes her husband, Martin, as well as her daughters, Kate and Lucy. Nicki has a slightly older sister, Sally Ann, who lives close by. Of course, she had no memory of her grandfather, Charles, as his 1952 expiry predated Nicki's 1966 birth. Nicki and Sally Ann were the only living descendants of Charles and Eva Williams. However, Nicki shared with me that she was still in touch with a Fay Harman, daughter of Dorothy Denise Williams and granddaughter to Alfred's younger brother, Dennis. Thus, I anticipated that with any degree of good fortune I would soon be in contact with descendants from both Alfred's brothers.

Nicki shared that Bernard was a wonderful family man and overall impressive person. Along with his wife, Ann, Bernard had doted on his daughters and naturally turned into an excellent grandfather. He was a special man quick in intellect and impressive in physical stature. Professionally, he had written, travelled and founded institutions in relation to his profession. Sadly, I learned that Bernard had struggled with dementia for close to a decade, family members still reeling from his very recent death.

One more note: upon his retirement in the 1990s, Bernard had self-published an autobiography. To say I was excited to read his book is an understatement. On a sunny and hot July afternoon, the book unceremoniously arrived in brown envelope, a generous gift from my newly found family. After a quick dinner, I cordoned myself off in the living room and with a chilled glass of Riesling devoured my literary desert.

As would be expected, most of the book focused on the impressive, rich life of Bernard Williams. In addition to matching the facts of his obituary with his self-reported life details, the book filled in information regarding Bernard's personal life from the time he was a boy into young adulthood and finally, his golden years.

Bernard outlined the factors explaining his parents' rather late marriage, Bernard not being born until his father was in his forties. The true story of Dorothy Denise Williams and the kidnapping allegations were also explained. Details were sympathetic to Charles and Eva and rightfully so as I have no reason to doubt their accuracy. The information helped me to fully understand that Bernard and Dorothy Denise were more siblings than first cousins.

The late teen and early adult years are often the most exciting of a person's life story. In this case, Bernard did not disappoint. He shared stories of adolescent rivalry, career frustrations, motorcycle excursions and even broken love affairs, including a bride left at the altar.

In terms of the Williams family as a whole, the account offered a few items of interest. I learned that the same "Uncle George" from the letters to my grandfather was a fairly prominent figure in young Bernard's life. In one account Uncle George spends his last days in the living room of Charles and Eva's Staffordshire home. The general impression offered of Uncle George certainly matched the bombastic personality emanated through his letters. Another prominent remembrance was the account of Charles' early death. The details of which allowed me to place a person with the distant letters I had scoured over.

Also interesting was Bernard's mention of a Mary Ann Corbet. I immediately recalled a line from Uncle George's May 1944 letter in which he explains to my grandfather, "your grandfather belonged to a Shropshire Family at Shrewsbury Moreton Corbet Castle." In his well-written account of life, Bernard too posited that our very branch of the Williams family had descended, in part, from the Corbets at Moreton Corbet Castle. An oil painting of Mary Ann Corbet had dominated his family living room as a child and served as catalyst for many tales of family folklore. I made note to follow up at a later time, lest my focus further delve from my immediate mystery.

Overall, the autobiography cemented my impression of a successful career man and dedicated family patriarch, a proud member of the Williams clan. As always, however, my ultimate focus was on any details surrounding my grandfather. Although not mentioned more than once, and even then, not by name, my interest was piqued by the following passage: "It was a brother of Charles, from Canada I think, who visited England after the war. His intention was to find Dennis Williams. However, his efforts were unsuccessful."

I knew from letters that Alfred has been searching for Dennis in earnest both in the 1940s and in the latter years of his life, the 1960s. I assume his efforts spanned the in-between time also, but I have no evidence of such. This suggestion of the trip to England was new though. Immediately I asked my father about the possibility that Alfred visited England between the years of my father's birth, 1948, and Alfred's death in 1968. My father was reasonably certain that he had not. In addition to limited funds, my father couldn't recall any instance of his father being away for an extended period.

This opened up the possibility that Alfred may have visited at some earlier time. I allowed myself to fantasize that Alfred may have returned to England during the 1920s or 1930s, possibly even starting a family. I very quickly returned to reality, recalling the 1940s letters from Charles and Eva confirming that neither had any contact with Alfred as an adult.

The only possibility, then, was that Alfred returned to the United Kingdom between the final letter from England that I had in my possession, a 1946 letter from Uncle George, and the 1947, Vancouver, introduction to my grandmother, a tight window to be sure. My initial excitement doused, I reasoned that Bernard may have crossed details, the truth being far more likely that the enquiries were by letter only rather than in person.

Nicki and I continued corresponding almost daily, sometimes more than once. My mother and father also continued a regular correspondence. Also, my Aunt Shirley connected successfully with our new England relatives. It wasn't long before Nicki, along with her husband Martin and two wonderful daughters, Kate and Lucy, became...well, they became like family.

There were some realities I had to accept: bundle of long-lost letters? No. Stack of old family photos? No. Family legend and tales passed down for generations? Sadly, no.

While this was a welcome, exciting feeling, having new family in another corner of the world, it also sat somewhat uneasily. This was a feeling that I experienced to a far lesser extent through my connection with Linda Kenney. At times, I felt a little ruthless, uncaring, overly concerned with mining any snippet of information regarding my mystery that I could accrue. All the while, the innocent, caring individuals on the receiving end of my missives and demands wanted nothing more than a familial relationship. Not everyone shared my hell-bent obsession with finding my grandfather's missing years. I had to accept that and remember to be respectful. As I complete this story, some seven years after first making contact with the Branagan family, I can proudly report that we continue to be in touch and continue to share a warm, family bond.

There was one fairly robust mystery that Nicki was able to solve almost immediately. Upon reflection, "debunk" might be a preferable word to "solve," as the information she provided did nothing more than snuff out a potentially rich clue. The mysterious, mid-twentieth century class picture marked, "my son, Donald Roy Williams," turned out to be none other than a youthful Bernard Williams. No doubt, Charles had shared a picture of his son, only to be eventually mislabeled as my grandfather slowly descended into dementia. Cross that clue off the list.

Nicki offered a profound thought that put the value of our connection in clear perspective. Considering our initial attempts to connect were so unsuccessful and frustrating, it had to be prophetic that it took Bernard's obituary to reconnect the Williams from different parts of the world. As Nicki asserted, "it was my father's final act."

I had to agree.

# Calling Janet Fay Harman

**Saturday, April 30, 1910, 8:44 p.m.  465 West 21st Street, Manhattan Ward 16, New York, New York, United States of America.**

*Alfred half-heartedly writes to his family but doesn't figure he'll be in one place long enough to bother including a return address.  He assures his mother he is doing fine, even if the past four years haven't turned out quite as well as he'd envisioned.  Quietly, he hopes his mother is well, although by not providing a return address, he has no way of knowing.*

*In truth, Toronto had grown lonely with the Turley family returning to England.  Also, what good was leaving home if he was destined to stay in the same place for any period.  Now twenty, Alfred yearns for adventure which is exactly what New York City offers.*

*He's lucky to find a room at the home of John and Clara Willis, a middle-aged couple who never had children. Aware that owners are tentative to rent to young men, Alfred identifies himself as twenty-two, two years older than his actual time on earth.*

*Even though his new Chelsea neighborhood is known for its factories and industry, Alfred doesn't miss the hard labor at the Toronto Fire Brick Company and is able to find a better suited vocation this time. His salesman job allows him to use the tricks and tools of speech that he witnessed so successfully in his father and Uncle George. Alfred considers himself a type of modern day "horse trader" only it's jewelry he is attempting to hawk to financially comfortable New Yorkers. Dressing daily in a suit and tie, he fashions himself on the way to success. So confident is he, that he begins to court fellow lodger, Tollie Hoffman, a sophisticated, twenty-two-year-old New York native with a glamorous job as salesclerk at the new Gimbel's Department Store. Away from the confines and dirty conditions of the railway and his Worcester home, as well as the hot, brick factory and his Toronto lodgings, the future finally seems bright for young Alfred.*

While the most satisfying aspect of finding Nicki and her family was the close connection, she did provide another hot lead. She was in touch with a Janet "Fay" Harman, a granddaughter of Dennis Williams. Specifically, Fay, as she preferred, was the eldest daughter of Dorothy Denise Williams, whom you may remember as my grandfather's "once kidnapped" niece whose sad plight was described in her 1966 letter to my grandfather and in Charles' autobiography.

This was exciting, if for no other reason than it completed a set. As you know, my grandfather was one of three boys:

Charles, Alfred and Dennis. Making contact with Fay would mean that I was able to connect with ancestors from all three. Charles produced one child, Bernard, who gave birth to Nicki and Sally Ann, whom I was in contact with. Alfred produced two children, my father and Aunt Shirley. As far as I could tell Dennis had produced six offspring in total.

It seems Dennis's oldest, known as Charles Barrett may have been stepson to Dennis, delivered by Dorothy in 1918, prior to her 1919 marriage to Dennis. The aptly named Dorothy Denise was born in 1921.

Given experiences with my last two connections, the fact that Fay's mother, Dorothy Denise, was estranged from her immediate family, and the dismal information contained in Dorothy Denise's 1966 letter to my grandfather, I wasn't holding out much hope that Fay could assist me in my mystery, but...I could remain optimistic, couldn't I?

Another reason for my excitement was the fact that I possessed a hand-written letter from her long-deceased mother. I imagined it would be a special gift to receive some correspondence personally penned in a warm, familiar, but now distant voice. Conversely, I again reasoned that the very fact that I possessed a letter my grandfather had received almost fifty years ago meant that it was possible Fay would possess a letter her mother had received in the same time period. At least, I tried to convince myself there was a possibility, anyway.

I sent my first email in fall of 2016. Cognizant that Fay would likely not share much of an interest in finding my elusive grandfather, a distant, unknown granduncle, I decided to keep it light and focus on the family connection. Depending on the response, I could always bring up my grandfather in future.

*Hello Fay: I hope you do not mind me emailing. I was given your email address from Nicki Branagan. My father, Donald Roy Williams was first cousin to your mother, Dorothy Denise...I think that makes us second cousins. We have always wondered about family in England, so it has been very exciting for us to have made contact with Nicki and her family. I am a forty-four-year-old teacher and father of four living near Vancouver, British Columbia, Canada. My family and I are very interested in hearing from you. Sincerely, Ron Williams*

The response was almost immediate. Fay wrote that she "was delighted to hear from" me and shared she "saw Nicki and her mother Ann earlier in the summer." She explained they "try to keep in touch especially now that Bernard has passed away." Fay was sure to add that Bernard, "was a lovely man and more like an uncle to [her] than a second cousin."

The email continued to offer Fay's understanding of her mother's case. It was no different than previous reports. Again, I took notice of her reason that her mother, Dorothy Denise, first went to Charles and Eva's. She then explains it was because her grandmother "was not well after the birth of her fifth child and could not cope with a toddler at that time." According to my research, Fay's mother, Dorothy Denise, was only Dorothy's second child and Dennis's first. Also, it seemed that Dennis and Dorothy were able to cope with the ensuing four children in their home. Peculiar to be sure. Fay continued explaining, "then the war came and [her mother] lost all trace of [her family] after the bombing of London." She did surmise that perhaps my "research you could shed some light on this mystery." It did and I would soon share it with her.

Fay continued that she is "seventy-two years old, married to John for fifty-one years [with]...four children." She also proudly shared a Canadian connection, as she has a nephew in Ontario whom she'd visited a couple of time, boasting that a visit to Niagara Falls was included in each trip. I took note of another mention of Niagara Falls. The tone was certainly akin to my earliest messages with both Linda Kenney and Nicki Branagan. Even though our total time together was comprised of one sparse email exchange, once again, it felt like family.

Another email to Fay contained some information about myself and my family: where we lived, our jobs, ages of children, etc. I also couldn't help but share the family mystery I was working on. As expected, Fay wasn't able to offer anything to add to my case file; however, she did express admiration – if not interest - that I was working diligently on our family tree. I figured, if nothing else, that was an opening to discuss genealogy.

Finally, I shared what I knew about the Dennis Williams family. I included the names and birthdates of all the children: Charles W. Barret, born in 1918; Dorothy D. Williams, born in 1921; Eileen J. Williams, born in 1922; Daphne P. Williams, born in 1926; Vivian R. Williams, born in 1929; and Ken D. Williams, born in 1930. Attached to the email, I shared a 1939 census report that I had only recently found. The document showed that Charles, Eileen, who was now with husband, Daphne, Vivian, and Ken all resided at home. Without connecting the dots, I wondered what Fay would make of the fact that all other children, now ranging in age from nine to twenty-one were living under their parents' roof.

While the information was at odds with the picture painted of a family in dysfunction and chaos, in reality, the document didn't provide the whole story. In later years I would learn that all the children were fostered out at some point, this 1939 snapshot occurring at a time when the kids were a little older and possibly more manageable. After all, regardless of motive, it was true that Dennis and Dorothy had tried to get Dorothy Denise back in her teenage years.

Fay, along with her husband John, who seemed to be cultivating an interest in genealogy, were appreciative of the information but did not have much to add. In addition to building our personal relationship, it felt benevolent to share information with family members. I gained a sense that my hobby or obsession was doing some good for others. I was giving back in some small way.

Fay's line that "the war came and [her mother] lost all trace of [her family] after the bombing of London" resonated in my mind. It made me consider how challenging life could have been for Dennis and Dorothy with difficulties that could have included poverty, alcoholism, unemployment, and wartime. Also, from one of Eva's letters, there is suggestion that the three boys – Charles, Alfred, Dennis - may have experienced tumultuous treatment by their father. While I still pined to discover what my grandfather was doing during the missing years, perhaps not contacting family wasn't a large part of the puzzle. While I had been considering that a prison stay may have prevented contact, I now began to consider that it wasn't anything as grandiose.

Somehow, also, this thought made my grandfather a little more human. My grandfather had made a sincere effort, spanning three decades, to locate his younger brother, Dennis, even though he hardly knew him. When Alfred departed for Canada in 1906, Dennis was only eleven years old...still a young kid.

I realized that there was more to my grandfather than the abusive alcoholic who terrorized his wife and kids. Suddenly my father's act of kissing the gravestone didn't seem that unusual.

# Aunt Shirley Meets the Branagans

**Monday, January 5, 1920, 10:26 p.m. Exact whereabouts unknown, United States of America.**

*It's been close to ten years since he has written anything to his family and closer to fifteen years since he's heard from them. With some crude math, Alfred, having just turned thirty, expects his parents to be comfortably in their sixties, if neither has succumbed to illness. His older brother Charles, in his mid-thirties, should be a family man probably still toiling at the Kidderminster Railway Station, the same one Alfred left some fourteen years prior. His younger brother Dennis, the runt of the family, would be a man of twenty-six, likely married himself with one or more children. How he'd like to see them again, but even with the end of the war, Alfred knows it's unlikely to happen.*

*His World War I absenteeism was fortunate, and he feels lucky to have avoided participation. However, he no longer holds the same degree of optimistic promise about his bright future. At the age of thirty, Alfred is beginning to question his life. He already holds regrets, personal relationships that have not turned out well, in part, at least, due to his behavior. He's aware of the legal proceedings but confident in his ability to avoid consequence. In terms of his profession, he loves being on the street selling and makes enough for food and shelter. Don't forget the bottle of rye each day, either.*

*Maybe it's the shame of not going to war, or maybe it's the shame of not being settled that keeps Alfred from writing home. But of course, Alfred has a far bigger reason for his literary inaction, a secret he is keeping from everyone.*

M y efforts to uncover my grandfather's missing lost fifty-seven years continued in 2016 with a variety of both focused and unfocused efforts and avenues.

I am aware thus far that I have included my wife, my mother and my father in this encapsulating but frustrating project. I hope I've also made clear my Aunt Shirley's committed level of interest. For her, making connection with family was just as important as discovering the mystery. It seems possible that she didn't think the truth of her father would ever be revealed. I know I felt that way at times. By 2017, Aunt Shirley had developed a fairly close relationship with our cousin, Nicki Branagan. It was soon announced that she would make the acquaintance visual by visiting England.

This was exciting news for everyone. It would bring the family closer in contact with arrangements being made for

Aunt Shirley to meet up with, not only Nicki and her family, but also with Fay and her husband. A reunion of sorts, I suppose, if meeting for the first time can be considered such. Again, I wondered that family lines of the three brothers would be united: Charles, Alfred, and Dennis. I envied the opportunity and felt great happiness for my aunt. She's worked hard for years as a single mother of three and deserved this trip as much as anyone.

Of course, the sentimentality of the trip did not fully eclipse my wish that she could combine the visit with some research. I spent the next week looking up addresses and contacting various individuals, including email correspondence with a gravedigger. Luckily, my aunt was amenable to this, even requesting a list of locations and landmarks. I optimistically provided the following list:

Moreton Corbet Castle, Moreton Corbet, Shropshire: This is related to our family according to a letter from George Williams and Bernard Williams' autobiography.

Cookley House, Worcestershire: I don't have an address, but this is the small village just above Kidderminster where the three boys lived during their early years and where Alfred Victor Williams was reportedly born.

Hoo Brook, Stone, Worcestershire: This is a small place near Kidderminster and the birthplace of Emily (Crane) Williams. There is no address in census records.

64 Stourport Road, Kidderminster: This is the 1891 home of the Williams family. I am unsure if it is the same house.

18 Dog Lane, Bewdley, Worcestershire: This is the 1871 and 1881 home of the Williams family. Alfred Sr. and Emily lived there when first married. I believe this is the same house.

Lord Nelson Inn, 91 Blackwell Street, Kidderminster, Worcestershire: This is the 1911 home of the Williams family. I do believe that the buildings you will see there are newer and not the actual dwellings of the family.

25 Blackwell Street, Kidderminster, Worcestershire: This is the 1901 Williams family home. It looks like it is currently an Italian restaurant.

Kidderminster Cemetery, Park Lane, Kidderminster, Worcestershire: Several Williams family members are buried here. These include Emily Williams (Charles and Alfred Victor's mother), George and Mary Williams, (Charles and Alfred Victor's grandparents), and George Thomas Williams and Sarah Ann Williams (Charles and Alfred Victor's uncle and aunt).

#3 Brindley Street, Stourport on Severn, Worcestershire: This is the home of Alfred's Uncle George.

Looking back, I was able to offer a few specific addresses but not with any certainty that the same buildings would still exist. Most of the locations were vague and imprecise. Even I questioned the worthiness of visiting all the places. I do confess, my contact with the gravedigger was both eerie and full of suggestion. I pictured an older, haggard, one-toothed being with a fantastical knowledge and history of the area, who might just be capable of sharing a few Williams family mysteries. Too bad this wasn't a fantasy novel, I suppose. In truth, I had no idea how many of these places my aunt would have the time or opportunity to visit.

Maybe a little more realistic was the idea that something more tangible could come from her visit. To myself, I also hoped the fact that she would be visiting Nicki, Sally Ann, and Fay might provide some extra motivation for them to look through boxes, photo albums, maybe even do a little preparatory research of their own before my aunt's arrival. I envisioned one of them making a call to a distant cousin who may have gained possession of an old photo album containing long-lost pictures of Alfred and his family in younger years. Also, maybe sharing the information that a cousin from Canada would be visiting would jar a faint memory long held by a family member.

None of us had any idea what Alfred may have looked like prior to when he was approaching his sixtieth year. It was Charles who remarked in one of his return letters after receiving a photograph from Alfred, "if I were to see you on the street, I daresay I would not have recognized you." Once again, the chances of such were certainly remote, but the fact that I was able to gain possession of letters, photographs, and other documents made it possible that other such items existed also. Again, it would take only one old letter from my grandfather to blow the proverbial roof off everything!

My fantastic imaginings weren't confined to my aunt's trip either. The year previous Lana and I had occasion to visit Seattle, Washington where we found ourselves in an older, antique store. In one section of the quaint abode, was a twenty-foot-long bin containing a motley collection of thousands of used postcards. The images on the front spanned from the beaches of Hawaii to the monuments of England, and towers of New York City. Equally varied were the messages on the back, penned in various shades and colors of ink, including everything from surface greetings, "having a great time, wish you were here," to "I made a mistake...if I come home, will you take me back?" Amidst the nostalgia and intrusion, I imagined finding a postcard written from my grandfather to his mysterious Seattle friend: "Dear Lola – I miss Seattle. Please consider joining me in my new home in [insert name here]." Of course, no such postcard would emerge, and Lana would wonder why I was spending so much time in the section. Chagrinned, I declined to offer her the truth.

On a similar afternoon, Lana and I were perusing stores in the Commercial Drive area of Vancouver, a pedestrian-friendly mecca of pubs, restaurants, and curious new and used stores. In one long-standing bookstore, I found a modest collection of Mickey Spillane pocketbooks dated to the fifties and sixties. Despite the odds, and without any concrete proof, I purchased a couple, trying in earnest to convince myself that they were the very copies held in my grandfather's hands a lifetime ago.

Rounding back to my Aunt Shirley's trip, my dad dropped her at the airport, and she was off. With the exception of one or two hasty text messages, we were not to hear from her for two full weeks. Of course, I considered her situation from time to time during her trip, envisioning what exactly she might be doing, hearing, finding. And then, fourteen days later, there we were enjoying a pizza dinner in her townhouse, entertained by souvenirs and details of her momentous visit.

She happily reported that she, Nicki and Sally Ann were certainly long-lost cousins, and the family connection was strong and immediate. She also spoke of Martin, Kate and Lucy as family...which they certainly qualify. Additionally, Aunt Shirley was also privileged to spend time with Bernard's widow, Ann, as well as Fay and her husband John.

Together, they spent time in Nicki's home of Welwyn Garden City. They also ventured to the Norfolk area and rented a watercraft. The area held special significance to the family as it is the original place that Bernard had envisioned his retirement, a dream that he chose to forgo in order to stay closer to his grandchildren. The Worcester area also played host to my aunt's overseas jaunt. No, she wasn't able to check off all my suggested stops; however, she did manage to see a few including the Moreton Corbet Castle and nearby church, locations in Cookley and Bewdley as well as Blackwell Street, Stourport Road and the Kidderminster Cemetery. They were able to visit 25 Blackwell Street, the very home of the Williams family in 1901. My aunt reported an eerie uncomfortable

167

feeling, which I believe was real. Immediately I consider the timeless cliché, if only walls could talk.

In addition to providing the pizza she also brought back souvenirs and what might be considered some more special items. There was the usual, including playing cards with the Union Jack, and a deluxe copy of Led Zeppelin's untitled fourth album for Jack. One item I cherished was a copy of the *Kidderminster Shuttle*, the town's daily newspaper. Maybe I would have preferred a copy that was one hundred years old, but this one amused for some time also.

Nicki is a teacher with unlimited access to a photocopier, color photocopies at that. She and Aunt Shirley spent time making copies of pages from Bernard's personal scrapbook. Among the shots, I was able to enjoy the very images that painted a picture of Bernard's life as described in his autobiography. Bernard certainly was a man who subscribed to the phrase "carpe diem," each shot featuring adventure of some sort. With Bernard growing up so close to Dorothy Denise, there were also more than a few shots of her in her younger years.

Aside from the warm family connection, Aunt Shirley was most proud to be generously gifted the previously mentioned oil painting of Mary Ann Corbet which had played so prominent a decorative role in the childhood home of Bernard Williams. This seems like an ideal time to follow up on the whole Moreton Corbet Castle connection which I first became aware of in Uncle George's letter and Bernard's autobiography.

I began by looking into the Corbet family itself and was pleased to discover plenty of information easily available online. I learned that the Corbet family first entered England in 1066 along with William the Conqueror, the first Norman king of England who reigned from 1066 to 1087. Roger and Robert Corbet are listed in the Domesday Book of 1086, generally known as the first comprehensive survey of England. The Corbet family soon grew to be one of the richest

*Nicki Branagan bids farewell to Aunt Shirley with the painting of Mary Ann Corbet in the middle.*

and most powerful of the landed gentry in the Shropshire area. Basically, they were high-class landowners, members of nobility.

In terms of connecting these distant, ancient noble gentry to the current Williams family, I had the anecdotal clues from both Uncle George and Bernard. While I considered Uncle George's word could be somewhat dubious, I found it difficult to consider that Bernard would report anything not substantiated and precise. Back on *Ancestry.com* I was able to discover a marriage record dated October 22, 1825, joining Thomas Williams with Mary Ann Corbet. The location, Shropshire, matched both my own Williams family history, as well as the very Corbet family that inhabited Moreton Corbet Castle.

Certainly, the connection resulted in subdued excitement; however, in researching further, I was unable to definitively ascertain that the "Thomas Williams" listed had a direct connection with my own "Williams" family line. Likewise, I couldn't boast of any clear connection between the "Mary Ann Corbet" listed on the marriage record with the line of Corbets who once inhabited the castle bearing their surname.

While my rational mind offered skepticism that my own Williams family was in fact "castle-breed" through our connection to the Corbet family, I also couldn't dismiss any information offered by Bernard Williams. With that divergence from my research, I put the notion away, if not only temporarily, a likely topic for future curiosity.

To be certain, my aunt's trip was a total success. Not only did she have the opportunity to visit a part of the world foreign and distant, but she cemented the bond between the Williams family, past and present. While emails, phone calls, even Face Time calls are wonderful to connect, their impact cannot quite match a meeting in person. My aunt was welcomed everywhere as a member of the family. Additionally, she was able to set foot in the very locals that her father, Alfred Victor, roamed over one hundred years prior. If you recall from the introduction, I shared that I'm the type who relishes the opportunity to return to a former house or childhood park whenever presented with the opportunity. I can only imagine the innate thrill of standing at the edge of a property and envisioning my mysterious grandfather occupying the space as a young man.

For my aunt, this is what the trip was about, and I was pleased for her. That doesn't mean she didn't come through with a little to add to my research. Nicki had given her a small package containing papers that represented work Bernard had done on a family tree. I was a little perplexed, but also pleased to scan a rough version of Bernard's family tree, only to halt my gaze at two names: Don and Shirley. I was aware that Bernard's dementia had taken hold approximately one decade before his sad death. This would mean that the family tree must have been constructed sometime prior to 2006. I wondered how Bernard knew my father and aunt by name.

It was possible that his father, Charles, had shared the information. Charles and Alfred reconnected through letter in 1942 when Bernard was eleven. While I didn't have the letters to prove it, I assumed the correspondence continued until Charles' 1952 death, when Bernard would have been a twenty-one-year-old man. But could Bernard have remembered these names some fifty years later? I had to also consider that a working family tree may have existed since that time, taped inside a kitchen cupboard or hidden in a desk drawer. Or was it also possible that Bernard did possess some letters from my grandfather sharing such information? And if he did have these letters, what other information may have been shared? My independent mind began leaping to wonderful conclusions; however, my rational sensibilities reminded me that no letters had been reported.

One explanation for how Bernard was aware of my father and aunt may exist in a short note my aunt also brought back from overseas. It was a copy of a letter she had sent in 1968 to Dorothy Denise. The note read, "Hello. I have some terrible news to share. My father, Alfred Victor Williams, passed away on November 1, 1968. I am sorry to have to share this news. We will be having his service in the near future." Why this note remained while all other correspondences were discarded is curious, if not strange. For her part, my aunt does not recall writing this note. She no doubt gained knowledge of Dorothy Denise's address amongst my grandfather's possessions at the time of his death. Nor does my aunt remember any subsequent correspondence. She can't rule it out though, either.

In all, my aunt's visit proved precisely what we'd expected. Our English relatives were first class people all around. More and more I began to accept that my efforts at looking into my grandfather's life may be rewarded, not with discovery of his missing years, but with reuniting the Williams family after more than one-hundred years apart. Would this be enough for me to continue?

# In Appreciation of Mark Purcell

**Wednesday, November 18, 1931, 3:33 p.m. Exact whereabouts unknown, United States of America.**

*Alfred cannot believe his luck. While some tend to begin grieving their birthdays or foolishly spend in some doomed effort to stave off middle-age, Alfred is feeling younger than ever. The reason? He's met someone, a former beauty queen only twenty-one years of age. She's a little troubled, to be sure, recently coming off an unfortunate divorce scandal, but Alfred intends to take care of this one. Now that he's a little older, more reserved, it shouldn't be too difficult to behave, he surmises. He's aware the rye may pose a problem, but the fact that his new girlfriend regularly imbibes seems to forgive any of his overindulgence.*

*In this new state of bliss, Alfred wonders if "she's the one." If so, maybe it's time to be honest for once and tell her the whole truth. He didn't think it would matter with the last ones, reasoning that their acquaintances wouldn't last long. Now, with this one, Alfred believes it may be forever. Wouldn't it be better to be honest from the start?*

A ll this time, I was still looking at *Ancestry.com* a few times a week. More like daily to be honest. Besides minor discoveries, usually involving far-distant relations, I wasn't making much progress. There was definitely nothing relevant on Alfred Victor Williams, Alf Williams, Al Williams, Fred Williams, or Roy Hammond anyway. For some time now, my missing years had been narrowed down to 1910 to 1942. I figured there were two primary lines of research: online resources, and people. Yes, two separate lines both proving to be equally barren. I had to admit though, I was receiving some pleasure from searching, even if there were frequent moments of frustration.

Continuing on with 2017, I wasn't entirely sure where I'd find my next personal connection. I supposed I could have focused my pursuits on Lola LeDuke, but my online attempts so far had yielded no concrete leads. In life, though, they say that timing is everything and – wouldn't you know it – there came a day when the *Ancestry.com* gods came together and allowed me to make another fairly profound family connection. I was able to find a family tree for a "Mark Purcell" who listed himself as a grandchild of Dennis Williams.

How I stumbled upon this family tree is a mystery to myself. According to his profile, Mark had been a member of *Ancestry.com* since November 16, 2009, incidentally, my thirty-seventh birthday. Somehow despite all my numerous searches, none had turned up his tree until now. Realizing the valuable time that had already expired, I wasted no additional minutes messaging him.

*Hello Mr. Purcell: I came across your family contact information while completing a search for Dennis Williams. I believe that your parents might have been Eileen J. Williams and Michael Purcell. That would make your grandfather Dennis Williams (1894-1958). I am the grandson of Alfred Victor Williams (1889-1968), who was Dennis's brother. We share a great grandfather, Alfred Williams Sr. (1857-1934). I am in contact with other grandchildren of Dennis and would love to make contact with you and share some information. I look forward to hearing from you. Sincerely, Ron Williams*

Realizing that not everyone was as invested – obsessed – with researching the Williams family as I was, I wasn't entirely surprised that it took Mark nearly a month to reply.

*Hi Ron: Yes, I am the grandson of Dennis Williams. I don't have much information on his sons whom I believe are Charles and Ken. His daughters were my mother, Eileen, and her sister, Daphne. I recently found where my grandparents are buried in Stanmore Clamp Hill. They used to live on the same road, and I'm told my grandfather was the postmaster for Stanmore Post Office. I'd be interested to know more information about his sons if you can help. Regards, Mark*

With that we exchanged email addresses, and our relationship was off and running. The connection was fulfilling, but by this time, I held no grandiose notions of a potential bombshell connection, especially reading the incomplete rendition of family members. That didn't mean he wasn't connected to some other relative though and I was fully vested in pursuing every available angle. It occurs to me that I had begun to fashion myself something of a detective. It's fortunate I wasn't relying on any income from my pursuit.

It turns out Mark didn't know a heck of a lot about the Williams family in general or even his late grandfather. In his second email, he shared what I considered a fairly amusing anecdote. It was the only meeting that would occur between Mark and his grandfather, Dennis. Mark relates that he "must have been about seven and Dennis sent [him] to the nearby shop to get some pear drops (sweets) and said he was gonna' count them when [he] came back." Upon Mark's return, "Dennis said [Mark] had eaten one, which [he] hadn't." It took Mark a moment before he realized his unfamiliar grandfather was enjoying a joke at his expense.

Reading over the amusing situation, it immediately struck me as the very type of prank my own father would play. Also, I had to admit, it was a type of humor I seemed to be adopting more and more of as I grew in age. I was beginning to grasp some commonalities in my Williams clan.

I relayed above that Mark was somewhat fuzzy on family specifics. What he lacked in precise details, however, he made up for in family lore. Mark reported that his grandparents, Dennis and Dorothy, created a fairly rough home for Mark's mother, Eileen and her siblings. Apparently, Dennis had his hands all full with his wife Dorothy. Mark's mother, Eileen, had passed in 2000 but regularly reported that she never cared much for her mother. There were family stories that involved Dorothy sneaking out the window at night to enjoy a taste of the nightlife without her husband. This certainly matched what Charles Williams had reported in a 1940s letter when he wrote that Dennis had "married the wrong girl."

While Mark seemed aware of four children born to Dennis and Dorothy, I was able to correct him on the missing two. Whether it was his late mother's omission or Mark's incomplete memory, he had omitted Dorothy Denise, the oldest daughter and first child of Dennis and Dorothy, and Vivian Raymond, the second youngest child. When I shared the strange story of Dorothy Denise's adoption and subsequent kidnapping, he confirmed no knowledge of the tale. Mark was able to share that the oldest son, Charles, had one glass eye.

Mark explained in an email that his mother "was basically disowned for marrying an Irish man." I figured that may have accounted for the extremely limited interaction between Mark and his grandfather, totaling one solitary visit. I wondered the discrepancy regarding the Irish. My grandfather seemed to deliberately fabricate an Irish heritage, while his brother Dennis apparently despised their neighbors to the west. I thought back to a line from Eva's September 1943 letter to Alfred in which she offered that "there is one little bit of advice if you don't mind taking it." She cautioned that in his newfound correspondence with his extended family, he "don't say anything against [his] dad to them." This matched what I had heard from my own father, that Alfred Victor and his dad didn't necessarily enjoy a harmonious relationship. It was Eva's next line that sparked a connection here. She cautions that "Dennis was all his father." It makes sense that Dennis had adopted an anti-Irish sentiment from his father, while Alfred had purposely, stubbornly, taken the other point of view. I'd never know for sure, but I found it satisfying conjecture.

As we became better acquainted through email, Mark shared some details about his immediate family. I learned that his mother, Eileen, and father had ten children in total. Sadly, one boy, Chris, died in infancy. Mark further explained that his father, who passed in 1999 could best be described as a "mad Irish man" and "a bad piece of work," who drove his mother crazy. To another cousin, Mark shared that there were times when he and his siblings were relegated to foster care. Whatever their upbringing, it seemed that Mark remained close to a number of his siblings, and in the end, he described his late father as "an amazing guy."

I couldn't help but think of the commonalties between what little I knew of Mark's upbringing and my father's own upbringing. If the pear drop story helped construct a distinct,

"Williams" brand of humor, here was another, darker commonality: chaotic family upbringing. I now had several situations in which Williams family constructs simply fell apart due to circumstance and necessity. This realization made me admire my own father even more for the warm, stable home he and my mother created. At the same time though, I again considered that maybe it wasn't too odd that Alfred Victor was estranged from family for all these years. Maybe it was simply the "Williams way."

I had to accept that this also meant if Alfred did have a family in the United States, it would be equally natural for him to simply walk away from them. Thus, I needn't necessarily expect any photos, letters or other evidence of such if I were to continue entertaining the theory. It's possible he never left any evidence behind with sentiment or thought. The photo of the two girls looms large in my mind.

Finally, I had to consider what it was I actually hoped for. Did I want there to be no big reveal, that he simply roamed North America from job to job, just naturally estranged from his England family and never laying down any newer family roots? Or did I still pine for some deep secret, a family or a prison term? I couldn't ignore the alias, "Roy Hammond."

I guess I just wanted to discover the truth.

# Reconnecting Kenneth Williams

**Friday, September 14th, 1934, 10:41 a.m. City Hospital, Birmingham Union Workhouse, Western Road, Birmingham, England.**

*Waking on the strange cot in the strange recreational room, seventy-seven-year-old Alfred Williams Sr. is confused and weak. Unable to understand why he is not in the familiar bed of his Birmingham rooming house, Alfred realizes he has been stripped of his clothes, now dressed in unfamiliar robe. In some time, a kind girl visits with a cup of tea and some biscuits. After assuring Alfred his gold watch and chain are under lock in the office for safe keeping, she explains that Alfred has found himself in the poorhouse, the police delivering him in the late hours of the night after receiving reports of a man wandering.*

*His mind failing, Alfred attempts to rise and dress, frantic not to miss his employ at Mitchells and Butlers for the afternoon rush. Only moments later, his heavy body falling onto the hard cot, he realizes it has been quite some time since he was employed and now survives the life of a lonely old man, far from those he loved. Of course, his eldest son, Charles, visits the most regularly, making the trip from his home in Stafford, often bringing Alfred's very young grandson, Bernard, for the visit. Dennis, a little further away in London and preoccupied with a challenging family life, visits far more seldom. Now, aware of his imminent death, Alfred's thoughts uneasily turn to his middle son and namesake, Alfred Victor.*

*Almost thirty years since he saw him, and over twenty since he last read his letters, Alfred Sr. takes inventory of his regretful actions that drove his son away including the mistreatment of the boy's mother, and the harsh criticisms aimed to injure. Where Alfred Victor, now forty-four, is in the world or whether he counted as one of many who perished in the great war, Alfred Sr. realizes he will never know, as his breathing slows, and he descends to his death.*

B ecause Dennis and Dorothy bore six children, I reasoned there had to be more grandchildren out there. For the most part, I had given up finding living children of Dennis and Dorothy, what would have amounted to first cousins for my dad. This was hardly a surprise. My father's first cousins' birthdates ranged from 1921 to 1931, meaning that any living first cousins would be in their nineties. Not impossible, but unlikely. Owing to the fact that Alfred Victor became father to my dad at the age of fifty-eight, it was to be expected that all of my father's first cousins were born much prior to my dad's own 1948 birthday. On *Ancestry.com*, I had discovered that

179

Dennis and Dorothy's fourth child, Daphne, had passed in 1990. It seems she had married a man named Thomas Nethersole and together they gave birth to three daughters, Patricia, born in 1953, Sandra, born in 1957, and Lorraine, born in 1961.

It was another online tool that would prove useful this time: Facebook. It was Lana who first suggested Facebook could prove a valuable tool. It was true that *Ancestry.com* contained thousands of extremely useful documents; however, some such documents were controlled by moratorium, with no personal information to be released until a safe number of years had expired. With Christian names, surnames, birthdates and places of birth in hand, I scoured Facebook for a Patricia, Sandra or Lorraine who fit the bill. I can't recall the exact path of clues and discovery that led to the connection, but I eventually found a Sandra Thomson who fit the bill nicely. I messaged Sandra, explaining our connection as distant cousins.

Further to that, I shared that I was in touch with her first cousins, Mark and Fay. She was very polite and showed an interest in our shared family history but didn't ask many questions.

This constituted offspring from three of the six children born of Dennis and Dorothy Williams. I had found a daughter from Dorothy Denise, a son of Eileen, and a daughter of Daphne. As for the remaining three, I had deduced that Charles Barrett had married a woman named Esther in 1940. To date though, I hadn't been able to find any records of the two youngest children, Vivian Raymond or Ken. Little did I know that was soon to change, in a fairly substantive way.

It was during another routine *Ancestry.com* search for Dennis Williams that I stumbled upon a Kerr family tree, managed by a Peter Kerr from Hemel Hempstead in Hertfordshire. The name "Kerr" meant nothing to me. Additionally, I didn't recognize the majority of names listed in the small family tree. The name, "Dennis Williams," however, was prominent along with his spouse, Dorothy Halsey. Underneath, there were spaces for three children, Vivian Williams, and two spots identified as "private," which likely meant the manager had not entered a date of death. True to form, I didn't waste any time making contact:

*Hello Mr. Kerr: My name is Ron Williams. I live in Vancouver, Canada. I noticed that you have a Vivian Raymond Williams listed in your "Kerr Family Tree." I believe this is the first cousin of my father, Donald Roy Williams. My father is the son of Alfred Victor Williams (1889-1968). Alfred Victor and Dennis were brothers. It would mean a great deal to my father if he were able to connect with family overseas. Can you please let me know if you can offer any information? Thanks. Sincerely, Ron Williams*

In truth, I had hoped for much more, including establishing a correspondence, plying them for information and possibly sharing photographs or other documents. Three days later, I was pleased to receive the following response.

*Hello Ron: Thank you for your email. It's exciting news and certainly your records seem to tie in with mine. My name is Brenda Kerr and my father is Ken Desmond Williams, son of Dennis Williams. Unfortunately, I have no information on Vivian Raymond Williams, whom I believe was only a year older than my father. However, my father remembers him. The only relative of my father that we knew was Charles Barrett, his eldest half-brother, married to Esther Barrett. The other names of Charles, Vivian and Ken's siblings are Eileen Joan (Williams) Purcell and Patricia Williams. Hope this has been useful and many thanks. Kind regards, Brenda Kerr, Hertfordshire, England*

Although the message didn't include any new information, I keyed in on one line specifically: "my father *is* Ken Desmond

Williams." Was I reading this correctly? Was Ken Desmond Williams still alive? Was it possible my father had a first cousin, alive and well? According to my research, Ken Desmond was born in 1930, which would make him eighty-seven years old...certainly possible. I was desperate to respond, confirming the use of present tense; however, I was also a little apprehensive. Brenda closed her message, saying, "hope this has been useful and many thanks." Although very polite, that didn't sound like someone overly keen in pursuing the connection. I had also to accept the possibility that she failed to share in the excitement of potentially uniting her aging father with a first cousin. I determined I'd need to approach this carefully. Lana, on the other hand, urged me to respond right away. She suggested the time to strike was while the message was hot and that for all we knew, Brenda may decide on a hiatus from *Ancestry.com* at any time. The website was subscription-based and required a monthly fee after all. She had a point, but I think her real motivation was no different than mine – pure excitement. As usual, her wishes won out and I found myself offering the following response the very next morning.

> *Hi Brenda: Thank you very much for the reply...very exciting! My father, Donald Roy Williams, born 1948, is the son of Alfred Victor Williams (1889-1968). Alfred Victor was the older brother of Dennis. Thus, my father is your father's first cousin.*
>
> *I began family research about a year and a half ago, mainly for my father who always wondered about family in England, so this is quite exciting. I have also been in touch with two of your first cousins – who I think – probably live nearby. I believe that you also have two wonderful cousins right in Hertfordshire at Welwyn Garden City.*
>
> *Thank you for the information. I'd love if you gave me your personal email and I can send you some*

*photos/documents. Also, I know my dad would love to send a message to your dad at some point, if possible. Thank you, Brenda. I look forward to hearing from you. Sincerely, Ron Williams*

Unfortunately, this is one time my usually correct wife was in fact, wrong. I waited a day. Then I waited two days. Finally, a week passed by. Then two weeks came and went. I figured for sure that I'd scared Brenda off with my father left to pay the price. Thankfully, it turns out I was the one who was wrong, as I received the following response exactly two weeks after my message.

*Good evening, Ron: It's good to hear from you again. I apologize for the delay in my response as I have been away on holiday. I will be very honest. I started this journey out of my own curiosity, and I ambushed my husband's Ancestry.com tree, not thinking for one moment that I would find any of my father's family. However, I have to be mindful. Although I find the connection very exciting, my father has not seen or heard from any of his family since he was twenty-years old. Only the lovely Mr. Charles Barrett, who was a very wonderful person, was close to us, so I really feel that I have a clear responsibility to respect the sensitivity of our findings.*

*The good news is that it seems both of our fathers are equally excited about our findings and my father is happy for me to give you his email address which could be a good starting point of communication. If he does not respond, please get back to me. It will not be because he doesn't want to. It will be because he is a full-time support for my mother and has his own health issues. Kind regards, Brenda*

I felt a little ashamed of my own shortsightedness. I realized that I'd only been thinking of myself, of my own motives for making a connection without much regard for how my instruction would affect others. Additionally, I should have expected that "Ken," as we had begun referring to him, likely had not been in touch with any of his immediate or extended Williams family. Quite the pattern had now fully emerged.

I guess I figured if someone made their family information public, they must be open to a connection. Here, though, Brenda's words had me considering another option. Either way, I was thrilled at the response and couldn't wait to share the news with my mother and father.

On June 15, I was pleased to send an email to Mr. Ken Williams introducing myself and my family and including photos of myself, Lana and the kids as well as a separate photo of my parents. My dad wasn't going to let me monopolize all the attention for myself and before long, he and his cousin were regularly emailing one another. I couldn't have been more thrilled.

It turns out that "Cousin Ken's" story was, well, exactly as I'd expected. He was a man of utmost class and honor. Explaining his situation, he shared that he joined World War II as a young man. When the war ended and he returned to England, his family had simply disbanded...no more than that. From Brenda's original message, it seemed clear that Ken remembered all his siblings, save for Dorothy Denise. I left it as an unfortunate footnote to be followed up later.

Perhaps most exciting was a phone call that my dad set up to include Ken, my father and myself. England being several hours ahead of Canada, I set my alarm for 5:00 a.m. one early Wednesday morning in July and ventured to my parents' house prior to making my way to school. The connection wasn't necessarily ideal and both accent and age made communicating a little difficult. There was no doubt, however, that we were speaking with family. Ken outlined his life, sharing how proud he was of his beautiful wife, Edna, of almost seventy years and his two daughters Brenda and Deborah. After serving in the war, Ken enjoyed a long, satisfying career as a type of engineer with the Rolls Royce Motor Company. My dad was impressed by all of it and immediately considered his first cousin a gentleman of great success. I had to agree.

At one point in the call, my father and I steered the topic of conversation to family history. Ken was unable to add much that we didn't already know. Truthfully, he seemed much more interested in learning about us, which, suited me just fine.

In addition to sharing this news with my father, I was almost equally as excited to share the news with the nieces and nephews of Ken Williams whom I'd been in touch with. This included Fay Harman, Mark Purcell and Sandra Thomson. Probably more exciting, though, was the prospect of bringing all these cousins together to meet their Uncle Ken and Aunt Edna. With each discovery, I had shared both information and email addresses with all parties and I was pleased to see a correspondence emerge between them. In one such email, Mark Purcell wrote to his newly discovered Uncle Ken:

*Hi Uncle Ken: I am your nephew, Mark, your sister Eileen's son. She always spoke of you with affection and wondered where you were. She said she would love to see you again and said Charlie had a glass eye. This is from my mother's lips. They lived in Clamp Hill, Stanmore, Belgrano Lodge and are now buried in Clamp Hill where I visited their graves.*

*Ken, I would love to meet with you to fulfil my mother's dreams through my eyes and get an insight to how things were in your days and get an understanding how things were with the family. You are the last one left, my only surviving uncle on both my parents' sides. You are very special to us. I live in London, NW7, very close to you and I would really love to meet you. Regards, your nephew Mark*

185

*The lovely Dennis Williams family united at last. (From left to right) Ken Williams, Brenda Kerr, Janet Fay Harman, Maureen Purcell & Mark Purcell.*

It was almost natural that someone set up a reunion, which is exactly what Mark's older sister, Maureen, did. The group agreed to meet on August 20, 2017. To sum up, there was a possibility of reuniting members from four of Dennis and Dorothy's six children. The only ones omitted were Charles Barrett, whom it seemed had no children, and Vivian Raymond, whom I had no record of past birth. As preparations for the reunion came together, I took great pride in one of Mark's rallying cries he included in an email: "Let's repair this Williams family!" At the risk of sounding boastful, I had to pause and pat myself on the back for orchestrating the reunion of this family, even though my efforts were based on more selfish, ulterior motives. My only wish was that I could have boarded a plane and joined in the festive occasion.

August 20 came and went. I thought about the family on that day, wondering how the visit was proceeding, but also, what family history or even secrets may have been bandied about. Probably none. It seems we were unable to secure the participation of Sandra Thomson, but all the others reported they'd be in attendance. I didn't have to wait long for a report. At approximately 1:20 a.m. on August 21, I received the following email from Mark.

*Hi Ron: I just wanted to congratulate you on your fine work. We had our meet up today including Ken, his wife, Edna, his daughter Brenda and Brenda's daughter, Brooke. Also, there were Fay and her husband, John, as well as myself and my sister, Maureen, with her husband, Tim.*

*All this from the other side of the pond! They are our family one hundred percent. I have attached pictures. Regards, Mark*

True to his word, he attached several photos of very pleased family members posing with just enough emotion to reveal a true family connection. Looking over the photos, I had to say, they presented as a proper, even handsome, group with no trace of the turmoil and struggle many of them had faced as eventual offspring of Dennis and Dorothy Williams. The look on their faces was no different than the smiles on my father and aunt's faces at family functions: perseverance, contentment, pride. Looking at the photos, they reflected exactly how I felt to be a Williams: proud.

Some days later, I received a message from Fay Harman. Turns out she had some modest biographical information, if not just observations, that added to my understanding of the family history.

*Dear Ron: We met up with my long-lost relatives at a restaurant at Kings, Langley which is not far from Hemel Hempstead where my uncle Ken lives. It was quite an emotional time meeting my mother's youngest brother, but sadly he had no memories of her at all or even knew that she existed. The same went for my cousins, Mark and Maureen - their mother Eileen never talked about an older sister which I thought was strange as she would have been a teenager when my mother was summoned back to London with the ensuing fuss when she ran away back to Wolverhampton.*

To be sure, this was a surprise to myself. True to Fay's account, in her 1966 letter to my grandfather, Dorothy Denise reported that she had returned home for eight months. This would have been in 1936, when Charles Barret was eighteen, Eileen Joan was fourteen and Ken was six. Wouldn't they have remembered an older sister? For that matter, the existence of an older sister was never kept a secret. In another letter from Dorothy Denise, she provides updates on all her siblings, suggesting there was an ongoing relationship. It's possible memories and people were pushed aside in a conscious bid for mental and emotional peace or maybe the memories and people faded out of consciousness, an unfortunate product of the turbulence and chaos in a dysfunctional homelife. It certainly wasn't up to me to judge.

Fay continued her email expressing sympathy and understanding for the difficult life several of Dennis and Dorothy's children and grandchildren suffered. Further, she expressed relief that her mother was raised in the warm, caring house of Charles and Eva. She also reported a new understanding that it was, in fact, Dennis's wife, Dorothy, who was the difficult one with a reputation for being cold and harsh. The one photo I had of my great aunt seemed to support this opinion. In the end, Fay thanked me for the opportunity to not only meet these long-estranged family members but also to learn a little more about her dear mother's family. In her final words she concluded, "they are a very nice family."

All well and good, but, again, the entire ordeal offered little in my elusive quest to discover my grandfather's missing years. Yes, once again, I was left with a now familiar consolation: both the joy of bringing family together and the understanding that families grew apart in difficult times and that Alfred's estrangement wasn't necessarily an important factor in my mystery.

More and more, I was accepting that the above would form the conclusion of this book.

I was giving up hope of solving my mystery.

# Lola LeDuke: A Life

**Wednesday, October 28, 1942, 7:19 p.m. Exact whereabouts unknown, United States of America.**

*Lying alone on the hard bed of his rented suite, Alfred is feeling unsettled. He's unable to concentrate on the crossword puzzle in the day's paper. The entire population of the world is unsettled as well with World War II now going strong. He'd managed to avoid fighting in the first world war, and, at fifty-two years of age, hasn't been too keen to become involved in this one.*

*Also, the hard miles he's put on are beginning to take their toll. In the early days roaming the streets of the city selling his wares was an excitement, a challenge. Now, more and more, it's lethargy he feels and respite he craves. With no other options for employment, he marches onward. Also, the alcohol. Some late nights in lonely pubs, carousing with unattended, most often younger, ladies, but also quiet evenings listening to a boxing match on his radio with an ever-present bottle of rye. He fools himself that the alcohol will aid in forgetting his woes, but they're still there the next day.*

*It's now been over thirty years since he's had any contact with family members. He accepts his parents are likely deceased. It would be nice to hear from Charles and Dennis though, that is, if they both survived their military participation. A return to England out of the question, Alfred thinks of Toronto. William Turley should still be alive, and Alfred can't help but thinking that a return to his cousin and a reconnection with family might be what he needs.*

*When the local draft board contacts him to report for a physical, it gives perfect excuse for him to execute his homecoming.*

W ith the sad notion of futility overtaking the hope I had been holding, I knew I needed to pursue a different path, one that was not directly connected to the Williams family. It was certainly fulfilling connecting with family, but I had a mystery to solve, and it was clues that I sought. I figured discovering Lola LeDuke could possibly provide those clues. You may recall, Ms. LeDuke was author of a 1967 letter to my grandfather. Although it was possible, I had no evidence that she was a part of the Williams family, so, discovering the nature of her relationship with my grandfather could provide details as of yet unknown. I fantasized that Lola could be an ex-wife, ex-partner, stepchild, child! In truth, though, based on the details of her letter I shared in part one, I believed their relationship was based on geography rather than biography, and geography could provide the very information I was lacking.

If you recall, there were several clues offered in her brief correspondence. Lola was familiar with Alfred's kids, whom she referred to as "Donnie and Shirley." As well, even though the postmark and text revealed she resided in Seattle, Washington, she was familiar with and mentioned several British Columbia locals including the city of Burnaby, where a mutual acquaintance named Mona resided, and Vancouver Island, where Lola and her husband Bill intended to take a vacation in near future. Lastly, the opening salutation, "Dear Al," had me suspect that Lola knew my grandfather in Canada. This was based on the Turley affidavit claiming that my grandfather had went by the name, "Roy Hammond," while in the United States. I wasn't about to take that as gospel though, quite yet. Even if it was true, I couldn't rule out that Lola may have been one of only a select few who was acquainted with my grandfather in the United States and aware of his true identity. Almost sounded like a detective novel.

With that, I opened up the familiar homepage on my *Ancestry.com* account and got to work. I began with what I knew:

First and Middle Names: Lola
Last Name: LeDuke
Lived In: British Columbia
Lived In: 1967, Seattle, Washington, United States
Spouse: Bill LeDuke
"Search"

I was immediately rewarded with a matching record under the *Washington, U.S. Death Index, 1940-2017*. A "Lola J. LeDuke" of Seattle, Washington passed away on January 14, 1972. With the date of death only about three years after my grandfather, I had to consider that this Lola may have been roughly the same age, a clue I may have been on the right track.

Below, I clicked on a listing for the *U.S., Social Security Death Index, 1935-2015*, with matching name, death date and location. This second document listed a social security issue date of 1959/1960 and a birth date of March 10, 1919. The date of birth was somewhat surprising, putting her at age fifty-three at time of death. Also, this would put her as thirty-years junior to my grandfather, not typical of a friendship but not unheard of either. Immediately I considered the situation of my Oma who married Alfred despite a twenty-seven-year difference. No sir, the thirty-year age difference didn't rule out that Lola could have been a romantic partner, nor did it rule out the possibility of child. I pulled the horses back a little when I accepted I was not yet sure I even had the correct Lola LeDuke.

Nonetheless, I pursued the birthdate offered, and in the *1921 Census of Canada*, I found a Lola J. Shier, matching birthdate of March 10, 1919, born in Hamiota, Manitoba, Canada. By the time of the census, when Lola was a mere two years old, the family had relocated to Victoria, British Columbia, specifically on Vancouver Island. I naturally took note of the 1967 letter in which Lola shared her and her husband's intention to visit Vancouver Island for their holiday. Returning to a past home, perhaps?

I'm not entirely sure where my level of skepticism falls within the wide world of genealogy. Lana would say I am too skeptical, but I was scolded on one occasion by a potential relation for being too loose and free with my research. In this case, I felt pretty comfortable – for the time being at least - I had the correct Lola LeDuke or Lola Shier. The dates of birth and death fit with the narrative. Also, the familiarity with British Columbia and Vancouver Island felt right.

Continuing with said details, I found a 1935 newspaper article dated October 19, reporting on the death of a Johnston Harold Shier. From the *1921 Census of Canada*, I knew the name as Lola's father.  To be sure, Lola herself was listed as a mourner.  At age sixteen, Lola had lost her father to a motor vehicle accident in Vancouver.

The next clue was a voters list from 1940.  Lola, now twenty-one, was listed as a "spinster" residing at 796 13$^{th}$ Avenue, East with her mother and brother, Russell.  A 1957 voters list had Lola, now thirty-eight, in apartment #4, 3587 Rumble Street in Burnaby, neighboring city to Vancouver, this time listed as a widow.  I found it was curious that she was still using her maiden name and I was unable to find any marriage certificate online.

From the detail amassed, I put together the following crude timeline:

1919 – Lola Jane Shier is born in Hamiota, Man.
1921 – Lola (2) resides in Victoria, B.C.
1935 – Lola (16) resides in Vancouver, B.C.
1940 – Lola (21) resides with mother in Vancouver, B.C.
1949 – Lola (30) bridesmaid in Vancouver, B.C.
1957 – Lola (38) listed as widow in Burnaby, B.C.
1959 – Lola (40) applies for social security in U.S.
1967 – Lola (48) married to Bill LeDuke in Seattle, WA.
1972 – Lola (53) passes away in Seattle, WA.

I regretted not being able to fill in more for the missing years; however, that's all I was able to find for the time being.  Based on above, and assuming I had the correct Lola LeDuke, I was able to create a few working hypotheses.

First, my grandfather was acquainted with the Shier family in Manitoba around 1919.  At this point, he may have been a friend of Lola's parents, or he could have been Lola's father or stepfather.  Lola, for all I knew, could have been one of the two girls in the mystery picture from his wallet.  I recognized that this was, at best, wishful thinking, but I couldn't rule it out.

Second, I considered my grandfather originally crossed paths with Lola in British Columbia between 1921 and 1942.  This is at odds to what William Turley reported in his 1942 affidavit, but I had no corroborating evidence that he was accurate either. This would suggest Alfred had a relationship with Lola when she was between the ages of two and twenty-three. Again, it seemed most likely that he would have had some type of relationship with one of Lola's parents. It could have been a friendship; however, I reminded myself that Lola's mother was a widow from 1935 leaving open the possibility of a romantic tryst. I tried to rule out that my fifty-three-year-old grandfather would have been romantic with a twenty-three-year-old Lola. If my grandfather had lived in Vancouver between 1921 and 1942, it could explain why he returned in 1947.

Third, my grandfather may have been acquainted with Lola in Vancouver between 1947 and 1959. Again, this could have been a romantic relationship, friend, neighbor, or co-worker. All three would fit the tone of Lola's 1967 letter. As well, it was the only theory in which I could absolutely place both in the same area. I had to admit that this theory seemed the most likely but also the least helpful or exciting. Such is the reality of a genealogist, I suppose.

What to do next? Attempt to prove or disprove each hypothesis, of course. I began with online records from Manitoba in the early 1900s. I knew my grandfather was in Ontario until the later part of the first decade. Was it possible be moved west to Manitoba for a time? Not according to any online documents I could find. Moving to my second hypothesis, I was pretty certain I'd searched for my grandfather in British Columbia numerous times, covering not just the years I was certain he was a resident, but previous years also. My certainty was confirmed as no new records for British Columbia between the years 1921-1942 presented themselves.

With no luck on *Ancestry.com*, I decided to pursue a connection with a relative. As far as I could discern, Lola had no children of her own, so, I'd have to rely on some less direct family member, specifically one who remembered a relative who died about fifty years prior. I managed to connect with a Rachel Johnson from Minnesota. She had Lola Shier listed in her family tree, and they looked to be third cousins as they shared a set of great, great grandparents. Ms. Johnson showed an immediate interest in my cause when I explained the mysterious reasons behind my search for Lola LeDuke. In fact, she sent me no fewer than eleven messages containing various information about my grandfather and Lola. Maybe her most useful contribution was finding that the "Mona" mentioned in the letter was actually a cousin of Lola's who had spent time back and forth between Vancouver and the United States also. In the end, Rachel suggested I look for a Sharon D. LeDuke, born in 1940. Although she was the child of William LeDuke's previous marriage, Rachel suggested that, if alive, she may remember something of her father's second wife.

Having found no evidence of Alfred and Lola connecting prior to them both being in the Vancouver area between 1947 to 1959, I had to accept that they likely came into contact during those years. From the feeling of Lola's letter, it seems they were coworkers or friends of some sort. From her playful tone, it seems like she considered him an older uncle type.

There is a saying in life that one can be defined by the company they keep. It seems Lola dealt with instability and death at an early age, followed by living her adult life as a single woman, before marrying late and passing before her time. Is that what attracted Lola and my grandfather to one another, a shared misery and difficult past?

I considered they had that in common. Also, I couldn't ignore that it was looking more and more that if I ever were to solve my mystery, the answer may rest in Seattle.

# The Beloved Elizabeth Zelbel

**Monday, November 16, 1942.    351 Ashdale Avenue, Toronto, Ontario, Canada.**

*The Toronto of 1942 that Alfred encounters is much different from the Toronto of 1909 that Alfred left. That's the result of his thirty-three-year absence, a period that most certainly comprises Alfred's prime years.   He's comforted but knows there will be challenges ahead.*

*First, there is the matter of immigration. With no legal identification bearing the name, "Alfred Victor Williams," a British subject by birth, Alfred acts upon advice given by his cousin, William, and contacts Francis Peddie of McNish and Peddie. Well-studied in the practice of immigration law, Peddie immediately contacts the Canadian Immigration Department, making arrangements to have Alfred's radio examined against federal regulations, a necessity in war time, as well as taking an affidavit from William Turley, confirming the identity of this new arrival. Although strange to Alfred, Peddie insists they are transparent, maintaining that they must be honest about using a false identity and hope they can remain vague when it comes to details.*

*Second, there is the matter of his name. Relinquishing the title of "Roy Hammond" and re-adopting his given name will be something of a challenge, if for nothing else than remembering to provide the correct title when asked. However, he finds it easy to assume his old name and vitals when completing his National Registry card, an essential step in preparing for possible military service. It's been a while since Alfred responded honestly to a government form, even recording his birthdate to the best of his knowledge. He pauses when he reads the line, "can you handle horses?" remembering back so long ago to his Worcester trips with his father and Uncle George. Now, some forty years removed, he responds with a simple, "no."*

*Third, he has decided to reconnect with his estranged family. He expects that his mother and father will both be deceased but looks forward to connecting with brothers Charles and Dennis, if they remain alive.*

B y 2018, I was refreshed and spending more time researching than ever before. It seemed that for approximately every twenty hours I'd spend online, I'd make a new discovery, albeit a usually modest discovery. Yes, this could be frustrating, but I also accepted it was because I had already amassed a fairly impressive amount of information, including a few new pieces that I hoped held some promise.

I made the time to follow up on an old card found in my grandfather's possessions. It was a two by three inch, soft, weathered, identification card in yellowed stock, titled "Dominion of Canada, National Registration Regulations, 1940." Below the title, underneath the subheading, "this is to certify that," I read, "Alfred Victor Williams residing at 351 Ashdale Avenue, Toronto, was duly registered under the above-mentioned regulations this 16 day of November 1942."

Upon completing some cursory research, I learned that filling in the National Registry was a wartime requirement between the years of 1940 to 1946 for all persons sixteen years or older. Basically, individuals had to register so they were ready to be called to World War II if the necessity arose. While there was no information of interest on the card my grandfather carried, I learned that there was a long form that I could request, for a nominal fee of course.

Weeks later I received my grandfather's completed long form from the federal government offices, but sadly it too was to prove a disappointment. While the questions, aimed at judging what wartime contributions a person may be capable of making, were comprehensive enough, my grandfather's responses could best be judged as lacking. In the vital statistics section, my grandfather accurately listed his place of birth, his father's place of birth, his mother's place of birth and his racial origin. I had to laugh that he had his birthdate correct, November 23, but again he erred one year to his advantage in birth year. Sections for marital status and children were left blank.

It was in the occupation and craft section, which held the most promise, that I was most disappointed. For occupation, he simply listed, "salesman" and "thirty years" experience, reporting he had worked forty-nine weeks during the past twelve months. Here is a sample of his responses to several other prompts:

What other work can you do well? [left blank]
Who was your most recent employer? [left blank]

Nature of business where you were employed. [left blank]
Describe training or experience. [left blank]
Have you worked on a farm? No
Can you handle horses? No
Have you previously served in any Naval, Military, or Air Forces? No
Have you ever been rejected for military service? [left blank]

I couldn't have expected him to add much more than quick responses for the queries regarding farm or military experience. However, seeing as he had just reentered Canada, likely that very day, any mention of a recent employer could have been a huge boost to my efforts.

At this point, I realized I'd tracked and researched over one-hundred family members. Included in that, were personal email correspondences with multiple strangers. I had made contact with offspring of those close to my grandfather. Then it occurred to me. I hadn't looked at the one person who may have been closest to him, the one person who may have known more of his secrets than anyone else: my Oma.

I guess I was fairly confident that tracing her life wouldn't provide much in the way of clues about my grandfather. I knew the circumstances of their meeting. I understood their complicated and estranged relationship. What could studying her life add to my efforts? My recent connections and research of people and ancestors in my grandfather's life had failed to yield any monumental clues; however, with the information gleaned from each person's story, I was able to gain insight into the times and circumstances of the world my grandfather inhabited. I was slowly understanding the personal and societal forces that may have influenced his strange life and, in the process, gaining a better understanding of the man.

More specifically, from researching William Turley, I understood that my grandfather was attracted to men of style, active in pursuing worldly adventure and the company of women. Connecting with the Dennis Williams family, I had learned that the Williams family came from difficult conditions, it not being that unusual for individuals to choose personal survival over the long-term maintenance of family ties. Researching Lola LeDuke, I considered that my grandfather was well-suited to keep company with the wounded and deprived. What could I learn about Alfred by researching the only woman I could be sure he had ever married?

Similar to the case with my grandfather, I had heard only rumor of my Oma's background. It was at a family dinner at Lana and my first house that my Oma retold the story of her harrowing escape that eventually led her to Canada. The tale involved a hasty, secretive, midnight departure and a life-threatening boat ride through enemy waters before she ended up in a German concentration camp which almost cost her life. I didn't ask many follow-up questions and carried around my confusion for years, wondering why she, a German, would be housed in a German concentration camp. So, not totally convinced it would assist me in uncovering the mystery, it was in the still rainy month of April 2018, that I began to look into the life of my Oma.

Elizabeth Zelbel was born September 2, 1916, in Tashkent, the highly populated capital city in the country of Uzbekistan. It was the place her parents, Reinhold Zelbel and Anna Katherine Keil, were married some eleven years prior. Readers, while I have done my best to be accurate with what I am about to share, I am also cognizant of being brief and possibly simplistic. While the political and geographical history of the region is rich and vital, I am including only cursory details that will illustrate my Oma's story as I understand it.

*Pictured holding my father, my Oma's life was fraught with struggle and survival.*

In early 1900's Tashkent, my Oma, along with her parents and two older sisters, Regina, born in 1906, and Olga, born 1914, were a family of German heritage and custom living in Russian controlled Tashkent. While families of German descent had occupied the area for some time, it seems this Zelbel branch was relatively recent, with Reinhold reporting his parents place of birth as Poland and Anna reporting her place of birth as Klarus, Russia.

I read of the "Volga Germans," families of German descent who were initially recruited to occupy land within Russian borders along the mighty Volga River in efforts to populate otherwise vulnerable, unoccupied Russian land. These families enjoyed the fruits of Russian farmland while retaining their German customs until the early 1900s when they were forced from their land due to Russian cleansing.

My Oma's home in Tashkent was some distance to the east of the most populous Volga German settlements. However, I have borne witness to at least one source that grouped those

Germans in Tashkent with the Volga Germans. In any event, my Oma, along with her family, was no longer safe in Tashkent by the early 1920s.

As related by a Zelbel cousin, the family was forced to flee their home in the middle of the night via dogsled, sticks and other weapons used to fight off predatory wolves. Finally, the family transferred to some type of watercraft, resuming their harrowing escape.

I was able to find an online copy of a *Journal of the American Historical Society of Germans from Russia*, dated Spring 1988. The journal featured an article titled, "Refugees Arriving in the Heimkehrlager at Frankfurt/Oder in 1922," by Edward R. Gerk. Along with the article was an accompanying list, where I spotted the following:

Zelbel, Reinhold
Zelbel, Anna (wife)
Zelbel, Regina (child)
Zelbel, Olga (child)
Zelbel, Elisabeth (child)
Zelbel, Lidia (child)

The "Heimkehrlager at Frankfurt/Oder" was a refugee camp for Volga Germans returning to their ancestral homeland. From what I read, it had served as a concentration camp during World War I and was now being repurposed.

The family was listed as arriving from Reinsfeld, although a question mark was added after the name. This confused me as the area is to the west of Frankfurt, while documents showed me the family travelled from Tashkent which sits to the east of Frankfurt. I had to suppose that their escape may have taken them far west before doubling back to Frankfurt.

Also confusing was the listing for "Lidia." My research on *Ancestry.com* showed that my Great Aunt "Lydia" was born in Canada in 1925. Narrowing my focus to the different spellings of the two names, I remembered an old story that my Oma had suffered terrible injury as a child when she banged heads with one of her sisters. I was told that the collision was so injurious that it proved fatal to one. I realized now, it was the original "Lidia" who succumbed to the injury, to be honored in name by Reinhold and Anna's next daughter called "Lydia." Although she lived for only a short time, I was pleased to be able to honor her memory by adding her name to the family tree.

As reported by my Oma, life was not easy in the camp; however, the family was forced to remain for some considerable time, my Aunt Marie being born there in 1924. My Oma reported terrible conditions, including children being separated from parents and a lack of food throughout. Thus, it was good news when in 1924 the Canadian Catholic Church Members Society arranged to sponsor seventy-six Volga Germans for Canadian immigration. It was in March of that year that Reinhold boarded *The Montrose* on his journey to Vibank, Saskatchewan with an opportunity to earn as a farmhand. One year later, he had amassed enough to send for his family. The Zelbel females arrived as a group of five. On immigration papers, they listed their home as Berlin; however, their citizenship was marked "statenloss" or "stateless." It was there in Canada that Marie, would have met her father for the first time.

The arrival in Canada did not mark the conclusion of strife for the Zelbel family, which would add Lydia in 1925 and Helen in 1926. As immigrant farmers, it's no doubt that both Reinhold and Anna, along with their girls, were expected to dutily conduct the long, back-breaking work of farmhands. At some point prior to 1930 the family managed to move far west to Vernon, British Columbia, likely in pursuit of improved employment conditions. In a *1945 Canadian Voters List*, Elizabeth Zelbel, my Oma, is listed as "homegirl" residing with her parents in Kelowna, a small town not dissimilar to Vernon.

*1925 immigration document showing my Oma, along with her mother and sisters, joining Reinhold in Canada.*

You may recall that I began this book explaining that my grandparents had met at the Astoria Hotel in 1947. Family legend had it that Elizabeth's brother-in-law, Albert Widmer, owned the Astoria Hotel and was happy to provide lodging and a modest salary in exchange for chambermaid duties. Information on the infamous Astoria Hotel is available plenty online, but I failed to see any mention of Albert Widmer involved in ownership. This caused considerable doubt on my part for some time until I finally decided to call Albert's son, Bob Widmer. My first cousin once removed explained that his father was involved in ownership of various Vancouver hotels and rooming houses in the 1940s; however, he clarified that there were other times in which his father, Albert, served only as manager with no ownership stake. When I mentioned the Astoria Hotel was formally known as the "Toronto Rooming Houses," he confirmed familiarity with the name. It no longer seemed confusing that I couldn't find Albert Widmer listed as an owner.

No doubt the Toronto Rooming Houses offered an opportunity for my now twenty-nine-year-old Oma to leave the family home and make a life for herself. In the *1947 Vancouver Phone Directory*, I locate the following two listings:

ZELBEL, Eliz. clk r 769 E Hast
WILLIAMS, Alfd V r 769 E Hast

*My only picture of my grandfather and Oma together.*

It was in June of that year that Elizabeth would become pregnant with my father, Donald Roy Williams. The rest, as they say, was history.

From political persecution to deadly escape, to a concentration camp, death of a sibling possibly involving herself, to the difficult life of a farmer in a strange country, to being a German living in Canada during World War II, my Oma's life was full of turmoil and struggle. Not yet thirty, she finds herself a young mother, away from family in a physically and emotionally abusive marriage to a strange man the same age as her father. What I'd learned definitely provided me a better understanding of my Oma. All she had known was to do whatever it took for personal survival. Rest in peace, Oma.

Again, the information didn't reveal any secrets that would assist in my mystery, but it did spur some thought. While I accepted that Lola was likely a friend, I saw some similarities between her and my Oma. Both dealt with struggle and change in their early lives, and both were alone until marrying at a later age. Also, both were much younger than my grandfather.

If my grandfather did in fact attract those whose lives, at times, may have lacked stability, is that an indicator that my grandfather's middle years were also dominated by instability with minimal long-term commitments, addresses, relationships? When I considered how this would affect my chances of tracking his missing years, it didn't feel good.

# The Intersection of Logic and Intuition

**Thursday, November 26, 1942, 11:42 p.m.   351 Ashdale Avenue, Toronto, Ontario, Canada.**

*Dear Charles – I am sure you'll be quite surprised to hear from your long-lost brother or "Major" if you still remember.  However, if you can find it in your heart to read this letter and forgive an old man, it would mean very much to me.  As you can see from the address, I am now back in Toronto, Canada for the first time in many years.  I believe I must have some of the gypsy in my blood, for life has taken me in many different directions and I have been fortunate to see much of this new world.  I should like the opportunity to share this with you some time.*

*I would very much like to hear about you also. I chance to guess you are still happily employed with the railway. Sometimes, I think I should have remained in that employ. Are you married? Do you have any children? How is Dennis doing? Are you able to provide me his address so I may write? I am ashamed to be ignorant, but I assume that our dear mother has passed. I remember well her being in ill-health. Is father still alive and if so, how is he doing? What other information can you provide about our dear aunts and uncles? I remember Uncle George well and would enjoy very much to rekindle his acquaintance. I imagine that much has changed and I am certain that I would not recognize the old streets any longer.*

*I do hope in earnest to hear from you soon and I sincerely hope you can forgive my poor behavior in allowing our relationship to be estranged for such an extended period of time. As always, your affectionate brother, Alfred*

A t this point, solving the mystery of my grandfather had been taking up to eight hours a week for approximately three years. I had exhausted all possessions, letters, family trees, names, and pursued connections with anyone I could think of. I had learned plenty about the Williams family and had certainly succeeded in connecting family members, or "fixing the Williams family" as Mark Purcell so eloquently described.

As for my mystery, I suppose I had discovered some information, mainly Alfred's life prior to 1910 and some information between the years of 1942 and 1947 which wasn't known before. I also had some leads to follow in both Ontario and Alberta during those latter years; however, my initial goal was to discover his missing first fifty-seven years. I still couldn't account for his actions or whereabouts between the years of twenty and fifty-two, what I'd consider the bulk of a man's adult life.

I felt it time to turn to a desperate measure. DNA. I was well aware that a simple DNA test could provide me with all the information I was seeking. If Alfred had fathered any children, it was likely to be exposed in DNA matches, if not from a child directly then from some other family connection. Why hadn't I done this before now? On one level, it felt like cheating. I didn't want this to be easy. I was enjoying it. I wanted to one day feel the pride and accomplishment that my dogged efforts and clever deductions were to receive credit for uncovering the mystery. It seemed to me that the immediacy as well as the impressive scope of a DNA test would deprive me of that. But there was another reason also.

In truth, I had come close to ordering a DNA test years prior as a Father's Day gift for my dad. I had read that it would be best to have the oldest living relative complete the test. I suppose my dad's DNA was closer to Alfred's than mine. In truth, though, the idea scared me a little. No, I'm not a conspiracy theorist who worries the government is hoarding DNA data in an effort to control mankind. Rather, I was thinking more of the potential for unwelcome skeletons emerging from the closet, not related specifically to my father either. In discussing with my mother, she had to agree, and another jigsaw puzzle was purchased for my father that year. Sorry dad.

By 2018, however, it was my dad himself who regularly brought it up. I was still a little tentative for the two reasons above, but I had to agree that it felt like the right time. Other leads seemed to be drying up. What did I have to lose?

If you've never had the pleasure of completing a mail-order DNA kit let me assure you that it's quite painless. After ordering the kit from *Ancestry.com*, a small package arrived a few days later. Opening the box, we took care of the red tape first, which basically meant linking the code on the kit to my *Ancestry.com* account. Once done, we moved to the practical steps, meaning my dad spit in a small tube which was then shaken and sealed. Our last task was to place the tube in the enclosed envelope and deliver to the mailbox. Pretty easy.

In the four weeks we anxiously awaited the results, my mind diligently conjured various, wild results and possibilities. I suppose the relationship I was most interested in for my father was a half-sibling; however, with my grandfather being of age to procreate in the very early 1900s, I had to accept that his secret may be exposed with the presence of a half-niece or half-nephew, or even a half-grandniece or half-grandnephew. Furthermore, not fully understanding the rich, confusing world of DNA evidence, I contemplated that any early offspring my grandfather had could have been exposed any number of ways with a variety of distant relationships possible. It was all for naught. In the end, the results came in failing to provide me any long-forgotten secrets or so it seemed.

In reality, it was difficult to understand exactly what I had. I suppose I found the "Ethnicity Estimator" simple to digest. According to the brightly colored pie chart, my father's DNA could be predominantly broken into two world regions: England (33%) and Northwestern Europe (31%). This, of course, made total sense based on the family heritage of my grandfather and my Oma. The remaining thirty-four percent was shared between several regions including Sweden and Denmark, Wales, Eastern Europe and Russia and even Ireland at three percent! Maybe my grandfather wasn't lying about Ireland after all; although I am pretty confident that if we were to test the DNA of the pigs in Dublin, their Irish ancestry would he measured considerably higher than the results of my father.

The area I was most interested in studying, DNA Matches, could best be described as overwhelming. The exact number of DNA matches was not provided; however, the site did tell me that my father matched three-hundred and fifteen people who qualified as fourth cousins or closer. Perusing this list, the number of matches deemed "distant" was in the hundreds, if not thousands. Within those three-hundred and fifteen people considered "close" there were very few familiar surnames. In fact, the only surname I immediately recognized was "Keil," which was my Oma's mother's maiden name. The total number of Zelbels was zero. The total number of Williams within the close matches was two, and I didn't recognize the given names.

At the risk of stating the obvious, I began with the matches that shared the most DNA with my father. A couple of the names were easy to identify as they included "linked trees" to their DNA profiles. I was able to see easily how they fit into my family tree. I wasn't surprised that the Keil connection continued to show its head. Perhaps, I'd look more closely into the Keil clan when my work with my grandfather was complete. That is, if I ever did complete my work with my grandfather.

Paul Poli was a name that appeared high on the list. Together, he and my father shared 410 centimorgans of DNA, approximately six percent. The site suggested Paul and my father may be first or second cousins. However, after clicking on the centimorgans, I learned that other relationships were just as possible, including "half-grandnephew." Half-grandnephew was the connection I was most interested in finding. In this scenario, Paul Poli would have been a grandson of my father's half sibling. Paul's profile identified him as falling under the age category of fifty to fifty-nine, meaning he was born between 1959 and 1968. This meant that Paul's grandparents could have been born early in the 1900's, easily matching the time when my grandfather was of age to procreate. Yes, I was growing excited.

Other details provided cause for further enthusiasm. Paul wrote that he "was adopted" and was raised in Scotia, California. Based on what I'd learned about the lifestyles of my grandfather's family as well as those my grandfather was close to, it made sense to me that any lineage born from my grandfather may not have been raised by biological parents. Also, Paul's profile showed a middle-aged man sporting a grey baseball cap and large dark sunglasses proudly leaning out the window of a large semi-truck. Have I mentioned that my father was a long-haul truck driver? Maybe driving a large truck was in the blood.

With no helpful linked family tree, I clicked "message" and made my first contact with Mr. Poli. My missive was brief and to the point:

> *Hello Paul: It looks like you are a fairly close DNA match to my father, Donald Roy Williams. I am researching the mysterious life of my grandfather, Alfred Victor Williams. As you stated that you were adopted, I am wondering if you could be related by birth through that connection. Your profile struck me as my father was also a long-haul truck driver, at times through northern California.*
>
> *I look forward to hearing from you. Ron Williams*

In all my correspondences, I made sure to include a request or demand at closing. This was a technique that I'd first learned in Mrs. Ruffeski's grade seven class at Cedar Drive Elementary School. It had served me well over the years.

This was my first attempt at connecting with a DNA match. I waited patiently, checking the site more than once daily, hoping against skepticism that his response would include a detail or two that could confirm my wild suspicion. Perhaps he would say that he was told his grandfather was "Alfred," or "Roy" or maybe he knew that one of his parent's surnames was "Williams," or "Hammond." I waited and waited and waited, but no response was forthcoming. Strangely, this was somewhat comforting as it meant I couldn't rule out the possibility, a possibility I entertained in my mind regularly over the next few years. I didn't know at the time that it would take until 2023 to make the definitive connection between Mr. Poli and my father.

Making my way down the list, there were plenty of other options for half-nephew or half-niece or even half-grandnephew and half-grandniece. None offered any substantial clues of surnames or locations that were cause for excitement. I drafted a generic message that read something like this:

*Hello: I see that you are a fairly close match to my father, Donald Roy Williams. I am researching the secretive life of my grandfather, Alfred Victor Williams, originally from Worcestershire, England, but also Toronto and parts of the United States, possibly using the name, "Roy Hammond." Please feel free to look through my family tree. I am keen to discover how we may be connected. I look forward to hearing from you. Sincerely, Ron Williams*

I attempted to offer just the right amount of information, hoping not to scare potential readers away with a lengthy message, but provide enough to pique interest or attach to a detail. Clever and tactical, I thought, but also largely ineffective.

The results were equally few and disappointing. Many of my messages went unreturned. Rather than relegate those experiences to rudeness or passivity, I recognized that in many cases individuals may not have maintained a monthly subscription after receiving their DNA results. While *Ancestry.com* is extremely valuable it does come with a financial cost. The messages that were returned were most often polite and encouraging, but generally void of any potentially useful information. It struck me how little most people seemed to know about their family, a condition I was all too familiar with prior to my interest in genealogy.

I decided to begin an Excel spreadsheet where I'd planned to list all DNA matches along with geographical and other notes, with the goal of finding commonalities and making connections of my own. Make sense? I didn't really know, but it seemed like the right thing to do. Another feature I began working on listed "shared matches," allowing me to identify threads of connection by other cousins we had in common. For example, I didn't know who "Christi Lewis" was, nor did she maintain a family tree or respond to my message. However, seeing that we listed several "Keils" as shared matches, I could identify that she was a cousin connected through my Oma and rule her out as a potential clue to my grandfather.

The spreadsheet turned out to be an exercise in awkwardness and confusion, resulting in more head scratching than "eureka" moments. Nonetheless, I was able to create a few "DNA groups" that seemed to come from similar lineage. I noticed that several unknown relatives showed shared matches with "Wolfe, Erwin, and Webb" surnames. I decided to cleverly tag these individuals as the "Wolfe, Erwin, Webb" group. It required patience and an extended amount of time scrolling before I was able to find a DNA match with a substantial family tree related to the group.

Here I discovered that the "Wolfe, Erwin, Webb" group and my own "Williams" family tree shared a common ancestor. Florence May Williams was my grandfather's first cousin, her father being Alfred's Uncle Edward. Through searching her name, I learned that Florence ventured from her Liverpool home, arriving at Ellis Island in New York on October 17, 1920. She married Roy Martin Berg a day later on October 18, 1920, in Manhattan, before eventually becoming a homemaker and mother of five in Oklahoma City, Oklahoma. Seeing as Mr. Berg had served overseas in World War I, I had to accept this as a war-time romance. My reaction was paradoxical, both pleased and disappointed at the same time. I was pleased to have made the connection but disappointed that it revealed nothing towards my mystery.

It wasn't always this easy though. A second common group I identified was the "Sinclair, Ozolins, Cheslin" tree. Scanning family trees of "Sinclair, Ozolins, Cheslin" members with shared matches yielded no familiar names. Not always convinced of the accuracy of other amateur genealogists, I went as far as to create my own family tree for one of the members, an "Elizabeth Ozolins." I was able to build a fairly complete family tree going back three generations. From that point, holes began emerging. My findings failed to yield any obvious connection and after beginning trees for a few more names, I sadly abandoned my pursuit of the "Sinclair, Ozolins, Cheslin" group.

Another evening, I was excited to make contact with a Steve Hughes. Despite the late hour at his England home, we moved to Facebook Messenger and began attempting to analyze our connection. Scientifically related, he shared that his father was born in the early 1900s, an illegitimate child from Worcestershire. That perfectly matched the time and location when my grandfather originally left England. Was this the real reason why my grandfather left his home in 1906? Had a sixteen-year-old Alfred gotten a girl pregnant and left the country to evade any financial and personal obligations? That could further explain why he would eventually change his name and immigrate to the United States. In the end, we failed to find that piece of evidence or detail that would explain the match. It was an enjoyable evening, even if the exact nature of our connection remained elusive.

Perhaps the connection I spent most time researching was one, Shirley Erwin. Ms. Erwin shared one-hundred and five centimorgans or two percent DNA with my father. Clicking on the data, I saw that there was a twenty perfect chance that she has a half-great-grandniece. She reported her age to be "sixty plus" and her home to be Ontario. Her shared matches revealed members of the "Wolfe, Erwin, Webb" group, so I was confident she had some Williams blood in her. Coupled with the fact that my grandfather had spent time in Ontario in at least two separate decades, I was intrigued by what connection the DNA match might reveal. I sketched out a crude but potentially accurate joint family tree, positing that

Alfred Victor could have contributed to the conception of a child in Ontario in the very early 1900s. I was able to ascertain that the relationship could matchup with potential birth years. Again, I mused that an unwanted pregnancy may have been the motivation behind my grandfather's immigration, this time from Canada to the United States around 1910. Ms. Erwin did not have any substantial family tree connected to her profile; however, before long I recognized that her daughter, a Ms. Kelly Bernard boasted a private family tree featuring thirty-thousand names. I was certain that if granted access, I could find the connection.

Kelly and I began communicating through *Ancestry.com* messaging. Before long, we had shared unrestricted access to one another's family trees and were in regular correspondence with ideas and possibilities. Over the next four years, we explored a number of possible connections but were unable to make a definitive link. We did both have ancestors that went back to the Worcestershire area of England in the late 1800s but none of our relatives seemed to intersect by marriage. This led to suspicions that our connection was in the form of an illegitimate child, but we were not able to find evidence of such. The second place our family trees seemed to intersect was Toronto, Ontario in both the early-1900s and mid-1900s. The potential was there but the exact connection remained elusive.

I would be remiss if I did not add one mitigating factor. The identify of Alfred's maternal grandfather is unknown. This, of course, means that up to one quarter of Alfred's family tree remains empty. I'd spent considerable time attempting to identify Alfred's maternal grandfather, but my efforts were all for naught, a major obstacle for sure. With that in mind, I would put my focused search of DNA clues on hold, only to be revisited with irregularity in the ensuing years.

Another avenue I pursued around this time was turning to a professional. Again, this was a move I'd contemplated but thus far rebuffed in the spirit of "wanting to figure things out for myself." But, alas, it was a tool whose time had come, and I found myself turning to Google, looking for genealogists for hire. In the spirit of beginning with what I knew, I decided I'd look for someone to perform a deeper dive into my grandfather's time in Ontario. I chose this path partly out of default. I didn't think hiring a professional to look into the entire United States would be very fruitful, especially as, aside from the William Turley affidavit, I still had no concrete evidence that he was in that country. As well, if I accepted that his time in the United States was truth, what name would I have the researcher pursue?

Also, I felt that there were unanswered questions to be revealed through a more detailed professional look at Ontario. Was it possible that he had fathered a child there, either in the early 1900s or when he returned in the 1940s? If he did, in fact, immigrate to the United States around 1910, when and where exactly did he leave Ontario? Where did he identify his final destination when he crossed the border? What about phone books? I hadn't been successful in finding any record of a border crossing. Was he living with anyone in Ontario in the early 1900s? Then there was the mysterious "Clara" whom he listed as his wife in an unmailed income tax form in Alberta. Did Clara actually exist, and if so, did he bring her from Ontario? If I could learn Clara's true identity, maybe I could trace them to a place my grandfather occupied before returning to Ontario in 1942. Lastly, near the end of his time in Ontario, his mailing address changed from his cousin's home on 351 Ashdale Avenue to a nearby address at 23 Park Road. Was this Clara's house?

With the confidence that there had to be some answers asleep in the province of Ontario, I contacted my selected genealogist, Ms. Ann Logan, who represented a genealogical company called Ontario Origins. Near the end of 2018, I contacted Ms. Logan, providing some biographical information I had as well as a couple of documents. In my email, I provided a modest list of specific questions I was hoping to have answered:

> During my grandfather's first residence in Ontario, did he live anywhere else besides with the Turleys? At this time, did he have a job in Toronto? Was he married during his original time in Toronto? When did he leave for the US?

> Did he return to Toronto at any time during the 1910s, 1920s, or 1930s?

> When he returned to Toronto in 1942, why did he need to see a lawyer and contact immigration services?

> Why did he move to 23 Park Road? Was he renting? Did he own? Did he move in with "Clara" or someone else? Who was living there at the time?

I wasn't too uneasy, but I was concerned that Ms. Logan may reject my request, sharing that she felt it wasn't likely anything would be revealed. Thankfully, that wasn't the case, and I received her reply in quick order. For a little more than one-hundred dollars, Ms. Logan promised a thorough search into several avenues of information including phone books, voters lists, marriage records, and even a trip to the original Christie Street Hospital where my grandfather had worked during his second stint in Ontario. Without my prompting, my parents immediately transferred the fee. Ms. Logan was transparent that some of the above were available online, but I chose to defer to her expertise in the comfort I could be satisfied fully that no detail was missed.

When I received Ms. Logan's report approximately one week later, she had done all that she promised and more. The details reported included the following. First, there were several phone book entries listing Alfred Williams, but none that matched the addresses provided or contained any corroborating details such as middle name, initial, or place of employment. Second, it seems Alfred's second address on Park Road was a rooming house of sorts, Alfred most likely renting a room from the owner. Third, no marriage or birth records concerning Alfred Victor Williams were uncovered. Fourth, no personnel records were available for the Christie Street Hospital at time of my grandfather's employ. Other details were added such as an entry for an Edmonton phone book containing the same address I had read in income tax documents as well as his appearance on Vancouver voter lists from his later years.

I was mildly disappointed no shocking evidence was revealed. By this point, though, I had learned to temper my expectations. It was reassuring to know that I hadn't missed anything in Ontario, and I could close that open volume of possibility in my mind.

Having now leaped into the world of both DNA and professional assistance, the third avenue of consideration was a little more unconventional. My famously rational father suggested we visit a psychic. It was a sunny Saturday morning that my father pulled his beige Dodge pickup truck into my Maple Ridge driveway. With the assistance of my mother, he had conveniently chosen a psychic that operated not far from my house. Michelle Osbourne identified as a "professional psychic medium and teacher." Prior to the visit, I studied her website where she explains that she "learned to trust her intuition and began to embrace her keen ability to communicate with the Other World."

In a word, I was skeptical. I couldn't see how this uncertain science had any part in my efforts to solve this genealogical mystery, reasoning that any discovery or piece of the puzzle needed to be scientifically, not spiritually, corroborated. Thus, while I appreciated my parents' effort, I was having trouble appreciating any potential value in the exercise. On the other hand, if any clues were offered, it would be easy enough to substantiate and support with supplemental research. In this case, any potential clues offered by Michelle could prove extremely valuable. I suppose my main objection was that I remained unconvinced an individual could "communicate with the Other World," through "intuition." I didn't believe anything she shared with me could be accurate.

Well, that changed as soon as we sat down in the stylish basement of her well-maintained town home. She began by asking if either of us had ever had a premonition or "strange feeling" that ended up coming true. I instantly remembered a time, not long ago, when for no particular reason, I thought of an old classmate as I entered a nearby shopping mall. To my astonishment, I found myself face to face with that individual some fifteen minutes later. The fact that I hadn't thought of the person at any point in my recent memory seemed a coincidence of massive proportions and I shared it with several at the time.

Michelle explained that she believed we all had the gift of intuition, but most stifled the ability, dismissing the feelings as random and coincidental. Conversely, Michelle offered that she welcomed her feelings of intuition and fully explored their intrusions on more practical matters in her mind. That explanation was satisfactory, and I began listening to her fully with open intention and acceptance.

My father and I started by explaining our mystery as well as providing background information about my grandfather. Her follow up questions were thoughtful and before long, she began adding details that we hadn't shared. Without providing specifics of Alfred as a father, Michelle offered to my dad that Alfred "has a deep regret about something...the way you were raised." Again, turning to my dad, Michelle shared that Alfred never stopped "loving your mother." As we reacted with confirmation, Michelle shared that Alfred was now present with us in the room.

With Alfred now guiding the mysterious conversation, Michelle shared that "water" would be a key clue to identifying his missing years. My father and I remembered a strange piece of U.S. Navy jewelry we found with the belongings in my Aunt Shirley's box. Was this an angle we should further pursue? Moving on, Michelle explained that Alfred was showing a picture of two younger girls. If my father and I were impressed so far, we were fully astonished at this point, remembering the unusual photo of the two girls discovered in my grandfather's wallet. Was this the piece of evidence of which I should be focusing my research efforts?

The conversation continued well past the thirty minutes my parents had funded. Michelle continued to provide small details that matched both the facts I had learned and the assumptions I had made regarding my grandfather's life. While she didn't offer any concrete dates or locations for immediate study, I had made several mental notes regarding questions and angles to follow up. Continuing to listen, it occurred to me that research was largely based on intuition. Each search I completed or document I pursued began with a "feeling" that there could be a connection or match in an as of yet unknown area. Intuition.

As our spiritual experience continued, Michelle began to wrap up our conversation in a natural and professional way. I really was impressed with her contribution and couldn't wait to return home and share the experience with Lana and the boys. With my father, however, there are never any quick goodbyes, and before exiting her studio, my dad felt inspired to add one last comment.

"Dad, we're going to find out where you were all those years." Immediately Michelle offered Alfred's curt response.

"It won't be easy...good luck."

# Journeying a Familiar Path

**Sunday, January 7, 1945, 2:18 p.m.   Home of Mr. and Mrs. Williams, 10130 155 Street, Edmonton, Alberta, Canada.**

*With the ceremony and circumstance of Christmas and New Years a week behind them, Alfred and his wife are able to look to the new year with a truly optimistic sense.  Approximately six months in their new home and province, they find themselves both comfortable and settled as well as excited about this new place.  The bumps seem to have ironed themselves out.  As well, there is talk of World War II nearing an end adding to their optimistic, hopeful, psyches.*

*This afternoon the bright Alberta sun offers a respite from the harsh snowfalls they've experienced of late. The couple, fifty-five and thirty-two respectively have been together some time now and have grown comfortable in each other's presence. Mrs. Williams eschews the idea of a car ride, instead suggesting they stay at home and take care of errands. Alfred agrees and sets the first task as a walk to the grocery in order to pick up some treats for relatives in England. Upon his wife's encouragement, not having posted any Christmas gifts, and with a little extra money in hand, the couple procures some tea, cheeses, and small cakes, all non-perishable, to send to Charles and Eva, as well as Uncle George. It's a pleasure for Mrs. Williams to bestow small gifts on family members, especially as she has no family remaining of her own.*

*Now early afternoon, she holds an iron in the living room, preparing her dress for her weekly shifts in the women's clothing section of the nearby Zellers retail store. Next to the dress are the scrubs, washed and ironed, that Alfred is expected to wear at the Provincial Mental Hospital. Alfred comfortably rests on the sofa reading a "Mike Hammer" novel by his favorite writer, Mickey Spillane, and is soon to be interrupted to assist with dinner preparations, a proper Sunday roast, which he insists is cooked, "just right."*

M ichelle had given me some ideas I meant to pursue but I didn't suspect anything groundbreaking to emerge. Thus, I had to accept that as the calendar turned to 2019, I lamented the absence of a clear focus or plan of attack. I'd spent considerable time on some traditional avenues, including online research and family documents and possessions. As well, I'd opened my search to DNA evidence, professional help and even a psychic! What was there left to do?

DNA was one area that I had not totally given up. At least once every couple of weeks, I'd log on to check for any "new relatives." There were always plenty listed, but none of the "close family" variety I was seeking. Usually, I made sure to have a pencil and paper nearby so I could sketch potential lineages that involved half-grandnephews or half-grandnieces. At times, when a connection seemed ripe with potential, I'd share my sketch with Lana, who had grown quite adept at advising why I should or should not pursue specific connections.

Both Seattle and New York continued to be places of interest. I had reason to believe that my grandfather may have spent considerable time in each, knowledge of which provided a structure for my search. Consulting all documents available on *Ancestry.com* and exploring outside the site to look at phone book and Google searches, I was able to identify some potential leads, only to abandon each when I found evidence that eliminated my grandfather, or I simply couldn't locate information that would verify a connection.

I began an Excel file titled, "potential matches" that listed research routes for future attention. When I ceased attention to the list, it contained thirteen individuals as potential matches, based on census, voter, and employment records from places such as California, Saskatchewan, Kingston, Ontario and other places. Each potential match boasted a close variation of the name, "Alfred Williams" of English birth of similar year and an immigration date that could be considered partly accurate. Rather than comfort me that my search was far from dead, the list haunted me with the notion that one of the matched individuals could, in fact, be my grandfather, with the information idling in eternal suspension for lack of corroborating evidence.

I found a July 1924 immigration document for a 5'6" 145-pound "Alf Williams," born in 1888 and employed as a fireman aboard a ship called *The Princess Mary*, which was entering Seattle, Washington via Victoria, British Columbia. Michelle had suggested that "water" could be a determining clue in my pursuit. In addition to the age almost matching and a physical description that seemed potentially accurate, I was especially interested in Victoria as the Vancouver Island one-time home of Lola LeDuke and, of course, the mention of Seattle that had come up more than once in my now years-long search.

Adding to the lead above, I found a 1913 immigration document listing a man of similar description and birthdate entering Port Townsend, Washington from Vancouver, BC, employed as a 2nd mate on a ship named, the *David Evans*. I contemplate this could be the same "Williams" as above with matching birthdate, employment and general sailing route. One cause for concern was the man's name, listed as "A.L. Williams." Was this in fact the same person as above? If so, could I rule out my grandfather on both documents based on the middle initial of "L"? Or should I consider the middle initial a typo of sorts? Was it enough for me to abandon the lead?

Another possibility that enthralled me for days was the case of the "Dole Fruit Man." I termed him as such, because this "A. Williams" also identified in corresponding documents as "Alf Williams," was employed by the Dole Fruit Company. I was able to amass several immigration documents in which the gentleman in question travelled on ship between Cuba, Honduras and New Orleans for his employ. He was listed as both a carpenter and a fireman on separate documents. His birthyear matched my grandfather. Also, I was particularly interested in the vocation as some type of ship hand. Perhaps most intriguing was that this employ seemed to match with the grand, "life of adventure" my grandfather reported in his 1940s correspondences to England. Efforts to identify corroborating evidence again remained elusive and the potential match continued to wither in an unfortunate type of research purgatory. Time marched onwards, but my research success stalled.

By 2020, the world was dealing with Covid and life as we all knew it no longer existed. My situation was no different.

With our own and our kids' schedules now void of recreational and social commitments, along with my teaching job transitioning to "work from home," I had plenty free time on my hands. Lana and I missed meeting with friends and family but basked in this added time with our boys by enjoying increased family dinners, games nights and leisurely walks around the now quiet neighborhood. At the same time, though, I felt an inner urge to use the time to my advantage and to accomplish something concrete. Sadly, this meant, in part, focusing my time away from this mostly non-fruitful mystery.

To begin, I researched and created a tree for my mother's paternal side of the family, the Hoffert clan. This was not without some personal scruples, as my mother's father had walked out on the family prior to the birth of my mother. However, his extended family had not, and so many of my mom's stories and remembrances involved Hoffert aunts, uncles and cousins. With my research, I heard stories that involved both unwavering family connection and care, as well as brutal alcoholism and abuse of all types. There were cousins I learned of who lived in my very city as well as at least one missing person.

I also found the time to write drafts of two separate books. My first, a nondescript novel, told the unoriginal story of a middle-aged man experiencing a type of mid-life crisis. Although I completed the seventy-five-thousand-word draft, the text remains in solitary storage on my desktop, unlikely to ever be shared with the world. My second book was a personal memoir in which I shared my thoughts and experiences growing up as a dedicated follower of a certain rock and roll band. This second attempt was self-published and reached a fairy large audience. Once released, the book gained a little traction and I was both pleased and humbled to have been featured on websites, podcasts and even on the cover of our local newspaper. Additionally, I was able to connect with many old acquaintances and friends mentioned in the memoir. It was a project I was equipped to start and finish to completion. It was great fun.

Not fully forgetting my interest in Alfred Victor and the Williams family, I was pleased to present my father with a personalized Christmas present that year. Using family photos I had gathered from my grandfather's possessions, as well as information learned from my studies, I created two separate family posters. The first featured a photo of a family of three, which may or may not have been my great grandfather, great grandmother and a young child, posing outside the Nelson Inn, where Alfred's father had both lived and worked in the early 1900s. Above the photo, I included text mirroring the information I spied in the window of the hotel, "featuring Dunsville Whiskey," and the address, "25 Blackwell Street."

The second framed poster featured the title, "Williams Brothers Horse Dealing," with the subtext, "for fair trade in horses." Also featured were photographs of my great grandfather, as well as the infamous Uncle George. My father was especially pleased to receive both framed prints originally believing them to be authentic reproductions of original advertisements from England of one hundred years ago. I explained that I had created them myself but that they were factual. This seemed to please him, and I am happy to report that both still reside proudly on his office wall.

On one uneventful, Covid-influenced evening devoid of plans, my son, Jack, and I decided to undertake the forty-five-minute drive and venture to my grandfather's old Marpole neighborhood for an evening stroll. As we walked his streets in quiet, peaceful solitude – a little rain unable to damper our contentment – we basked in the neighborhood's history, pointing out old houses and even an ancient firehall that had been converted to some type of arts center. The highlight was the ten-minute section up Granville Street to the long-standing Fraser Arms Hotel, exact destination of my grandfather's frequent jaunts to retrieve a bottle of rum or rye.

I tried to imagine the sights and sounds of the late 1960s. I suppose it was a literal attempt to walk a mile in his shoes.

In time, I found myself canceling the automatic renewal of my *Ancestry.com* account. The calendar had turned first to 2021 and then to 2022 and I could no longer justify the fairly modest monthly fee based on the frequency and duration of my research. This did not mean that I had lost interest entirely in solving the mystery of my grandfather's missing years. However, the notion previously entertained, that my efforts would result not in discovering what my missing grandfather was doing, but in discovering and connecting with the lost Williams family, was becoming more and more likely in my mind.

In the summer of 2022, with the influence of Covid lessening, Lana had planned an east coast vacation for us to travel to Montreal for two days, before visiting the Atlantic Canadian provinces of New Brunswick, Nova Scotia and Prince Edward Island. Lana was most interested in taking in the extensive scenery and had planned visits to some of the country's most beautiful landmarks as well as several hikes in the vicinity. Knowing my love of live music and fine dining, she had made sure that most days were capped with ample opportunity for both. For our accommodations, she booked most stays at older hotels or bed and breakfasts with unique architecture and history. Her diligent work and my excitement about the holiday kept us occupied many evenings leading up to our August vacation.

Ever concerned about my happiness, Lana added that there was an immigration center in New Brunswick, that offered not only displays and artifacts but also trained assistants to help discover information about family members who may have arrived in New Brunswick decades or even centuries prior. You may remember that my grandfather's entry to Canada occurred on April 13, 1906 in the very New Brunswick harbor we'd be visiting.

*Visiting over 100 years after my grandfather's brief stop, my trip to Saint John provided a cryptic directive.*

Our ten days exploring the provinces did not disappoint. Both our daytime excursions and nighttime revelry exceeded expectations. The immigration center was as expected, stationed with keen, knowledgeable staff who were regretfully unable to add to my research findings. The displays at the immigration center were a highlight. In addition to artifacts including items of clothing and various trunks, there were hundreds of pictures depicting life for an immigrant new to Canada. In one particular picture, I spied the familiar Port of Saint John, a ten-minute walk from our accommodation and the site of our dining the evening before. While we enjoyed a quiet, picturesque setting during our meal, with the sun going down and the moonlight casting a brilliant light on the still water, the photo now in front of me divulged an image of chaos as tired and worn immigrants warily made their way from the packed, uncomfortable temporary homes on ship across the Atlantic to hopefully more favorable spaces in a new, alien country.

As I did with the postcards in Seattle, I found myself foolishly scanning faces of the young men, looking for an image I could attach to my grandfather. To clarify, I wasn't directly looking for my grandfather's face. For starters, I had no concept of his appearance as a young man. Furthermore, I wasn't sure the date of the photo presented. I think now what I was looking for was a likely image I could attach to the vision in my head of my grandfather arriving at that very port. Soon, I was interrupted, and my pretend exercise was all for naught.

Later that evening, Lana and I returned to the bay. We were well-fed with more than one glass of Merlot to ease into the late evening. We would be leaving in the morning, and I was determined to have one final look at the bay, where, in part, this very tale all began. Standing on the shore far above where water meets sand, I conjured the photo I had studied hours earlier and envisioned my sixteen-year-old grandfather laboring up the steep wooden steps, his arms full with suitcase and his head full with dreams.

My dreaming is interrupted when Lana asks if I'd like to stop at one of the nearby public houses, a quick nightcap before bed. We begin the traverse up the subtle incline in the cobblestone roads, eyes darting to both sides of the lane in search of an appropriate establishment. Turning the corner and continuing upwards, I spy a plaque commemorating the early twentieth century offices of the CN Railway. I realize I've traced the exact steps my grandfather likely walked some one-hundred and twenty years prior.

Has my grandfather purposely led me here? I know I have to solve the mystery.

# PART III – TRUTH AND DISCOVERY (2022-2023)

# A New Approach

**Friday, August 23, 1946, 5:32 p.m. Room #218, CN Rooms, MacDonald Hotel, 100th Street & Jasper Avenue, Edmonton, Alberta, Canada.**

*In his copy of today's Edmonton Journal, Alfred reads some disappointing news about the woman he once called his wife. He doesn't care. Lately, he doesn't care about much. It's another weekend of voluntary confinement in his very modest room. Alone. He has a new Mickey Spillane novel to keep company and he'll maintain his supply of rye as needed. And there's a boxing match he can always go downstairs to watch, if he's up to it.*

R eader, if you've come this far, I want to thank you for your patience in accompanying me on this sometimes indulgent and always frustrating journey. In the introduction,

I shared that I was very satisfied I was able to solve the mystery, as are my wife, my father, and my aunt. I also ascertained that you wouldn't' feel robbed, tricked or disappointed with any addendum added to my promise in a bid to fulfil my words. I now renew my lofty pledge and reassert, with a mixture of excitement and trepidation, that we are about to get to the good part.

Experiencing my epiphany in New Brunswick, I now felt a renewed, transformative commitment to solving my mystery. I could no longer refer to my unknown as the "lost fifty-seven," as I'd been able to illustrate a reasonably comprehensive picture of his life until age twenty. It was the thirty-two years between his twentieth and fifty-second birthdays, roughly 1910 to 1942, that remained unknown. After approximately eighty-four months of research, I knew I'd need to roll up my sleeves and dig deeper. Simply put, it was time to double-down and go the distance.

I began with a few leads I had avoided thus far, casting them off as "long-shots" unlikely to offer any clues. For starters, I sent away to Social Development Canada, filling out three online freedom of information applications to obtain information from my grandfather's social insurance number, similar to a social security number in the United States. I suppose I was hoping to form a clearer picture of his time in Canada, likely 1942 until his death, but more importantly any other time he may have resided in the country. To be more specific, I was crossing my fingers for employment history, social benefits, addresses, and maybe even dependents: a wife and/or kids. True, this would only be "Canadian" information, but I wasn't yet satisfied that I knew all about his time in my country or even that he hadn't spent more time in Canada at some point or points unknown. Also, I wholeheartedly believed that any information I could add would only give birth to more options for research.

I felt I had done a decent job of completing the forms and was pleased to receive an email the same day thanking me for my request and providing other useful information. I realized I had rejoiced too soon when I received an email from Claire Aline Alexandre, a Junior ATIP Officer, explaining that "to process [my] requests, [I] must provide more detail ...unfortunately the wording...is too broad." Being a writer, or attempting to be a writer, I was a little chagrinned but also thankful this bureaucratic government agency was taking my humble requests seriously.

I replied instantly, being more specific in the aforementioned information I was seeking including employment history, social benefits, addresses, and maybe even dependents: a wife and/or kids. I thought about adding shoe size and hobbies but held back. Satisfied I had been more specific, I hit "send" and once again patiently awaited response.

It took only two days for Jihan Wehbe, a Senior Analyst no less, to respond to my queries. This time instead of simply suggesting or requiring that I reword my requests, Ms. Wehbe took the liberty to reword my requests into more government "user-friendly" language. I was asked to confirm the edits were suitable, a request I quickly and thankfully adhered to.

One day later, I was to receive a second email from Ms. Wehbe, this time informing me that one of my requests was now being accessed under the *Access to Information Act,* as opposed to whatever original act I had first requested information.

Over the next week, I received three additional emails, as well as a personal phone call, from Ms. Wehbe. She took the time to walk me through the process, correct my errors and ensure I would be able to access the information I hoped to gain. Rather than be annoyed or impatient with the government "red tape," I was thankful she took the time to assist a novice researcher such as myself. I found comfort in the fantasy that because of the multiple precautions taken, there was almost certainly a great secret about to be revealed, a secret so monumental that the government had to ensure all necessary steps were handled with accuracy and attention.

About a week later, my inbox chimed, and I was pleased to see I'd received an official response from Employment and Development Canada. They had completed a search in response to my request and were pleased to offer me the following information:

First Name:      ALFRED
Middle Name(s): VICTOR
Family Name(s): WILLIAMS
This SIN record shows that the individual is: DECEASED

My reaction, of course, was one of disappointment. However, I convinced myself that there would be more useful information revealed in the other separate requests I had submitted. I received my answer a few days later in two separate emails containing the following explanations: "I regret to inform you that a search of the records under the control of ESDC has revealed that no records exist in response to your request," and "following a thorough search of our information holdings, I regret to inform you that no records were found that respond to your request." The messages were worded quite kindly and although I was provided direction for any complaints I may have desired to launch, I was satisfied there was nothing to be gained. I did, however, wonder why there was no information forthcoming, as the purpose, as I understood, of a social insurance number was to keep track of employment, pension and government assistance.

Around the same time, I had a wild, fantastical illusion that the Turley house at which my grandfather spent considerable time in the early 1940s, may hold a secret. In what I realized was a desperate attempt, I delivered the following to the local post:

*Dear Sir or Madam: My name is Ron Williams. I am researching my very mysterious grandfather, Alfred*

*Victor Williams (1889-1968). I have documents showing he lived at 351 Ashdale Avenue between 1942-1944. I believe the home was owned by George and Agnes Turley, who were Alfred's aunt and uncle.*

*I thought I would contact you to see if perhaps there are any old clues around the house or yard. Any personal possessions found? Any writing or carvings on walls or floors? Any land or building documents?*

*I would be very grateful if you could contact me by the email address above or the mailing address if preferred. Even if the message is to say that there are no clues, it would allow me to cross off one lead.*

*Thank you very much for your time. Sincerely, Ron Williams*

If nothing else, I had learned that – for the most part – people are pretty decent. I had no idea who lived at 351 Ashdale Avenue at present; however, about a week later, I received the following email from a thoughtful woman named Tanya De.

*Hi Ron: I believe you sent below letter. Unfortunately, we don't have any information that may help you. Nothing of interest was found in the house. Maybe the neighbors or previous owners. All the best and sorry I couldn't be of more help. Regards, Tanya*

It was also during this time, that I realized I had thus far ignored almost two dozen potential clues uncovered at the time of my grandfather's 1968 death. I'm talking about the notes and scribbles he had a habit of recording on various envelopes and papers loitering around his house. True to form, I began a Word document providing the source and content of each note and scribble. The meaning behind much of the content was obvious. An example was the note offering "model number, SDR 10-75-1, McClary Refrig" that appeared on the December 1942 envelope received from his brother Charles. When I read another notation, with the address for a "MacDonald Appliance" at "1140 Boundary Road," it wasn't too difficult to deduce my grandfather needed a part for his refrigerator. There were also the names, "Tom Hulbert [and] Gordon Hoy" whom my father explained were two of his roommates for a time.

Other notations could not be explained either through basic interpretive skills or my father's expertise and were thus left for imaginative conjecture. On an envelope from a 1943 letter from his Uncle George, Alfred copied "Nattie McNaughton, C6 608 Church." I notice that he had actually crossed out "Naughton" and recorded "Nauton" below. Relying on Google to guide me, I learned the address was for the Church Street Rental Apartments on Church Street in Toronto. What was my grandfather's connection to this person and address? Could it hold a clue? I conducted searches for various versions of the name, "Nattie McNauton" both at 608 Church and in more general terms. Although I found a few, "Nettie MacNaughtons" none offered any evidence that they were connected to my grandfather in any way, and I had to abandon the search. The name "Nathan Riddell," recorded on an April 1944 envelope received from Charles and Eva Williams was researched. I employed all tools to find a match to the name, but none made an impression. Another source of potential clues searched and exhausted.

At this point, I broke down and once again turned to a source I had hoped to avoid, another professional genealogist. This time though, I wouldn't be asking for any specific answers, meaning the likelihood of the individual hired discovering any groundbreaking clues would be minimal. This time, my plan was to meet with someone in person, go over what I had, and ask for some general guidance and direction. After a fairly brief search for "Vancouver genealogists," I settled on Celia Lewis. Ms. Lewis's profile identified her as a "genealogy consultant, writer, counsellor, grandmother, happily retired and ready for more adventures. Canadian." She runs an informative and enjoyable blogspot titled, "Twigs and Trees," in which she blogs about her own family research all while offering ideas and tips for beginners like me. Perusing the site, I was struck by one impressive missive in particular: "there are at least nineteen clues or questions to ask on every document you find." If she was capable of pulling that much data out of a single document, I was confident she'd be able to help me extract further clues from my mosaic of information.

In May of 2022, I sent the following email:

*Hello Ms. Lewis: I am an amateur genealogist researching my grandfather (1889-1968). I have documents from his early days (1889-1910), and documents from his latter days (1942-1968). However, despite a few clues, the years between 1910-1942 are a total mystery.*

*I am wondering if you provide consultation. I'd like to meet with a genealogist for an hour or two, show what I have, and receive some guidance for my next steps.*

*Do you provide this service or something similar? What might be the approximate cost? Thanks for reading. Sincerely, Ron Williams*

Again, I found the world of genealogy to move swiftly, and I received a quick reply:

*I'm happy to help you, Ron. And yes, I have done this. For genealogy research/consultation, I charge $35/hour. The first hour meeting is always free, as it takes some time for us to go through the known information, and also to assist me in evaluating how challenging it might be for me to help you successfully.*

*The first information pieces I'd be interested in knowing are the places your grandfather was born, lived, married, died, his parents, siblings, and his wife/children. It can be challenging finding people after 1920 because of redacting those documents formed after that time (legal privacy issues). So necessarily then we would be looking at other than the usual resource groups of censuses, birth/death/marriage records, military. Cheers for now, Celia*

Studying her response, I was immediately at ease I'd made the correct choice. I appreciated the way she dove headfirst into the challenge, offering immediate areas of focus as well as potential obstacles. In sharp contrast to my own often discombobulated research efforts, this was a lady who clearly knew what she was doing. I responded with a comprehensive timeline I had created for my grandfather as well as some other corresponding documents. We arranged for a Saturday morning meetup at her home, which I was pleased to discover was in the Marpole neighborhood of Vancouver, only a block or two away from my grandfather's house on Hudson Street. In fact, my grandfather, as well as Jack and I during our aforementioned Marpole evening stroll, travelled past the very apartment complex on the way to the Fraser Arms Hotel. It had to be a sign.

The very next Saturday, I jumped in my Jetta, travel cup of coffee in hand, and made the forty-five-minute drive to the now fairly familiar area of Marpole. Arriving a few minutes early, I visited the nearby Safeway in successful pursuit of a pen and note pad. Minutes later, I was being buzzed in the front door, my workbag filled with all that I'd accumulated. Ms. Lewis greeted me at the door and led me into her sizeable apartment, clearly the home of a prolific genealogist. I was impressed by a well-stocked workstation including monitor screens and printers on two separate desk areas as well as charts and documents neatly organized on the wall and bulletin board areas. I was offered a brief tour of her abode, with the explanation that with several current projects it was important to have her materials spread out for reference. Now comfortably seated, we focused on the task at hand.

It was clear that Ms. Lewis had spent considerable time perusing my documents and began with a series of clarifying questions, including "do I have any definitive evidence he was in the United States," and "how thoroughly have I studied the closest DNA matches." I provided more details regarding each avenue of research I had undertaken. As well, I went through my online files as well as the documents I had amassed. She shared that she was impressed with what I'd done, a compliment that I readily accepted with pride. Near the end of our time, she left me with two prominent thoughts.

First, she shared that I was fortunate. "You have a mystery," she explained, "not a lot of genealogists encounter this opportunity." She outlined that she had completed her family history – on all sides no less – years ago, with no discernable secrets, mysteries or puzzles to discover. "It was all straightforward and it's all right here," she professed, pointing to a set of one-inch, grade-school-type binders. Although I'd never considered that point of view, immediately, I knew I felt the very same.

Second, she rebuked my wild theories about a long prison term, a long-lost family or other grandiose tales. "It's likely that your grandfather's early life was no different than what we know of his later life." In this case that meant strained, possibly short, relationships with younger women, and a series of temporary, maybe transient sales jobs.

Third, she placed her warm hand on the tip of my knee and with chin lowered and eyes focused, she assured, "you have all the data you need to solve this mystery. You need to first follow up your father's DNA connections to ensure there are no relatives undiscovered. Then you need to carefully go through all United States and Canadian census reports...you must complete these two steps no matter how long it takes."

.

# Revelations of a Wife

*Saturday, June 15, 1947, 10:02 a.m. Toronto Rooming Houses, Astoria Hotel, 769 East Hastings Street, Vancouver, British Columbia, Canada.*

*What a difference two weeks can make. Only recently considered "down and out," Alfred, once again, finds himself in a new city, beginning a new life. After the places he's been, and lived, Edmonton never seemed quite...right. With his previous stop in Toronto, he was ready for a place on the west coast with more forgiving winters. Vancouver seemed the ideal option.*

*While tired of Alberta, he has also grown weary of hospital work. Yes, serving as an orderly had its advantages for a fifty-seven-year-old man. The security, the comfortable routine, and steady paycheck were all appreciated, but the work was also monotonous and dull. If Alfred is determined to reclaim some element of youth in a new city, he feels he ought to get back to the work that makes him feel alive, challenged.*

*His room, conveniently situated on busy East Hastings Street, is the perfect home base for his new life. Inspired by the youth and vitality of the city, Alfred finds a sales job with The Vancouver News Herald, not the biggest daily on the Vancouver streets but large and respected enough to please him.*

*With so much to be positive about, Alfred feels confident and has his eye on a pretty, young, German chambermaid from an orchard family also newly arrived in the big city.*

I left my meeting with Ms. Lewis optimistic but also a little skeptical. Could all the answers I so desperately yearned for really be in DNA matches and census reports, both readily available at my fingertips? I had to admit that even though I'd spent considerable time on both, often when I caught a snag or progress stalled, I'd minimize the problematic window on my laptop and pursue another more accessible line of research. I knew I needed to undergo a comprehensive, systematic, exhaustive search.

Just then, it happened again. My mind was invaded with a refreshing, welcome distraction. I remembered recently becoming aware that there was a comprehensive, searchable set of Edmonton phone directories available on the Internet. I believed I had searched similar on *Ancestry.com* in the past, but I had never attacked the records directly. Thus, I pulled up the Google home page and typed in "Edmonton phone book 1946." The first match was to a site maintained by the Peel Library at the University of Alberta. I was immediately directed to *Henderson's Greater Edmonton Directory 1946.*

For a set of tired eyes on a mundane weekday afternoon, this seemed a quick, easy search to provide my mind a break from the mental strain of beginning a comprehensive search of all available census reports.

I may remind that I was certain my grandfather had lived in Edmonton in the mid-1940s. He had identified the time as October 1944 to July 1947 on his 1959 old age security application. Moreover, the February 1945 letter from Uncle George was addressed, "Mr. A.V. Williams, Sub Post Office 23, Edmonton, Alberta, Canada." While I had learned not to definitively accept the word of my grandfather, I couldn't see any reason he'd lie to an uncle about his address, and, after all, the very fact that my grandfather was in possession of the letter shows that he was in Edmonton to collect it. I clicked on the link provided for the 1946 directory and opened the document search bar. Looking at the specific address my grandfather had entered in the old age security application, I typed "Alfred Williams." The result was instantaneous:

WILLIAMS, A V attndt Prov Mental Institute r 10130 155 St.

Even though this couldn't be considered any monumental discovery, or hardly even a surprise, it was always rewarding to see something confirmed in official print. Remembering my grandfather identifying a "Clara" as his wife on an unmailed 1946 income tax form, I went the next step by performing a type of "reverse search" with my grandfather's address. Again, the results were instantaneous.

WILLIAMS, A V attndt Prov Mental Institute r 10130 155 St.
FIELDER, Clara clk Zellers r 10130 155 St.

Finally, an undisciplined stray from my immediate research focus paid off. I found the elusive and mysterious, Clara. Instantly my mind raced with possibility, my greatest hope to discover information about the woman I now could identify as Clara Fielder that would lead back to my grandfather pre-1942. With Clara's surname, I could now complete a number of more detailed searches that I was unable to endeavor in the past. I recalled that my dad had petitioned both Toronto and Edmonton jurisdictions for marriage records concerning Alfred Victor Williams. Was it possible that my grandfather married her under a different name? Even discovering where Clara Fielder came from could provide a geographical location to search my grandfather: Alfred Victor Williams or Roy Hammond.

There were circumstances that dictated some realism, however. For starters, the listing in the phone book revealed that Clara did not take the Williams surname. Does this mean that they were not legally married? That would negate a marriage certificate and any information offered in said marriage certificate. Additionally, if my grandfather was honest in family correspondence – and it seemed he was – he reported himself as single and unmarried in family letters from Toronto earlier in the 1940s, so there was a good chance he had met Clara during his latter days in Toronto or possibly even in Edmonton. If either case were accurate, learning more about Clara may not expose any secrets during my grandfather's missing years prior to 1942. It was well-worth the chance though, so I had no choice but to pursue it.

With anticipation, I proceeded to the next step, checking the 1945 directory, where I spied the following two entries:

FIELDER Clara clk Zellers r 10130 155 St.
155 Street, 10130 Williams Fred

I found it noteworthy that Clara appeared only in the "name" section of the directory and was not mentioned in the "street" section of the directory. The opposite was true for my grandfather, who appeared in the "street" section, but not the "name" section. Was this done intentionally, a weak, veiled attempt to mask a shameful, unofficial domestic arrangement? Or maybe it was circumstance, unworthy of further thought?

Relying again on the 1959 old age security application, I note my grandfather reports his time in Edmonton as beginning in October 1944, possibly too late to be included in a 1944 directory. True to his word, a check of the 1944 directory shows the address occupied by an "Edward McGee." Similarly, a search of the 1947 directory shows a "Samuel Moore," occupying what details would suggest is a rental unit. If I wasn't fully convinced before, I'm now certain my grandfather was in Edmonton during the dates he self-reported. Now I could focus on the mysterious Clara Fielder and what clues her story may hold.

With no other choice but to temporarily pause my full-scale attack of census reports, I turned my full attention to my grandfather's one-time partner, if not wife. On *Ancestry.com*, I'm not surprised to discover some potential matches. In a 1915 World War I Attestation document, I see a Clara Fielder listed as wife to a Percival Fielder, both residing in Ontario. Birthdates seem to matchup, and I consider whether it possible my grandfather first met this Clara in Ontario prior to 1911. I am able to follow this lead to a 1929 border crossing, in which her son, John Fielder, enters Washington State to attend college. I note that his next of kin, in this case his mother, Clara Fielder, is listed as residing in Vancouver, Canada now. I am especially interested in the geography, with Washington State being home to Seattle. I'm unable to find additional supporting documents and the lead dries up.

It was on *Newspapers.com* that I found a wedding announcement originally featured in the *Edmonton Journal* on Friday, August 23, 1946 that immediately caught my attention. The announcement featured a wedding photo of the happy couple, she in white veil and matching dress, a large bouquet of flowers held tight in her hands; he standing proud and erect behind, with dark suit and satisfied smile. Really, it looked no different from any other wedding photo one may come across. What caught my immediate attention was the caption below the photo:

*Mr. Patrick Stanley and his bride, the former Miss Clara Fielder, who were married in a recent ceremony in the vestry of McDougall United Church. The bride is a daughter of the late Mr. and Mrs. W. Fielder, of Toronto, and the groom is a son of Mrs. G. Stanley, of Edmonton, and the late Mr. Stanley. The newlyweds have taken up residence in Edmonton.*

While the details of text seemed to match, the photo of Clara Fielder showed a much younger woman than the fifty-six years my grandfather would have been at the time. Rather than cast doubt this only strengthened the possibility I had the correct Clara Fielder, based on the rather large age difference between my grandfather and my Oma. As well, the fact that Clara reported to be from Toronto piqued my interest, accepting that as the city my grandfather had traveled from two years prior. If this lead was correct, I could expand my search to include the surname, Stanley. My mind sought a little more confirmation before allowing me to proceed.

If I can be permitted a quick, undisciplined divergence from the immediate text around Clara Fielder, while on *Newspapers.com*, my wondering mind drove me to enter "Fred Williams" in my 1944-1946 searches of Edmonton newspapers which yielded the following story in the September 17, 1946 edition of the *Edmonton Journal*:

### WALLET MISSING

*City police Tuesday was investigating a report from Fred Williams, resident of the CN rooms, that his shirt and a pair of trousers containing a wallet and around $25 cash had been stolen soon after midnight Monday. Mr. Williams said he was absent from the room at the time of the alleged theft.*

Whether this was my grandfather or not is difficult to prove. However, I found familiarity in a few details. First, he would have no longer been at 10130 155 Street with Clara in late 1946, so it made sense he would move to a new location. Cognizant that he began his stay in Vancouver in 1947 at the Toronto Rooming Houses, it made sense that he may have resided at the CN Rooming Houses during his latter days in Edmonton.

Second, in a 1968 letter to my father, Alfred reported he was in difficult financial state due to some stolen government cheques. Thus, this would not be the last time my grandfather would report a theft of funds.

Third, as it was well-known that my grandfather frequently enjoyed a drink, or three, it would make sense that as a single man not yet enjoying his golden years, he may be out on the town on a Monday night. Whether the "Fred Williams" in question was or was not my grandfather, I found the article an interesting aside.

Now back on *Ancestry.com*, I completed another round of searches for Clara Fielder, this time adding the alternate surname, Stanley. I was fortunate to find a "Province of Alberta, Registration of Marriage" for Patrick Stanley and Clara Fielder. I attacked the brief document with ravenous fury, looking for a singular detail that this Clara was the same Clara who lived at 10130 155th with my grandfather and was employed as a salesclerk at Zellers. I found it. In the section aptly titled, "Bride," the following information was entered:

Name in Full: Clara Fielder
Occupation: Salesclerk, Zellers
Spinster, Widow or Divorced: Spinster
Age: 26
Religious Denomination: Presbyterian
Place of Residence Before Marriage: 10838 124th Street, Edmonton
Place of Birth: Toronto, Ontario
Name of Father: William Fielder

Name of Mother: Margaret McVicar McCurdy

I was immediately both struck and pleased to read "Salesclerk, Zellers." The mention of employment at the well-known Canadian retailer confirmed beyond all skepticism that the Clara Fielder listed as living with my grandfather in 1945 and 1946 was the very same Clara Fielder who married Patrick Stanley in August of 1946. The overlapping dates did not cause any strife, accepting that information printed in city directories is likely gathered early in a calendar year or possibly even in the year before.

I may remind of my extended interest in this brief partner of my grandfather's. My goal was quite simple. I wanted to discover all that I could about Clara from before her arrival in Edmonton. The marriage announcement shared that Clara hailed from Toronto, but I wasn't prepared to accept that as definitive truth, nor the initial meeting place between Alfred and Clara. If Alfred and Clara had met prior to their Toronto residencies, it could tell me where my grandfather was living at some point in the remaining missing years.

Rather than immediately jump into her past, I chose to begin with efforts to connect with any family that might be remaining between Clara Stanley and Patrick Stanley. Reasoning that with matching 1920 birth years both Clara and Patrick were almost certainly deceased, I went in search of their obituaries. It's in the February 21, 1999 issue of the *Edmonton Journal* that I read the following:

*Stanley, Clara: On February 17, 1999, Ms. Clara Stanley of Edmonton, beloved wife of Pat Stanley, passed away at the age of 85 years.*

*She leaves to mourn the loss besides her loving husband; three sons, Al of Edmonton, Peter of Fort McMurray, Roger and his wife, Sharon Lange of Peace River; three grandchildren, Joanne, David, and Brittany; two great grandchildren, J.T. and Cohen.*

According to the obituary, Clara's date of birth was 1914. That was at odds with her 1946 marriage certificate in which she listed her age as twenty-six, promoting a 1920 birth year. The names of the children and grandchildren were especially noteworthy. I could use these names, as well as geographical information, to track them down. As Clara's death was some twenty-three years prior, I expect there may be more grandchildren also.

The next step was something that Lana had taught me. I again jumped on to my ancient, seldom-used Facebook account and began looking for Stanleys in the three areas of Alberta mentioned, Peace River, Fort McMurray and Edmonton, cognizant that there had likely been a customary degree of migration amongst family members, especially the younger.

I both found and messaged a number of Stanleys with the following generic greeting:

> *Hello [insert first name] – I am sorry to bother you. I am presently conducting some family research and I'm wondering if your grandmother was Clara (Fielder) Stanley who lived in Edmonton in the mid-1940s. I'm at a real stand-still with my findings and I'd be very interested in any information I can find. Thanks.*

With a very impressive sixteen-minute turnaround time, I received the following on Facebook Messenger from a Brittany Stanley:

> *Hi there, that does sound like my grandma. Wow, that is very cool. We also have tried doing some research! Here is my mom's number who is doing research for my dad, 782-623-8436*

Maybe I'm skeptical by nature, but the whole thing seemed a little too easy. I hadn't given any of my information or suggested any connection and I was given someone's private phone number. Brittany indicated that Clara may have been her grandmother, which suggested that Brittany's father was either Al Stanley, Peter Stanley, or Roger Stanley. With Clara and Patrick marrying in 1946, I figured these three were somewhere between the ages of sixty-six and seventy-six, not necessarily an age range for the elderly and vulnerable, but I did worry about making what was essentially a cold-call to an older-aged stranger to discuss family matters. I didn't want a repeat of my father's initial call to Bernard Williams' widow, Ann. For no other reason than Brittany mentioning her mother, I guessed she was the daughter of Roger Stanley and his wife, Sharon Lange, so I responded with the following:

> *"Hi Brittany – thanks for the response. I think your mother is Sharon. Is she aware I will be calling? Thanks."*

Brittany's response was immediately forthcoming:

> *"Yes. Thanks. My parents are looking forward to hearing from you."*

Adding to my scruples about cold-calling an older-aged stranger in hopes of discussing personal family matters, I knew that any correspondence would include the uncomfortable reality that Clara had lived with an abusive alcoholic some thirty years her senior, not necessarily the picture you want to offer of someone's dear, deceased mother or grandmother. I couldn't help wonder at the instantaneous manner of the events. I was far more used to my small discoveries emerging only after hours of fruitless research. It was only an hour later I found myself, strangely, in the once-familiar asphalt parking lot of the same suburban strip mall I had taken guitar lessons in some forty years earlier.

"Hello, Ms. Lange?"

"Yes?"

"My name is Ron Williams. Thank you very much for taking my call. I have been researching my late grandfather and I believe that he may have lived with your late mother-in-law, a Clara Stanley."

"Yes, that certainly could make sense. My husband and I have been trying to research his mother, but we have not gotten very far." She offered the last almost apologetically, maybe extolling her modesty. If only she knew I was very much a novice genealogist also.

"Well, I was able to find entries in the 1945 and 1946 Edmonton city directories that showed my grandfather and Clara, your mother-in-law, living at the same residence, on 155th Street in Edmonton."

"Okay." She paused, waiting for more information.

"It lists your mother-in-law as a salesclerk at Zellers."

"Okay, yes. That is correct. She worked at Zellers for a long time."

The conversation continued in a sort of slow, quizzical way, each of us offering small pieces for contemplation, requiring a few moments to reassemble the narrative we thought we knew about our family members. Sharon, along with Roger in the background, shared that Clara was a wonderful mother and grandmother who was fiercely protective of her family. She was a kind, benevolent woman who won the hearts of all those in her circle. She had maintained that in the spring of 1946 she and a girlfriend had travelled from their homes in Toronto for a western adventure, placing them in Edmonton for what was supposed to be a brief stop. The brief stop, as Clara reported, turned permanent when she met her future husband, Patrick Stanley. Soon they were in love and married, as they would be for the next fifty years plus. Apparently, Clara rarely spoke about her early years in Toronto and maintained that she had no living family remaining.

I couldn't necessarily offer any directly contrasting evidence other than to share that my research showed Clara did not arrive in Edmonton in the spring of 1946, but rather in 1944 when she proceeded to live with my grandfather for parts of the ensuing two years. Other than the common address, the only real evidence I could offer was the letter from Uncle George addressed to "Fred and Clara" and paying respect to Alfred's wife, as well as my grandfather indicating that Clara was his wife on the unmailed Alberta tax form of 1944. These last two points demonstrated that Alfred and Clara were not simply roomers in a shared accommodation. Certainly, Sharon and Roger were surprised at this news, but acknowledged that they were not shocked, further explaining that Clara seemed somewhat secretive about her past.

Rather than seeming fragile, Sharon and Roger were both curious and forthcoming, so I felt it my burden to offer some information about my grandfather. "I believe he was a lot older than your mother-in-law, likely thirty years to be exact." I further explained that he had married my Oma in 1947 despite their thirty-year age difference. Next, I offered that my grandfather, "struggled with alcohol and was abusive towards my Oma." Sharon confessed that a relative once bore witness to a modest fight between Clara and her husband Patrick, in which Clara offered something along the lines of, "I was mistreated by my last husband, I'm not going to stand for it again here."

We finished the thirty-minute call with an exchange of email addresses and a promise to share what information we had about our once-connected and now deceased relatives. In my email later that evening, I shared PDF clippings of the phone book entries, as well as the information and timeline that I had composed. Both Sharon, along with Roger, and myself were fully convinced our respective family members were a match. I was hoping that my level of interest would be contagious, and she could provide some information on Clara...information that could lead to my grandfather's earlier years.

While on this journey, I had paused several times to briefly contemplate the basic benevolence of humanity. Sharon and Roger further proved my observations. In quick time, she returned my email along with a document sharing the information she had amassed regarding her mother-in-law who was shaping up to be as much of a mystery as my grandfather.

Sharon shared Clara's birth certificate, which included some interesting, if not confusing, information.

Name: Clara McCurdy Johnson McConnell
Date of Birth: Aug. 3, 1913
Mother: Margaret McCurdy, single
Father:

The fact that no father was listed, along with what appeared to be three surnames suggested that "Johnson" or "McConnell" may have been Clara's father. Further to that, the name, "Johnson" was actually crossed-out for whatever reason. Nonetheless, I was thrilled to have some potential surnames to further research. The birthdate, too, seemed to confirm that the information in her obituary was correct, but that she had been untruthful at the time of her marriage to Patrick Stanley. Also, Sharon had a 1937, T1 income tax form which listed her address as 279 Gerrard Street, East Toronto. Lastly, Sharon provided a May 1938 receipt from Adams Furniture Store, listing the delivery address as 265 Bleecker Street. This rounded up the official documents she had in her possession. I mentally juxtaposed her three artifacts against the papers and possessions my grandfather left and felt fortunate.

At this point, I was interested in how Clara came to take on the "Fielder" surname. In her 1946 marriage certificate she identified that she was a spinster and that her father was a Mr. W. Fielder, deceased. If this was the case, why did she have completely different surnames in her birth certificate?

In addition to documents, Sharon had been busy on the Internet and had found several entries in the Henderson directories for the Toronto area:

1937 - Clara McCurdy, 279 Gerrard St Toronto
1938 – C. McCurdy, 265 Bleecker St Toronto

1939 - Clara McCurdy, 265 Bleecker St Toronto

Sharon shared that in 1938 and 1939 the address of 265 Bleecker, which doubled as an automotive garage, also listed William Fielder, Linda Fielder and Norman Fielder as residents. With this new information and based on the data Clara entered in her marriage license, I surmised that Clara was born to Margaret McCurdy and an absentee father whose surname was either Johnson or McConnell. I guessed that, at some point, Clara's mother, Margaret, had married William Fielder, whose surname Clara adopted, either formally or informally. I also had to consider that maybe William Fielder was Clara's actual father. This could explain why Clara is living with the Fielder family in 1938 and 1939 without her mother, Margaret. Perhaps there was a reason he was unlisted on the birth certificate and Clara simply moved into his house at a later date. The identity of both Linda and Norman would have to be confirmed later. Although I was somewhat murky as to what potential clues may await, my interest in my grandfather's one-time partner was strong. It was a lead I was confident would pay dividends.

I needed to learn more about William Fielder, the seeming patriarch of the Fielder family. Back on *Ancestry.com*, I found a family tree containing information for a William Richard Fielder. It seemed that William Fielder was born in 1890 in London, England. This put him at age twenty-three in 1913 when Clara was born. Next, I found an immigration document, showing that William Fielder departed his home in England in late May 1913, traveling across the Atlantic on the *Franconia* and arriving in North America on June 4, 1913. Based on the information provided in Clara's actual birth certificate, this eliminated the possibility that William Fielder could have been Clara's biological father as he was not in North American to contribute his part to her conception in November 1912. Also, to further complicate matters, I learned that Linda, rather than a daughter, was actually William Fielder's wife.

Continuing to study the family tree, I learned that at the time of Clara's marriage in 1946, William Fielder was alive and well and would continue to be so for another fourteen years, until his death in 1960. If Clara was fond enough of him to list him as her father, why make up the fact that he was deceased? I now favored the theory that Clara was somehow taken in by the Fielder family, only to have things go awry at some point, leading to her permanent estrangement. Despite some discovery, I continued to admit ignorance as to the exact circumstance that resulted in Clara McCurdy taking the Fielder surname.

I realized I was descending into a rabbit-hole with the potential to steal my research time and alter me from my target. However, I carried a strong feeling that this mysterious woman held some clue to a missing part of my grandfather's life. I decided to switch focus and look into the life of Clara's mother, Margaret McCurdy.

Once again, it was *Ancestry.com* that I would consult. I learned that Margaret McCurdy was born in Scotland around 1890. She immigrated to Canada as a single, twenty-one-year-old in 1911, planning to find work as a servant in Toronto. Two years later, she was an unmarried mother, giving birth to Clara. There was a 1916 marriage to a John Towers that produced a half-sister to Clara. Sadly, Margaret passed away in 1919 at the young age of twenty-nine. With Margaret's premature 1919 death, she would have had a small window to cohabitate with William Fielder, especially when you factor in that Margaret married and bore child to John Towers during that time. With the knowledge that Clara did not appear to live with the Fielders prior to 1938, I could now eliminate that Clara became a Fielder because her mother, Margaret, had been enjoined in some way to William.

It was back to the drawing board in my efforts to discover exactly how Clara McCurdy came to be a Fielder. At this point, I figured it was again time to look forward, this time on the Fielder side. In Norman's obituary, he listed his children as

Veronica Peete, married to Nigel Peete, and Eleanor Davis, married to Paul Davis. Norman's grandchildren were listed as Allyson, Patrick, Ryan, Tim, Lara and Sean. Armed with several names, I figured it wouldn't be too difficult to fall back on my Facebook skills in a bid to make contact. On a plain sheet of paper, I sketched a rough family tree including the six grandchildren with the surnames Peete and Davis. Fortunately, I found a few whose Facebook "friend" lists were public allowing me to confirm I had the correct individuals. Once identified, I sent the following familiar message:

> *Hello – sorry to bother you. I believe that you or your husband may be related to the late Mr. Norman Fielder. I am in the process of researching family members and I believe that my grandmother lived with the Fielder family in the 1940s. I'd very much like to get in touch with someone who may be able to help with some family information.*

Although Clara Stanley was, at best, my step-grandmother for a short time, she was still, technically, a type of grandmother. I believed this would carry a little more weight towards credibility in my message and I promised myself to be fully truthful should any further contact be made.

Within thirty minutes, I received a message from someone with the Facebook name, "Lori-Oreo," whose byline read, "Saving the Universe One Hamster at a time." I identified her as the daughter-in-law of Eleanor Davis, one of Norman Fielder's two children. She sent me the following message:

> *Hi Ron – We're not too sure about that far back in history with the family line but I can give you one of our elder's contacts that would definitely be more helpful. Please reach out to Eleanor via email as she will definitely know more than Ryan or me. This is very exciting, and I cannot wait to hear more about how our families may be connected.*

I thanked her immensely for her help and immediately emailed Eleanor Davis, wishing to strike while the iron was hot, so to speak.

I titled my message to Eleanor, "Family Mystery," hoping to appeal to her curiosity. I began by introducing myself and providing a little information about my quest to discover my grandfather's missing years. Once complete I switched to the purpose of my contact. "My step-grandmother was born in Ontario in August 1913 as Clara McCurdy. Her early life is a mystery, but phone book records show that in 1938 and 1939, Clara, twenty-five, was living at 265 Bleecker Street, with the Fielder family, including your father who would have been twenty-three years old." I made sure to attach the phone book pages to support. Finally, I ended with my request for help: "I hope I have not confused you too much. I am really curious if you have any information about my grandmother living with your father's family or why she would have adopted the Fielder name. I'm pretty desperate for information and would really appreciate this. Thanks!"

I had been so fortunate in receiving responses that I half expected Eleanor to reply that very day. However, that did not happen, nor did it happen the next day either. In truth, I secretly applaud people for taking their time with electronic communications, envious at not allowing email and other technology to dictate the pace and commitments for the day. Candidly, though, it was difficult for me to wait, and I was guilty of checking my email several times each day in hopes of a response from Eleanor. Finally, on the fifth day after I sent my message, Eleanor's response was forthcoming.

*Hi Ron: Thanks for your email. I have been away, hence the late reply. You have supplied me with a lot of information related to your step grandmother and I thank you for the phone records. They are enlightening. I knew a lot of the information but had totally forgotten about my relatives' occupations.*

*You say you are desperate for information. I'm assuming there are gaps in the family history. Perhaps your grandmother put my grandfather's name on her marriage certificate because she was estranged from her parents. I'm interested in continuing this conversation. Sincerely, Eleanor Davis*

I immediately felt a sense of gratitude for Eleanor taking the time to respond so graciously. I was disappointed that she wasn't able to offer any concrete information. From my research, I knew her father, Norman, was born in 1914. I could assume that his daughters, Eleanor and Veronica may have been born between 1935 and 1945, which could be within the years 1938 to 1939 when Clara lived with the Fielder family. Of course, the birth years were simply assumptions, even guesses, but I had to accept it was possible Eleanor or Veronica would have been aware of Clara. Nonetheless, Eleanor's closing promise that she was "interested in continuing this conversation" was certainly reason for optimism and I received it with great delight.

In order to preserve continuity, I tactfully waited two or three days to respond. When I did, I kept my message brief. I thanked Eleanor for her thoughtful response and asked if Eleanor was aware of the family taking on renters. Finally, I ended by complimenting her family, mentioning that Clara must have cared for her grandfather to list him as her father. Eleanor's response, which I received after another short delay exceeded all my expectations.

To begin, citing a mixture of curiosity and nostalgia, Eleanor asked if I was able to forward a copy of the furniture receipt I had alluded to in an earlier email. Lastly, Eleanor dropped what I would consider to be a something of a bombshell:

*I was speaking to my sister, and she has some information you would be interested in. When we cleaned out our mother's house after her death a few years ago we uncovered some papers and have since reviewed them. Our father was apparently married to a Clara Fielder but divorced her in 1944 due to adultery with an Alfred Victor Williams.*

*Would he be your grandfather?*

# A Question of Paternity

**Wednesday, March 3, 1948, 2:07 p.m. St. Paul's Hospital, 1081 Burrard Street, Vancouver, British Columbia, Canada.**

*It's finally happened. Alfred is father to a boy, and he couldn't be any prouder. For now, he's achieved his dream: a new bride, a healthy baby boy, a nice house in a family neighborhood. In addition, he is comfortable in his job working for Mr. Gaisford in the Circulation Department of The Vancouver News Herald. At fifty-eight years old, Alfred acknowledges it took much longer than he originally expected when he arrived in Canada at age sixteen some forty-two years earlier, but Vancouver has been good for him, offering much more happiness and good fortune than previous stops.*

*Knowing him as a proud man, Elizabeth is partially*

*surprised their baby is not bestowed with the middle name of "Alfred," the father opting instead for the unfamiliar "Roy." The temporary thought is almost immediately lost in passing, the couple optimistic about their days as a family.*

T his was certainly a shock. My secret hope had always been that there were documents hidden in a drawer somewhere in North American that would divulge the entirety of my grandfather's mysterious years. In my quiet hours I would use my powers of imagination to devise a machine that would complete a clean sweep of all papers and files across the continents for a physical, "Google-like" search for all documents pertaining to "Alfred Victor Williams, DOB, November 23, 1889" or "Roy Hammond, DOB unknown." These divorce papers didn't quite live up to my fantastical musings, but it was a step in the general direction.

Over the past few weeks there were times I felt I was diverging from my focus by pursuing Clara's connection to the Fielder family. It was nothing more than intuition that motivated me to continue pursuing this angle. My trust in our one-time psychic, Michelle Osbourne, was growing.

I desperately pined for a copy of the divorce papers, but the tone of Eleanor's email told me to tread lightly. I decided the most practical and possibly advantageous position would be to put Eleanor Davis in touch with Roger Stanley and Sharon Lange. They were the parties who shared the closest bond, as both their fathers were married to Clara McCurdy, not at the same time, of course. I communicated my plan with Sharon who was delighted to continue the correspondence. Soon after, she forwarded an email she sent to Eleanor. In the warm message, she identified herself and provided some background on Clara. I recognized the content as the very same she had forwarded me only a few weeks prior. Sharon explained that she and her husband suspected that Clara had been married prior but lacked any concrete details. Of most import, Sharon requested a copy of the divorce papers, explaining that any information provided would help fill in the details of her mother-in-law's mysterious earlier years.

In her return message, Eleanor shared her theory that Clara began as a boarder in 1938 before marrying her father, Norman, in 1939. According to the divorce papers, the brief marriage ended abruptly in 1944. Eleanor also explained that her father never mentioned Clara to her or her sister and that they only discovered the existence of a first marriage at the time of their mother's death. Finally, in regard to the divorce papers, Eleanor explained, "I am not at liberty to send the actual divorce papers. I only know that Clara and Alfred Williams were the adulterers. You have done a lot of research. I hope the divorce details help you. Sorry I can't be of more help."

While both Sharon and I were disappointed, I had to respect Eleanor's wishes. She had been both pleasant and helpful thus far. Additionally, for someone who preferred not to share the divorce papers, I had to give her immense credit for sharing their very existence. It would have been far easier for her to simply bury the document. That didn't, however, mean that I couldn't surmise potential reasons for not sharing. I responded to Sharon that there may be some disparaging charges against Eleanor's father, possibly mental or even physical abuse. Of course, it was equally plausible that Eleanor was protecting Sharon and Roger from disparaging detail about their late mother. Either way, I had to accept her wishes. That wasn't going to stop my curiosity, however, and it wasn't going to stop Sharon either.

In her next email, Sharon rejoiced that she was able to obtain a copy of the divorce papers directly through Ontario Records. She added, "it's been bothering me that Eleanor wouldn't share divorce papers. I do believe there is more to it! After eighty years I'm not sure what she was hiding but guess we'll find out!" I had to applaud Sharon's moxie and was thankful she'd pursued the document. All I could do now is wait.

It was a cold December, Friday afternoon when I returned from work in a rush to attend a pre-Christmas night out with some close friends. My preparations for the evening would have to be put on hold, however, as I noticed an email from Sharon Lange simply titled, "Divorce Papers." What was attached was a fifty-two-page document, containing some twelve separate legal briefs, if that is the correct nomenclature. On the first page of each document, it listed the plaintiff as Norman Richard William Fielder and the defendants as Clara Fielder and Alfred Victor Williams. I found it interesting that my grandfather was listed as an official defendant when he was not, in fact, legally involved in the marriage; however, I soon discovered that the plaintiff was pursuing the cost of legal services to be paid by my grandfather.

The first document, dated May 6, 1944 was a "Writ of Summons." In the writ, Norman Fielder petitions the court with the following: "the dissolution of the marriage solemnized between the Plaintiff and the Defendant, Clara Fielder, on or about the 20th day of May 1939 at the City of Toronto, in the County of York, on the grounds of the adultery of the Defendant, Clara Fielder, with the Defendant, Alfred Victor Williams."

It seemed pretty self-explanatory.

The second document, dated the same day, was an "Affidavit of Plaintiff Verifying Statement of Claim," in which Norman Fielder offers thirteen sworn statements for the court. Highlights included that Norman and Clara were originally married "in the Province of Ontario on the 20th day of May 1939," that "before her marriage the Plaintiff was Clara Johnston McCurdy and...was a divorcee residing in said City of Toronto," and that the couple lived together in two separate locations between June 1939 and March 1944.

According to Fielder, "early in the month of April 1944 and May 1944 the Defendant, Clara Fielder...committed adultery with the Defendant, Alfred Victor Williams, and the Defendant, Clara Fielder, is now residing with the Defendant, Alfred Victor Williams, at 23 Park Road in the City of Toronto as his wife and has assumed the name of Mrs. Williams." I noted the Park Road address matched what I'd read on the final family letter to my grandfather in Ontario. Also, I saw that the family letters began being addressed to Edmonton early in 1945. The dates all matched, I observed with some pleasure.

Further down the PDF file was a "Notice of Trial," dated May 29, 1944, stamped, "this notice of trial was served by me on Clara Fielder and Alfred Victor Williams." A solicitor whose name seems indecipherable explains, "Norman Richard W. Fielder and Clara Fielder et. al. Defendant, required to sit down for trial at present non-Jury sitting, at Toronto." I must admit the wording seems peculiar and I cannot be one-hundred percent certain I have copied the line correctly. In any event, the document seems to verify that both my grandfather and Clara were aware of the trial and the expectation of attendance.

It seems the actual trial commenced on June 23, 1944. The court noted that the trial proceeded, "in the presence of Council for the Plaintiff, no one appearing for the Defendants although duly served with the Writ of Summons...and with Notice of Trial." I was hardly surprised that neither my grandfather, nor Clara, showed up for the trial. Further down it noted, "this court doth order and adjure that the marriage between the Plaintiff and the Defendant, Clara Fielder...be dissolved by reason of the adultery of the Defendant, Clara Fielder, with the Defendant, Alfred Victor Williams, unless sufficient cause be shown to this Court within six months from the date hereof why this Judgement should not be made absolute." Lastly, the judge adjudicated that "the Plaintiff do recover against the Defendant, Alfred Victor Williams, his costs of the action forthwith after taxation thereof." Lastly there appeared a stamp that the document, once again, had been safely delivered to Clara Fielder herself.

Immediately, I recall a resignation document from amongst the possessions kept upon my grandfather's death. Locating the frayed, worn card, I examine the details. The card identifies that Alfred is resigning from his position of "hospital nursing orderly" at the Christie Street Hospital, citing "ill health" as the reason. I take note the date of the resignation, June 30, 1944, one week after he and Clara learned of the divorce and the expectation that Alfred pay Clara's former husband's court costs. I recall the modest sum of twenty dollars charged to my grandfather for services related to his 1942 reentering of Canada, but that hardly allows me to estimate the cost of a divorce, including the filing of no fewer than twelve legal documents.

In a separate "Statutory Declaration" also recovered at the time of my grandfather's death, he reported his 1943 income to total $1193.40. Thus, if he was on the hook for even one-hundred dollars of legal fees, that would represent almost ten percent of his yearly earnings, a formidable sum! My grandfather reported that his last shift at Christie Street Hospital was to be July 7, 1944, but whether he fulfilled his promise shall remain a mystery. On the same unsent 1944 Income Tax Form in which he identified Clara as his wife, my grandfather noted that he began working at the Alberta Provincial Mental Hospital on July 20, 1944, so it is possible that he completed his final shifts in Ontario before making the journey west.

This information impacted both Clara's family and my own. To Sharon and Roger, the information came as quite a shock, having no idea the woman described as a "sweet old lady" could be involved in such an affair. Thankfully, I was able to draw upon my earlier discoveries regarding hard-times and survival. Knowing that Clara was born to a single mother and seemingly estranged from all family at the time of her 1946 wedding, I suggested to Sharon and Roger that Clara was simply doing what she needed to survive. It was possible, although I had no proof, that conditions in her marriage to Norman Fielder were unsatisfactory, even unsafe. At the time, it's possible my grandfather offered her what she needed, even if it was only temporary. The world of 1946 was far different than the comfortable existence many of us are privileged to enjoy in 2023 and Clara's legacy as a dedicated and supportive family mother and grandmother is unblemished.

The information certainly helped me piece together my grandfather's time between his re-entry into Ontario and his eventual, long-term relocation to British Columbia. I could confidently state I knew the reason he fled Ontario. On a larger scale, while this information didn't help me directly fill in my grandfather's missing years between 1910 and 1942, it did provide some evidence for further consideration. I recalled what Celia Lewis had told me, "it's probable that your grandfather's early life was no different than what we know of his later life." I reminded myself what this likely meant: strained, possibly short, relationships with younger women, and a series of temporary, maybe transient sales jobs. His time with Clara seemed to support this theory. More and more I was doubting the prison or the United States family angle and figuring my grandfather's life was going to be as expected, that is, if I ever discovered the truth.

We arrive at the point that could reasonably be considered the final appearance of Clara Fielder in my genealogical search. However, my interest in Clara would have two further intrusions in this tale.

First, having come this far with Clara, I found I couldn't simply allow her story to fade to the background. Also, Sharon and Roger still had questions about Clara. It's possible I was experiencing a kind of vicarious wonder at a mystery that I believed could be further solved.  Maybe it was a substitute for my own seemingly unsolvable mystery.

I was interested in learning more of Clara's younger life, from 1913 to her marriage to Norman Fielder in 1938.  It didn't take long on *Ancestry.com* before I discovered a family tree owned by a "marlenn," from Brockville, Ontario, that seemed to contain our Clara.  I report that it "seemed" to contain our Clara because the information didn't quite match up.  According to marlenn, Clara McCurdy was adopted by family at a young age and became "Jean Clara Conway," before marrying a Charles Pratt and finally passing on in 1984.  Soon after the discovery, I sent "marlenn" the following:

> *Hello Marlenn: I am very impressed with the work that you have done on the McCurdy family.  I am researching my step-grandmother who went by the name, "Clara Stanley" when she was married in Edmonton in 1946. Upon her death, paperwork showed she was born Clara McCurdy in Toronto around 1913.*
>
> *When I look at your information for Jean Conway, born "Clara McCurdy," it seems that both our Clara's match-up before the 1940s.  However, yours went on to marry Charles Pratt and live until 1984, while mine went on to marry Patrick Stanley and live until 1999.*
>
> *I guess I'm wondering how sure you are of the name change and adoption.  Also, I noticed that you have her born in 1913 but the photo of her gravestone says 1923.*
>
> *I've got a real mystery on my hands with lots of loose ends.  Any thoughts you could give me would be greatly appreciated.  Thanks*

Reading over my message, I was attempting to be both courteous and light; however, I was skeptical of the accuracy of her details in addition to the conflicting dates of birth entered in her tree.  Also, I could find no corroborating evidence that Clara was adopted.  Any doubts to the veracity of marlenn's research skills were put to rest when I received her very timely response.

Marlenn, who signed off as "Marie" explained that the tree I had found was a type of "work in progress," explaining she was aware of some conflicting information and that she had intended to mark the tree as private. Marie explained that she had been researching the life of her grandmother, who was adopted at a young age. She shared that her "grandmother died twenty-seven years ago and for twenty-seven years [she's] been trying to find out" the identity of her grandmother's birth mother. She continued that "through DNA and a ton of research, [she] figured out 99.9%" that her grandmother's birth mother was Margaret McCurdy. If accurate, this would make my Clara and Marie's grandmother sisters or at least half-sisters.

Marie confirmed what I had found in my research, that Margaret had died in 1919 due to the Spanish Flu. Through 1921 census reports, Marie was able to trace her grandmother and Clara to Margaret's parents' house but, mainly due to the moratorium on census records, no further. Marie had been told by a relative that Clara was adopted by an aunt and uncle, taking on the name, Jean Conway. With my information, Marie was able to learn that Jean was, in fact, a third sibling, entirely separate from Clara. Learning that I was in touch with Clara's son and daughter-in-law, Marie was keen to connect and enthusiastic about confirming the connection through DNA.

I immediately shared this new connection with Sharon and Roger. In the scope of a few weeks, they had learned plenty about their dear deceased mother, resulting, I'm sure, in a multitude of conflicting emotions. Now I was able to connect Roger with a first cousin, once removed. The details and documents matched, but a DNA test would be necessary to confirm.

In early January of 2023, I received a pleasant greeting from Sharon Lange, who began with "Happy New Year to you," before continuing, "Roger did get his DNA results and Marie was one of his matches." I was overjoyed for both Marie and Roger, essentially first cousins, who were able to confirm their connection. At the same time, I heard from Marie, also sharing the exciting discovery or at least confirmation. In her message, she thanked me for helping put the family together, reflecting at the bottom of the message that I "should have been a detective." Both humbled and a little chagrinned at the remark, I considered what I'd help accomplish with the family.

At this point, it occurred to me that there was at least one additional thread that called for attention. Lost amongst the information I helped gather were the birthdates of all three sons born to Clara and Patrick Stanley. Roger and his brother, Peter, were actually twins, a year or two younger than their older brother, Al Stanley, born on March 3, 1947. Immediately, I took note that Al and my own father shared the March 3 birthdate, albeit one year apart, my father entering this world in 1948. It wasn't necessarily the March 3 aspect that most ignited my curiosity, but rather the 1947 part. While math was never my strong suit, I worked backwards and deducted that Al must have been conceived in mid-1946, the very time my grandfather and Clara are listed as residing at 10130 155 Street. My curiosity was obvious: was Al Stanley possibly my grandfather's child?

I retreated to my records to see what else I may have gathered about either my grandfather or Clara during 1946. The recording of their names in the phone book was fairly unremarkable, as I reasoned the information could have been recorded early in 1946, later in 1945 or it may have even been an automatic "roll-over" simply based on the previous year's data. I was privy to the fact that Clara married Patrick in July 1946, meaning she would have been pregnant at the time. The address on her 1946 wedding license was 10838 124th Street, different from the home she shared with my grandfather. I wasn't able to link the address to either my grandfather or

Clara's groom, Patrick Stanley, the residence seemingly a rental complex of some sort. Was the marriage planned in haste, with the young couple already expecting a baby or was this a move by a pregnant and possibly desperate Clara to escape life with my grandfather and find a man more suitable in both age and temperament to raise a family?

Complicating the issue was the fact that, despite being only one year older than my father, Al Stanley had sadly passed away in 2016, both eliminating the possibility of questioning him on the subject and the prospect of my father having a half-brother out in the world. However, I was aware that Al's legacy on earth included at least one child, a son named Greg. In fact, Greg was one of the relatives who had responded to my original Facebook message that led to my initial contact with Sharon and Roger. Was it possible both he and I were Alfred's grandsons?

Quite comfortable in my relationship with Sharon and Roger, I decided to broach the uncomfortable subject with them, rather than contacting Greg myself. I should admit, it was Lana who diligently persuaded me, but I made the contact, nonetheless. Having spoken on the phone only once during our initial contact, I drafted an email to Sharon and Roger outlining some of the dates and sharing my suspicion, "do you think it's possible Al was my grandfather's child and not the son of Patrick Stanley?"

Roger's response, "absolutely."

Naturally, my next question for Roger and Sharon was whether they felt comfortable asking Greg to complete a DNA test. Roger's response? He thought it was a good idea, but preferred to wait until the timing was right. Apparently, Greg was slated to visit in the summer at which time, the opportunity may arise. I'd have to be patient.

Patience was "okay" by me if there was no other alternative. That doesn't mean Lana felt the same way though and if there's one thing you need to know about my wife, it's that she tends to get her own way. Finally, in September of 2022, her powers of persuasion proved too much, and I decided to contact Greg directly. I had recently read, *Finding Family*, by Richard Hill, a book I would recommend that outlines the author's decades-long search for his birth parents. Operating largely in the days before commercial DNA testing was widespread, he had found success in the unobtrusive practice of writing letters to prospective family members. So, I decided to do just that. Locating his address in an online Manitoba directory, I filled out an old-fashioned paper envelope and hand wrote the following:

*Hello Greg: You may recognize my name from the brief contact we shared on Facebook Messenger some months ago. In researching my family, I have been in contact with your Uncle Roger and Aunt Sharon, and we have shared a great deal of information. It seems that your grandmother, Clara, lived with my grandfather, Alfred, in Edmonton between the years of 1944 to 1946. In fact, they are listed at the same address in both the 1945 and 1946 Edmonton phone books.*

*The date is of interest to me, as I understand your late father was born in the early months of 1947. I wonder, with respect, whether it is possible that my grandfather, Alfred Victor Williams, may have been your father's birth dad.*

*I have heard many positive things about what a great family woman your grandmother was, and I sincerely hope this letter does not cause any upset. However, it would mean a great deal to my father if there was any family connection to be enjoyed.*

*If you are interested or open to exploring this, my father and I would be very happy to pay for and send you a DNA test that would confirm such a match. Please do not feel any pressure, as I realize this is a profound request. Thank you for your time. Sincerely, Ron Williams*

I sent the letter in late February and anxiously awaited a response. However, one month later, I was still waiting. Feeling like I was too far committed to retreat, I jumped back on Facebook and followed up with another message.

*Hi Greg: Just wondering if you received the letter I sent you through mail. I fear I may have had the wrong address. I'm wondering if you'd be interested in doing a free DNA test. I'm curious as my grandfather is listed as living with your grandmother the year prior to marrying your grandfather. I totally understand if you're not interested and will let it drop. I figured I came this far in the research, so had to ask...thanks. Sincerely, Ron Williams*

Reflecting now, the words and tone accurately exposed my feelings at the time. I wanted to keep the message light – I was a little uneasy suggesting that his beloved late father was born an illegitimate child – but I figured I really owed it to myself to ask.

Lana will tell you this is just one of many times her continuous persistence was rewarded. Almost immediately, I received a response from Greg. He explained that he had recently moved and had not received any letter. Next, he enthusiastically agreed to go ahead with the DNA test. From his words, I'm not convinced he believed we shared a grandfather; however, he seemed excited about the prospect of discovering other relatives. That very day the kit was ordered with his correct address as final destination.

I was aware the results would take some time, up to two months was my understanding. In the meantime, Greg and I continued to interact and developed quite the rapport. Like me, he is a father of young athletes who enjoys watching sports and the odd Pale Ale or two. He expressed a profound pride in both his immediate and extended family. He reported that his grandmother, Clara, was a lovely lady, who along with her husband, Patrick, helped raise him. Greg also reported that his uncles, Roger and Peter were instrumental in his upbringing.   We were certainly becoming long-distance friends, if not half-cousins.

One particular evening, during a chat, Greg shared a couple pictures of his father with his uncles.  I was immediately struck by the likeness of both his dad and my dad, convincing myself beyond any doubt that they shared a father.  Greg also confirmed the presence of a small cleft in his father's chin, a sure sign of Williams' blood.  Lastly, considering the photo of Greg's father and uncles, I asked about his father's height. "That's the strange thing," Greg mused.  "My uncles are both over six feet tall, but my father was only five-seven."

My own father's height?  Five-seven.

Immediately, it became much more trying to wait patiently for the DNA results.

# A Gift From a Grandfather

**Friday, October 16, 1953, 2:31 p.m. 4141 Yale Street, Burnaby, British Columbia, Canada.**

*Elizabeth has left him again. "If you want to leave, you leave with nothing," he screams, in a fit of rage, scaring both mother and children. Don, five-and-a-half years old, goes out the door and briefly follows up the street. Shirley retreats to the comfort of the bedroom she shares with her older brother. Alfred, at sixty-three, really had tried, in his own way, to keep the family together. However, once again, the drink has proven too much, resulting in unprovoked attacks, always at the expense of his younger wife.*

*This time, Elizabeth has had enough, and Alfred holds the feeling she won't be back. Retreating to the front door, he spies Mrs. Blake, peeking from the corner of her window. The rage temporarily returns, and he attempts to scream out. Fortunately, something holds him back.*

*Elizabeth has left and Alfred must try to move on.*

T he calendar reminded that November 16, 2022 was to mark my fiftieth birthday. Upon my return from work, I was greeted with a cold IPA in a frosty glass and ordered to recline on the couch as Lana and the boys prepared a salmon dinner complete with Atlantic prawns and a delicious rice dish. For the ensuing two hours I basked in not only good food and drink, but the warm reward of a loving wife and children.

Hours later, the kitchen cleaned, I spent the evening in leisure, further enjoying the company of my family and generously feeling both proud and thankful. At some point amidst the wine and soft jazz, my mind, as it often did, wandered to thoughts of my grandfather. I attempted to picture what the evening of his fiftieth birthday may have looked like. Where was he on November 23, 1939? Surrounded by family, enjoying a quiet evening like me? Out celebrating in a lively setting? Or was he alone and regretful, no one and nothing to be thankful for?

In truth, my mind wandered plenty during these days. I was thankful to have discovered Clara Fielder and the possibility that my grandfather may have been father to her son, Al Stanley. I had to admit that my study into my grandfather's one-time domestic partner qualified as a detour in my specific task. However, I was satisfied that my efforts were worthwhile, having learned more about my grandfather's time in both Toronto and Edmonton as well as potentially identifying a son born to him.

However, while I was wholly determined to write this book, an ever-present, innate clock ticked away in my brain gently reminding what I was beginning to accept: my time on this project would need to come to an end at some point soon and

I still didn't have a satisfactory ending. My fear was that the final chapter would be a half-convincing, "in the end, my journey was about connecting with family, and strengthening relationships, the specific details of his life only secondary to what I was destined to accomplish."

Half-convincing at best.

Thankfully, the remaining part of my brain, less occupied with the innate, ticking clock urged me that it was time to definitively follow through with Celia Lewis's pointed advice. Thus, a few days after my fiftieth birthday I committed to a comprehensive search of all "Roy Hammonds" in available census reports.

While an overall study of census reports would certainly be onerous, I was fairly confident I'd be able to understand the data presented. I'd just need to be organized and methodical, which I believed were in my realm of abilities. If my working timeline of my grandfather's life was accurate, I couldn't expect to find my "Alfred Victor Williams" in any further available British, Canadian or United States census report. He appeared in the *1901 England Census* report, but immigration documents showed he was out of England by 1906, well prior to the next British census in 1911. There was a Canadian census in 1911, but again, his responses in the 1959 Old Age Security form suggested he had left Canada prior to that year. As for the United States census reports, I believed I had found him in New York in 1910 but had to consider that he was using the name, Roy Hammond thereafter. In any event, I determined that my best point of attack would likely be exhausting all Roy Hammonds in the appropriate United States census reports for 1920, 1930, and 1940.

Specifically, my plan was to focus on any results from the *1940 United States Federal Census* showing the name, Roy Hammond. For each match, I'd begin a further search including particulars such as birthdate, birth location, father's birthplace, mother's birthplace and family members, attempting to trace the Roy Hammond to 1942 and beyond. If there was record of the same Roy Hammond after 1942, I could be sure it wasn't my grandfather who had relocated to Toronto in that year. Conversely, using the same information, I would attempt to trace the Roy Hammond in question to prior to 1910. Again, if there was record of the Roy Hammond prior to 1910, I could be reasonably sure it wasn't my grandfather, as he had been going by Alfred Victor Williams in those days and living in Toronto.

In essence, I was looking for a Roy Hammond residing somewhere in the United States who seemed to both have no history prior to 1910 and disappear from records around 1942. While it seemed fairly straightforward on one level, there was an uncertainty that plagued my perpetually troubled outlook. I realized that my grandfather had likely stolen the identity of someone who was an actual person at some point, an admittance that could potentially render my search useless. I was desperate, but I knew I had to try.

I was off to what I'd considered a strong start. I bought a spiral-ringed notebook that I intended to use to list every Roy Hammond identified in the *1940 United States Federal Census*. In round one, I decided to focus on the 1940 census based on the fact that it was the 1942 Turley affidavit that stated Alfred had been living under that name until recently in the United States. Whenever I identified a Roy Hammond, I could then follow the lead backwards in previous census reports and other documents. Any Roy Hammond who couldn't be eliminated would be put aside for round two. Simple enough, or so I hoped.

With a tall glass of merlot at hand and warm slippers on feet, I cracked the window ever so slightly to allow the fresh evening air to intrude before opening *Ancestry.com* and beginning my formidable quest. I populated the search fields as best I was able:

First & Middle Names: Roy
Last Name: Hammond
Birth:1889

Gender: Male

I shuddered at the sight of the twenty-one empty search fields, the full visual effect of the limited information I had now fully realized. If he was untruthful about his name, I couldn't be confident he'd be truthful of any other details. Birth year was one measure in which I was reasonably sure he couldn't stretch too far from truth.

Selecting the circular, blue "search" button on the screen, I was met with, or faced with, 39,274 possible results. While daunting, it's precisely what I both expected and hoped for, accepting the comprehensive lists would contain enough matches of the *1940 United States Federal Census* as well as other documents, to keep me occupied for some time. If I had to look back, I likely counted on a couple months of documented inquiry to satisfy I'd done a comprehensive job or at least given it my best try.

With that, I clicked on my first target. Roy F. Hammond of Pine Bluffs, Jeferson, Arkansas, reported being born in 1891 in Texas. He was married to Myrtle Hammond and employed as a salesman of schoolbooks, the profession matching my grandfather's chosen method of financial preservation. Researching backwards, I learned Myrtle's name was actually Virginia Smith. They had raised two children, a daughter, also named Virginia, born in 1912 and a son, Harry, born in 1913. Roy's middle name was "Foote," and he listed his father as being from Michigan and his mother from Indiana. While none of the details strongly suggested he was my man, I was unable to rule out my grandfather at this point, so I diligently scribbled his information in my spiral notebook.

At this point, I moved forward, where I eventually found a death certificate for Mr. Roy Foote Hammond documenting his date of expiration as January 7, 1967. With the post-1942 documentation, I could be pretty certain this was not my man. Reflecting now, my process of elimination seemed swift and absolute. In actual time, however, events of the preceding paragraphs required almost a full hour. No, it wasn't going to be easy to go through the remaining thirty-nine thousand, two hundred something matches.

Match number two was Roy W. Hammond, born 1895, Iowa, residing in Mason City, Iowa in 1940. Again, he was a salesman, a clue that I was beginning to think would be too common to be helpful. His wife, Esther V. Hammond was born in 1887 and daughter, Maxine in 1927. These details, much like my first subject, offered some optimism. Moving backwards, I learned Roy and Esther were married in 1924 when they were both residing in Iowa and Roy was working as an automobile salesman.

I couldn't find this particular Roy Hammond in any 1920 census; however, in the 1910 census, I found a match showing his parents were John and Connie Hammond. Of course, this made it almost impossible this was my Roy Hammond, unless my twenty-one-year-old grandfather had somehow fooled John and Connie, taking on the identity of their fifteen-year-old son. Finally, I discovered that Roy had passed on May 27, 1941. I accepted this as convincing evidence that this man was not my grandfather, choosing not to entertain wild theories about fake deaths or the like. My spiral notebook now contained entries for two Roy Hammonds, both marked "Eliminated" in the margin.

Potential match number three was Roy C. Hammond, born in Pennsylvania in 1897, a little young, but who wouldn't take advantage of a few years when in the process of adopting a fictitious identity. In 1940, Roy was still residing in Pennsylvania employed as a tobacco salesman. I had learned from my father that Alfred had never smoked, but that didn't rule out the possibility that he made a living pushing the regrettable habit on others. He was married to a Helen C. Hammond, and they were raising two girls: Elizabeth was born in 1920, while Margaret J. was born in 1926. The two daughters, of relatively close age, made me once again consider the mysterious photo found in my grandfather's wallet. In the *1930 United States Federal Census*, Roy C., again residing in Pennsylvania, was working as some type of enumerator. So far, this seemed a fit. Moving forward, though, I learned in the *1950 United States Federal Census* that Roy and Helen continued to enjoy married life in their home state of Pennsylvania. This was at odds with my grandfather's 1942 arrival in Toronto and I quickly added a third, "Eliminated" to my notebook.

I'd been on my current task for only a few days. Information in my large spiral notebook comprised approximately six pages only, each potential match including a couple pages of dates, scribbles and other notes. Rather than discourage my efforts, any eliminations I had discovered offered a kind of satisfaction in the exercise. To begin, I was enjoying researching potential Roy Hammonds. Not sure how often I've mentioned, but genealogy, although frustrating at times, was more accurately a pleasurable hobby. Why else would I have spent this many hours attempting to solve this mystery?

In addition, there wasn't any urgency at this stage of my quest. I wasn't looking to discover anything in the next hour or even day. I knew I was in it for the long haul this time. Yes, it was slow, but I found solace in the idea that I was doing it right, knowing that my end result – whether it was to be success or failure – would be definitive and hopefully satisfying. If it was failure, I'd be able to conclude that I'd done my absolute best, but that the answers simply weren't available at this time. This is excluding the DNA angle that I'd eventually have to tackle.

Potential match number four in the *1940 United States Federal Census* was Roy R. Hammond, born 1890 in Indiana and married to Lucille. Before gathering too much information, I went straight to the 1950 census, pleased to see that Roy R. and Lucille remained alive and married. I wondered if that fact alone eliminated my grandfather. A wife could, after all, attempt to avoid the shame of a separation or abandonment by fictitiously reporting the presence of a husband. It could be, perhaps, safety-motivated, a single woman not wanting to advertise that she was living alone, vulnerable and defenseless. Once again, I marked the fourth Roy Hammond as "Eliminated," but with a little less confidence than I had done in past.

Roy F. Hammond from Irvington, Essex, New Jersey marked my fifth potential match from the *1940 United States Federal Census*. Again, I was intrigued at the "New York" connection. It made sense he may have entered the United States into New York through Toronto. Also, there was the 1910 census that I believed featured my grandfather living under his given name. Lastly, there was the frequent mention of Niagara Falls. This Roy F. Hammond was born in 1883, married to Naomi Hammond, ten years his junior and worked as an architectural draftsman. The younger bride certainly fit my grandfather. I was hesitant to accept his employment, but then again, my father had worked as a draftsman in the early seventies, and he wasn't required any special education. I had some trouble finding Roy and Naomi in the *1930 United States Federal Census*, so I jumped ahead. Sure enough, there were Roy and Naomi in the *1950 United States Federal Census*, both alive and well and not being my grandfather. Eliminated.

Five potential matches and five likely eliminations. At this rate, I considered there may not be any "round two" of further research for potential matches who couldn't be ruled out. That was actually fine by me.

Potential match number six came and went before I had a chance to really know him. Roy R. Hammond of Pendleton, Umatilla, Oregon was born in 1893 and married to Cressie who was a mere one year his junior. In 1940 they had a fourteen-year-old son named Loren Roy. I noted the pattern of matching middle names, my own father being bestowed the middle name "Roy." Beginning to hit my stride, I bypassed learning any more about Roy and Cressie until I checked them out in the *1950 United States Federal Census*. Once again, they were alive and well, likely enjoying their time as "empty nesters" with twenty-four-year-old Loren Roy out in the world on his own. Eliminated.

It was a cloudy Wednesday afternoon just one week after my fiftieth birthday that I retreated to my desk at work. The students were diligently working at their own desks, seemingly focused on their tasks. In a rare occurrence I was thoroughly up to date on both my planning and my marking. With nothing urgent to occupy the next two hours of my day, I reached down into my workbag and pulled out my little spiral notebook. Though it was unlikely I'd have time to fully research potential match number seven, at least I could begin on a target and finish later that evening.

Entering the now familiar "Roy Hammond" search parameters into my laptop, I was met with what was now beginning to establish as a familiar list of documents. Recognizing some of the same sets of names I'd researched above, I moved my mouse to click on a potential item of interest a little further down the list, not a record from the *1940 United States Federal Census*, but a *U.S. Social Security Application and Claims* record. This entry caught my attention, as the Roy G. Hammond listed shared my grandfather's birthday of November 23. Before I was able to click for the full record, a brief preview flashed on my screen, where the name "Emily Crane" registered in my eyes. Rather than become excited at the presence of my grandfather's mother's name in a "Roy Hammond" listing, I instantly assumed my cordless mouse had behaved on its own, as it's apt to do at times, and hovered to a record somewhere else on the screen I had already saved. This very phenomenon had occurred plenty in the past, resulting in brief unwarranted triumph giving way instantly to a cold, disappointing realism.

I repositioned my mouse, located the same *U.S. Social Security Application and Claims* record that matched my grandfather's birthdate and deliberately clicked on the precise line.

285

Reader, I am not sure how to adequately describe my reaction to what I saw on the screen directly in front of my astonished eyes. I can only relate that my body and all its facets temporarily shut down. My eyes were incapable of registering further information. My ears were incapable of hearing. My lungs incapable of breathing. My heart – I am certain – ceased to beat. With far too many synopses firing at once, I was both cut off from the outer world and incapable of any internal functioning.

But somewhere, far, far, back in the very cosmos of my being, a notion was ever so slightly beginning to formulate.

I'd done it.

I'd solved the mystery.

I'd found a record that matched my grandfather, Alfred Victor Williams to his alias Roy G. Hammond.

When I was able to come to my senses, I took a minute to double, then triple check what my eyes were slowly allowing my incredulous mind to ingest. With colors, sounds and my heartbeat slowly returning, I looked over the record I'd discovered:

Name: Roy G. Hammond
Gender: Male
Race: White
Birth Date: 23 NOV 1897
Birthplace: Niagara Coun, New York
Father: Frank Hammond
Mother: Emily Crane
SSN: 537091912
Notes: Jul 1937: Name listed as ROY G. HAMMOND

Now somewhat calmer, I was able to properly assess the information. The name, Roy Hammond, was the same as mentioned in the 1942 Turley affidavit; although, the initial, "G" was new. The birthdate, "November 23" was my grandfather's correct date, although the 1897 date was eight years more recent than my grandfather's actual 1889 birthdate. This didn't cause me too much concern, accepting that I'd probably afford myself the same advantage if I were to take on an assumed identity. The birthplace of "Niagara" sent a chill through my spine, having long since theorized the place held some meaning to my grandfather. Along with the birthdate, it was the mother's name, Emily Crane, that offered the strongest proof this individual was my grandfather. Lastly, the "father's name" was of no concern. In those days, I'm certain it would have been much more problematic to go by the surname, "Hammond," but list your father as a "Williams." In all, there were enough corroborating details for me to be satisfied this was my man.

Instinct told me to rush out to the hallway and share my news with Lana. That's not what I did. In a curious indulgence I'd first practiced decades ago as a young child on Christmas mornings, I trained myself to pause for a moment and bask in glorious anticipation when a moment of triumph is imminent. In this case, it was special that I alone was the only one vested in this project to know I'd made the connection. Selfishly, I wanted to experience it for a few moments for myself.

The basking didn't last long, and I soon found myself in the hallway anxiously waiting to connect with Lana. As I stood in the empty hallway, one eye through the side window so I could observe the potential havoc in my classroom, an unwelcome lump appeared in my throat as I began to share my triumph.

"Well, I did it. I found him."

"You what? You found...you mean your grandfather?"

"Lana, I found him. I found a document...he called himself Roy G. Hammond but his birthdate and his mother's name match...and it says he's from Niagara, which, you know, I always said was going to be part of the mystery."

"Slow down, slow down. What did you find? What is it?"

"It's a social security application with the name Roy G. Hammond, and including my grandfather's birthdate of

November 23, as well as his mother's name, Emily Crane. I found him."

Now minutes removed from my discovery, I desperately pined to return to my laptop where I could again verify that my connection indeed existed and then determine what further documents I could amass based on this new information.

The rest of the afternoon was spent in an intense match of telephone tag with Lana and I exchanging calls and texts every five minutes. Familiar with most of my personal passwords, Lana couldn't help but plug the new information into the search fields on *Ancestry.com* in a bid to beat me to the punch, so to speak. She had uncovered several documents showing where this Roy G. Hammond had been in those missing years. Having the advantage of superior intelligence and research skills, Lana was able to add to this new chapter in the narrative far faster than I was able to myself.

A mesmerizing two hours later, as the early winter sun began to retire, a golden lamp illuminated my desk in my den as Lana and I poured over our newly acquired treasure chest of discovery. In only a few short hours, we had learned more than I had thought possible. All it took was one matching document to act as a catalyst. At this point, we had a rough timeline of his whereabouts through the several missing decades, as well as multiple marriage and military records.

Settling into our second glasses of Merlot, the full wrath of discovery was beginning to set in. I was busy adding dates and details to the timeline I'd constructed over the previous seven years, entries for the 1910s, 1920s, 1930s and 1940s now miraculously appearing. While I was content to spend the remainder of the evening in satisfactory musing, Lana would have none of it and insisted I contact both my father and Aunt Shirley. It wasn't negligence or apathy that had prevented me from contacting them already. Rather, so proud was I of the accomplishment that I desired to make sure all my details were verified and in order before sharing. Lana listened attentively as I clearly explained my view of things. Then she ordered me to call them.

The first call was to my mother and father. I was pleased to be able to share the discovery in a fashion much clearer than my earlier phone call to Lana. I recall my mother being impressed but also sharing that she'd been confident all along the mystery would be solved. Not surprisingly, my dad was particularly delighted. He reminded me of what Alfred had communicated through our psychic, Michelle: "It won't be easy finding where I was...good luck." Approximately thirty minutes later I was on the phone to my Aunt Shirley. In addition to surprise and wonder, my aunt expressed sincere gratitude for our efforts.

A sense of pleasing contentment pervaded my body, knowing I'd been able to provide this gift, the gift of discovery and understanding. The gift of fulfilling a life-long wonder. I emailed my updated timeline to both my father and my aunt, hopeful that a visual would provide a clearer understanding of their mysterious father's life. It was a good night.

It was just after eleven when the hoopla surrounding the day's events died down, the kids retired to their bedrooms, Lana and I now relaxing on the couch. The feeling was probably no different than what anyone else may experience after solving a seven-year puzzle. As we sipped the last of our Merlot, Lana looked at me with a slight smirk.

"Hey, do you realize what day it is?"

I paused to consider.

"November 23, your grandfather's birthday."

Thanks for the gift, Grandpa.

# A Return to the Beginning

**Sunday, July 17, 1964, 4:01 p.m. 8168 Hudson Street, Vancouver, British Columbia, Canada.**

*Alfred has enjoyed the leisurely, warm Sunday morning. Dressed in full suit and hat, he's been at Callister Park, in East Vancouver, watching the Westminster Royals battle the Vancouver St. Patricks, a heated Pacific Coast League battle. The game of football, soccer, will remain close to his heart, a part of his time in England he can always hold special.*

*His heart is still warm from his visit the previous day to see Shirley, who looks an inch taller each time he sees her. In truth, he has missed the past two weekends, not quite feeling up to a visit. Yesterday, he made up for it, bringing a bag of treats, including her favorite – Cream Soda – as well as some medicinal drops for her infected pierced ears. He does cherish the time with his daughter, although it can be difficult to keep up with a fourteen-year-old.*

*It was at the soccer match earlier in the day that he had met Mr. Watson, another old British ex-pat, who suggests Alfred write to the Army Records Centre in London to enquire about his younger brother's records. Alfred, now an old man well into his seventies, still hopes to either connect with Dennis or learn the details of his sad fate. Either way.*

*On his way home Alfred stops in to see Mrs. Everett at Marpole Hardware, where he purchases some stationary for the planned correspondence, then it's a final stop at the Fraser Arms Hotel for a bottle to enjoy while he completes his missive.*

W aking the next day, my mind remained full of the pervading feeling of success garnered the day previous. Rather than retreat in my research, I was now spurred on, more intent than ever at discovering all I could, and the potential had just grown exponentially.

In truth, the social security number application didn't necessarily offer a plethora of details, but it was an invaluable starting point to say the least and missing details were conjured up in short time. What follows is the long-awaited story of my grandfather's mysterious life. Although my discoveries didn't necessarily follow a neat, orderly timeline, I offer the following in chronological order in a bid to add clarity to your reading pleasure.

I continued to cling to the notion that my grandfather entered the United States at age twenty in 1910, appearing as a lodger living in Manhattan, New York in the *1910 United States Federal Census*. In addition to the birthdate being close, he reported his occupation as salesman. As well, while

**Did Bertha know she wasn't marrying the man whose name is recorded?**

not Niagara specifically, it would explain the New York origins he reported in the newly discovered Roy G. Hammond social security application. Lastly, the 1909 immigration date listed on the census matched what my grandfather had reported in the 1942 registry and his unmailed 1959 social security application. Several years before conscription for World War I would begin, I could only assume he'd entered the new country in hopes of excitement or change.

I next found my twenty-five-year-old grandfather on July 6, 1915 applying for a marriage license in Salt Lake City, Utah. I considered how or what prompted my grandfather to relocate from New York to Salt Lake City, not necessarily a location desirable for a young man seeking fortune or excitement. I turned over this quizzical anomaly in my brain for several months, before I one day casually picked up my son, Jack's, copy of Kerouac's *On the Road*, and read on the opening page, "Dean...was born on the road, when his parents were passing through Salt Lake City in 1926, in a jalopy, on their way to Los Angeles." That seemed a likely explanation for my grandfather's presence in the Mormon headquarters, and future research would expose that he did eventually make it to California, if not Los Angeles specifically.

In the application for marriage, my grandfather, calling himself Gordon Roy Hammond, confirms his residence as Salt Lake City, reporting his age correctly as twenty-four. His intended is listed as Bertha Erhardt, also a resident of Salt Lake City, one year my grandfather's senior.

Marriage record 429308 of the State of Utah shows that my grandfather and Bertha became official on July 6, 1915. Marital bliss, however, did not last long. Barely a year after their nuptials, on July 13, 1916 an article boasting the sad headline, "Six Wives Beaten: Weather is to Blame," appears in the *Salt Lake Telegram*. It begins, "six men have been arrested during the past four days charged with beating their wives." Among the list is my grandfather, at this point, calling himself Gordon Hammond. The article continues "the crime of wife beating is not a usual one in Salt Lake," before explaining "general opinion has been expressed that the recent hot weather is really to blame." Further down, the writer describes a typical scenario, writing, "the husband comes home from work, tired and irritable from tolling through the heat of the day. The wife, who has been leaning over a tub or cookstove, is also in no present frame of mind. John throws his hat on the floor instead of hanging it on the hall tree where it belongs. The result – trouble."

I include this appalling account of domestic abuse as it is a regrettable but accurate detail of my grandfather's history, the same type of unacceptable behavior reported by my own father towards my Oma.

In June of 1917, with the United States enacting conscription, my grandfather fulfills his civic duty and registers with the draft board. In his papers, he lists his birthdate as November 23, 1890, another early example of his shaving time from his actual 1889 birth. He provides the familiar birthplace as New York State, this time in Buffalo, a mere twenty miles south of Niagara, and reports employment as a "constructor of concrete" with the Lock Point Pipe Company. Accurately recording his appearance as medium height and weight with brown hair and his characteristic blue eyes, he reports his marriage as the reason he is unable to participate in the great war. Whether or not his protest of matrimony was successful seems unlikely, as the October 7 issue of *The Salt Lake Tribune* includes a story titled, "Board No. 3 Calls for 99 More Men," listing Gordon Roy Hammond as required to report for "immediate examination." I am unable to find any record of him actually serving in World War I.

I learn that while my grandfather may have changed his name from his time in England, his chosen vocation eventually returned to what he knew: the railroad. A 1917 payroll docket from the Southern Pacific Company – Pacific System, Salt Lake City plant, lists my grandfather as a Signal Helper, a type of junior position, owed $27.34 for the month of December.

One year later, just before Christmas 1918, I find another mention of my grandfather and his violent behavior in *The Salt Lake Herald-Republican.*

### BEATS WIFE IS COMPLAINT

*Bertha Hammond filed a complaint yesterday in the third district court against Gordon R. Hammond, asking for a divorce. She alleged she had been beaten and kicked. She asks that she be allowed the furniture in their home at 336 W. Sixth North Street and that he be restrained from selling a talking machine which her mother and sister gave her.*

Again, I am disappointed but not entirely surprised. His abusive behavior was never kept secret from myself, and I suppose the fact that I never met him contributes to the detachment I feel at these reports. I do worry the effect on my father and aunt once I share these concerning details.

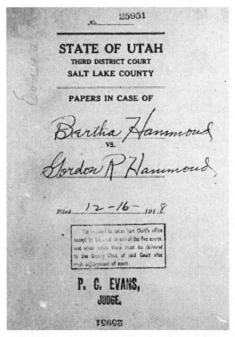

*The 1918 divorce papers were the first official record of my grandfather's poor treatment of women.*

Months later, I am successful in obtaining a copy of the 1918 divorce proceedings between my grandfather and Bertha, compliments of the excellent Salt Lake City Records Department. Dated December 16, 1918, the document, sadly, albeit predictably, proceeds in familiar fashion with Bertha, the complainant, outlining dates as well as specific details of the abuse she faced at the hands of my grandfather. In one instance she reports that my grandfather attempted to "choke her," making me think of the disturbing 1968 incident in which my grandfather, in some type of hallucinatory state, attempted to choke my own mother who had just recently began dating my father. It was all coming together.

Further in the document Bertha asserts she "was forced to leave the home at No. 336 West 6th, North Street...and to take refuge with friends." In addition to Bertha fearing for her safety, she shared concern my grandfather would "dispose of

295

personal property," including a Brunswick Talking Machine, which turned out to be a record player, as well as "furniture and furnishings," which were "mainly gifts to the plaintiff from the plaintiff's mother and sister." Additionally, Bertha reports concern that Alfred will squander "wages due...from the Utah Oil Refining Company, a corporation of this city where the defendant is employed." I took note of the change in employment, consistent with my grandfather's pattern of holding jobs for only a relatively short time. On that note, Bertha reports my grandfather earning approximately five to six dollars per day and asks that Alfred be required to pay fifty dollars per month alimony. Lastly, Bertha requests payment of one-hundred dollars for attorney fees.

Continuing to reason that the more I knew about the people around him, the more I'd learn about my grandfather, I determined it was time to find out what I could about the origins of Bertha (Erhardt) Hammond. Who was she? Where did she come from? In the *1913 Salt Lake City, Utah, City Directory,* I find the following listing:

Erhardt Anna, masseur Warm Springs Bath Co
r Warm Springs
-- Bertha, b Warm Springs

Despite my initial negative assumption, through research I learn that the Warm Springs Bath Company operated a type of community bathhouse innocently enjoyed by residents and families of Salt Lake City throughout the 1900s. I reason that Anna, whose presence is signified with an "r," is a resident and employee, while Bertha, signified with a "b" is a boarder. Considering the arrangement, I assume that Anna is Bertha's mother, though I cannot rule out a sister, likely older, as mentioned in the divorce proceedings.

While this marks the earliest entry in the city directory for any corresponding Erhardt, I do find a classified advertisement in the August 10, 1912, edition of *The Salt Lake Tribune*:

Mrs. Anna Erhardt Gives Massage
Just phone Wasatch 6649. 163 South 2nd East

Despite my efforts, I am unable to find any information for Anna or Bertha Erhardt in Utah prior to 1912.

Moving forward, I note that Anna continues to reside at Warm Springs Bath Company in the year 1914. Although the listing has changed slightly, with a notation added to Anna's name showing that she is a widow of "Chas," likely short for Charles. Anna continues to appear sparingly in the city directories, located at a residence separate from the Warm Springs Bath Company. Later, I locate a 1924 obituary that, although short on details, seems to match.

Back on *Ancestry.com*, I begin my search for the Erhardt family, including father, Charles, mother, Anna, and at least two daughters. Frustratingly, my efforts turn up zero quality matches. Birth, immigration, marriage, and death records are discovered with the "Erhardt" name, but I am unable to verify that any correspond to the Bertha in question. The best I can construct is that the Erhardt family arrived in Salt Lake City around 1912, either with or without father, Charles. My efforts are not totally without merit, however. With no official records in the area and the lack of a father, I consider that Bertha likely experienced challenges before meeting my grandfather, challenges that he may have used to his advantage. From the divorce documents, I note that she had a supportive mother and sister.

Without learning too much about Bertha's background, I determine to move forward. A return to the Salt Lake City directories contains listings for Bertha in 1920, 1921, and 1922, each indicating that she is a "widow" of Gordon R. I have learned that in these instances, "widow" can refer to a woman whose husband has passed or who is simply no longer cohabitating. There are no listings for my grandfather during those years.

I am surprised to see a November 7, 1922 article in *The Salt Lake Tribune* again featuring my grandfather. The article is titled, "Divorce is Granted: Three Actions Filed." The first paragraph shares a divorce finalized between Frank and Elizabeth Wagner; however, further down I read, "Gordon R. Hammond charges Bertha Hammond with desertion." Whatever his status was in 1920 and 1921, it seems my grandfather is back in Salt Lake City at the end of 1922. With that, I compose another email to the Salt Lake City Records Department, this time concerning a 1922 divorce. Once again, I find their services second to none, as I receive an email containing a twenty-page file consisting of several legal documents, many signed in my grandfather's unique, undeniable script consisting of block letters mixed with flowing cursive.

In these second proceedings it's my grandfather initiating the action. In his statement, he explains Bertha had a change of heart after filing her 1918 divorce papers, both forgiving and returning to my grandfather in February of 1919, a couple months removed from her initial legal action. My grandfather then reports that Bertha left some "six weeks later." Further, my grandfather swears "on many occasions" he has "endeavored to induce defendant to come and live with him as his wife, but that said defendant refused to do so." In the papers, my grandfather states that although he and Bertha have been residents of Salt Lake City for "at least one year past," they have not cohabitated for over three years, prompting my grandfather to petition the courts for dissolution of the marriage.

On the third day of November 1922, the papers are delivered to Bertha at her residence at the Kenyon Hotel. A month later, Bertha files a "demurrer" which seems to be an objection to the charges against her. Bertha claims that my grandfather "does not state facts sufficient to constitute a cause of action against" herself. Furthermore, Bertha denies my grandfather's alleged timeline, arguing instead that "on or about the 11th day of February, 1919," it was my grandfather who, "disregarding his marriage vows, willfully and without cause, deserted and abandoned the defendant and has ever since continued to live separately and apart from the defendant without any cause, or for any reason, and against the will, wish or consent of the defendant." Finally, Bertha asks for one-hundred dollars in attorney fees and an alimony of fifty dollars per month. I oddly note Bertha's claim does not include any details of the abuse she suffered at the hands of my grandfather. Perhaps not admissible when acting as a defendant?

The affair eventually goes to trial at the end of December, with the final results reported in the 1922 Christmas Eve issue of *The Salt Lake Tribune*:

### HUSBAND ORDERED TO PAY WIFE

### ALIMONY OF $5.00 MONTH

*On her cross-complaint in which she accused her husband of desertion, Bertha Hammond was given a decree of separate maintenance from Gordon R. Hammond by Judge Ephraim Hanson of the Third District Court yesterday. Mr. Hammond also alleged desertion in filing suit against his wife. He was ordered to contribute $5 month towards her support.*

Also of note, in both the 1918 and 1922 filings, my grandfather and Bertha maintain there were no children as a result of the marriage. Additionally, both claim poverty, petitioning the state to provide legal representation.

From his unfortunate union with Bertha, I can be absolutely certain my grandfather is in Salt Lake City, Utah in the years 1915, 1916, 1917, 1918, 1919 and 1922, during which time he is employed in the concrete trade with the Lock Point Pipe Company, as a signal helper with Southern Pacific Company and also in some capacity with the Utah Oil Refining Company. A succession of what could be entry-level jobs.

So successful had I been in finding details of my grandfather's time in the above years, I do wonder why there

| NAME | RELATION. | TENURE. | PERSONAL DESCRIPTION. | | | | CITIZENSHIP. | | | EDUCATION. | | | Place of birth of each person and parents of each person | |
|---|---|---|---|---|---|---|---|---|---|---|---|---|---|---|
| of each person whose place of abode on January 1, 1920, was in this family. Enter surname first, then the given name and middle initial, if any. Include every person living on January 1, 1920. Omit children born since January 1, 1920. | Relationship of this person to the head of the family. | | | | | | | | | | | | PERSON. | |
| | | | | | Age at last birthday. | Single, married, widowed, or divorced. | Year of immigration to the United States. | Naturalized or alien. | If naturalized, year of naturalization. | Attended school any time since Sept. 1, 1919. | Whether able to read. | Whether able to write. | Place of birth. | Mother tongue. |
| 6 | | 7 | 8 | 9 | 10 | 11 | 12 | 13 | 14 | 15 | 16 | 17 | 18 | 19 | 20 |
| Anderson Lynn R | Lodger | | M | W | 31 | S | | | | | YES | YES | Tennessee | |
| Hammond Gordon R | Lodger | | M | W | 30 | S | | | | | YES | YES | New York | |
| Swink Fredrick | Roger | | M | W | 71 | S | ✓ | | | | YES | YES | New York | |
| Springer Amos C | Clerk | | M | W | 37 | S | | | | | YES | YES | California | |
| Maynard Lewis R | Employer | | M | W | 57 | M | | | | | YES | YES | New York | |
| Gordon William | owner | | M | W | 74 | M | 1858 | Na | 1858 | | YES | YES | Ireland | Irish |
| Finch James C. | Superintendent | | M | W | 65 | S | | | | | YES | YES | Missouri | |
| Reeves George N. | Steward | R | M | W | 80 | S | ✓ | | | | YES | YES | New York | |
| | wife | | F | W | 31 | M | | | | | YES | YES | N.J. Ill | |

*The 1920 U.S. census finds my grandfather in San Francisco reporting his correct age but a false birthplace.*

are no city directory, employment, newspaper or even military records for my grandfather during the years 1920 and 1921 in Salt Lake City. I may have found the answer to my question in the *1920 Federal United States Census*. It's there I discover a listing for "Hammond, Gordon R." reporting as a thirty-year-old, single, white male, lodging at 153 Market Street in San Francisco, California. If I was correct about my earlier theory regarding his stop in Salt Lake City on his way to California, it seems it didn't take him too much longer to arrive in the Golden State.

In addition to the name matching, right down to the initial "R," New York is listed as birthplace, a detail that matches the fictitious Gordon Roy Hammond my grandfather has created. Also, birthplace for mother and father is listed as "Ireland," matching the unexplained predilection my grandfather seemed to hold for this land to the west of his actual English home. With all these matching details, and a hint at foreshadowing when I share that I would later discover more corroborating evidence, I am convinced this man can be none other than Alfred Victor Williams. Pulling out my timeline, I mark the years 1920 and 1921 as "San Francisco."

So, what exactly happened to Bertha and "Gordon" after the 1922 separation decree? For her part, it seems Bertha stayed put in Salt Lake City, at least for a time. Over the next four years, Bertha jumps between three addresses. In that time, she is self-supported. I find a classified ad in *The Salt Lake Tribune* from Sunday, November 22, 1925. It reads, "woman wants position as chambermaid in hotel or can operative an elevator. Miss Bertha Hammond, 895 West 2nd South." As evidenced by corresponding listings in the city directory, she finds work as a housekeeper mainly. The listings are sporadic after 1928 and I can only be sure of her habitation in Salt Lake City in the years 1933, 1939, 1941, and 1942. Where she was in between and whether she passed away in 1942 at age fifty-two remains unknown, my research proving fruitless. Recognizing I can be something of a rascal at times, I will share with you that Bertha Erhardt will appear at least once more before turning over the final page of this book.

Having placed my grandfather in the bay area of California in 1920, I pursued the vicinity in my searches. While he most certainly filed legal papers in Salt Lake City in 1922, the lack of any entrance in the city directory or employment records made me consider that may have only been a business trip, the one-day drive mandated to file forms, with the possibility that he was in California long term from 1920 onwards.

While I have been busy applauding my success over the past few thousand words, I must admit failure when reporting on the remainder of the 1920s. All searches on *Ancestry.com* and *Newspapers.com* failed to expose any valid information. There was a potential match for a "G.R. Hammond" living in Fresno; however, his inclusion in the 1920 directory eliminated the gentleman with my grandfather being two-hundred miles away in San Francisco.

Hoping the 1930 United States Census would provide a point in which to research backwards, I find a William Roy Hammond listed as "inmate" in the Buffalo State Hospital, which I learn was the state's first psychiatric hospital or "asylum" as it was then referred. The birthdate and location matches; as well, my grandfather had identified "Buffalo" as his place of birth in the 1917 World War I draft card, so it made sense that he may have returned to the place he considered home. Could the name "William" have been either a confused response in a temporary psychotic state or even a clever clue to his actual identity? I recall hearing that chronic alcoholics were treated in mental institutions in years past. Could this be why he was in the state hospital? Although I cannot rule out that my grandfather returned to New York, I cannot find any satisfactory corroborating evidence and thus I am forced to set the document aside, deeming its accuracy as "unlikely."

I consider the advice given by Celia Lewis regarding the census reports. Despite finding my grandfather in the 1891 and 1901 England reports, as well as the 1910, 1920 and eventually 1940 U.S reports, 1930 is the single census report of which I am unable to account for him. If this is truly the case, I wonder at his exclusion. For certain, he established an early pattern of not staying put for an extended time, but that doesn't preclude him from the other census reports. Was he out of the country working? *Unlikely.* Again, I consider incarceration but quickly remind myself that even prisoners are accounted for in the census. Perhaps he was travelling, on route to another city in search of another job and another woman.

# Moments of Romance, Moments of Loss

**Saturday, March 23, 1968, 2:11 p.m.    8168 Hudson Street, Vancouver, British Columbia, Canada.**

*Alfred awakes in bed, his full dress and the invading midday sunlight partnering to cause confusion in the old man's mind. It takes a few minutes before he recalls the sad state of affairs that have led to his troubled mind. Alfred realizes he has just been discharged from Vancouver General Hospital. It took some begging on his part, but he was desperate to return to his familiar walls.*

*How many days he has been home is unclear, with Alfred accepting that he may have unreasonably pushed for a premature homecoming. His entire body aches as he considers allowing himself to drift again to sleep. Suddenly, he snaps from his easy trance, accepting that he'll need to venture out of house as the cupboards are bare of food.*

*Soon Alfred finds himself on foot, stepping gingerly onto the curb. With no government cheque to cash, he is hoping he can rely on the kind benevolence of Mrs. Everett at Marpole Hardware for a temporary loan. Alfred reflects that it's nice to have someone to count on, even if he would prefer it was family.*

After discovering the social security application that cracked my case, the very next document I discovered was a November 28, 1931 marriage license and registration issued by the California State Board of Health in the city of Oakland and the county of Alameda enjoining my grandfather to one Thelma May Hastings. On the form, my grandfather identifies himself as "Roy" now without the "Gordon." More than ever, I accept that the "Roy" he bestowed on my father as a middle name was a tribute to himself.

He reports an 1896 birthyear, incorrect by seven years to his advantage, and that this is his first marriage, apologies to Bertha Erhardt. Again, he records New York as his birthplace, which it seems was at least the birthplace of his alter ego. Consistent with the social security application, Frank Hammond, born in Ireland, is listed as the father, while he is true to his mother's name of Emily Crane, birthplace, England. The latter details provide one piece of corroborating evidence that this is my grandfather.

Both my grandfather and Thelma identify their homes as Richmond, California in Contra Costa County, a distance of only about twelve miles from their wedding local. My grandfather lists his specific domain as Travelers Hotel while

*My grandfather's second known marriage to a bride twenty years his junior. The residence listed suggests he had just arrived in town.*

Thelma May provides a domestic address on the aptly named Richmond Street. This suggests that similar to his boarding house addresses he occupied in both Edmonton and Vancouver, his domain was likely temporary signaling that he may have just only arrived in the Richmond area.

His occupation? Welding. I mark that at actual age of forty-one, my grandfather, according to his own self-reports, has not yet begun his supposed life-long career in sales, a vocation he boasts of having no less than thirty years' experience in his 1942 national registration form he was required to complete upon his eventual return to Canada. My father is again surprised, unable to comfortably place my grandfather working successfully in any position requiring a degree of physical labor.

As for Thelma May Hastings, where do I start? I mark her middle name matches my Aunt Shirley's middle name, which could be nothing more than a coincidence, or not. In what may be the initial instance of the pattern he continued with both Clara Stanley and my Oma, the marriage license lists Thelma as twenty-one years of age, officially two decades my grandfather's junior. Despite her young age, she shares this is her second marriage. She further reports that she is employed

305

in "clerical work" and that her parents are natives of California.

I complete another Internet search, specifically looking for a "Roy" Hammond around the same Oakland area marked as his home eleven years previous in the 1920 census. It made sense that he likely stayed in the area. However, among the list of truisms I've learned throughout this search is the reality that things don't always make sense. In this case, even placing my grandfather in the bay area of California in 1931, I am still unable to find any trace of him in the immediate years previous. Interestingly, that's not the case with his new bride.

If there were no clues to garner, then I suppose it was pure curiosity that motivated me to learn all I could about Thelma May. It turns out, my search didn't take long. It's with some shock that I discover a 1934 entry in the *California, U.S. Death Index, 1905-1939*. Identified by her maiden name, Thelma is a mere twenty- four years of age at time of death and only three years removed from her marriage to my grandfather. My reckless mind is immediately filled with unlikely possibilities as to the cause of her death. I need to learn not only what led to her untimely death as well as any details of her time with my grandfather.

I begin with an article I find in the July 25, 1927 edition of *The Oakland Tribune*. At seventeen years of age, Thelma Ziem, listed with what I'll learn is her stepfather's surname, has been crowned Miss Richmond, and is competing in the beauty contest for the 1927 Miss Oakland title. Although noteworthy, I have trouble being impressed that my forty-one-year-old grandfather is successful in marrying a twenty-year-old beauty queen.

I learn that just two years after her reign as Miss Richmond, nineteen-year-old Thelma marries George Vidal in a January wedding. The headlines in the paper, however, are not of the announcement type, but rather of a missing person. Included on the front page of the December 19, 1929 issue of *The Searchlight*, out of Redding, California, I read the following:

### THELMA VIDAL, FORMER LOCAL GIRL, MISSING FROM HOME IN OAKLAND

*OAKLAND, DEC. 18 - Mrs. Thelma Vidal, 19, is mysteriously missing from her home here for more than a week. She is being sought by police, who believe she may be the victim of a kidnapper.*

*George Vidal, the woman's husband, reported that she had been followed on several occasions by a tall, dark man. She vanished after leaving the home of her parents, Mr. and Mrs. Paul Ziem.*

Any care or concern I may project into the long-expired event is quickly erased when I read a subsequent article published only days later.

### 'KIDNAPED' WOMAN IS VISITING FRENCH GULCH

*Mrs. Thelma Vidal Reported Missing by the Oakland Husband, Is at Her Grandmother's Home.*

*A woman "strangely missing" from Oakland since Monday has been found in French Gulch.*

*Mrs. Thelma Vidal was not "kidnapped" as an Oakland dispatch stated her husband feared.*

*She simply has quit her husband for good and come back to her old hometown of French Gulch to make her home with her grandmother, Mrs. Martinez.*

*Mrs. Vidal arrived in Redding on the Tuesday morning train. She went to the home of her old friends, Mr. and Mrs. Carl H. Van Cleave. Making known her desire to go to French Gulch, Van Cleave, a driver of the mail truck to Weaverville, invited her to make the trip with him and she did so.*

## THELMA VIDAL, FORMER LOCAL GIRL, MISSING FROM HOME IN OAKLAND

OAKLAND, Dec. 18.—Mrs. Thelma Vidal, 19, is mysteriously missing from her home here for more than a week. She is being sought by police, who believe she may be the victim of a kidnaper.

George Vidal, the woman's husband, reported that she had been followed on several occasions by a tall, dark man. She vanished after leaving the home of her parents, Mr. and Mrs. Paul Ziem.

The Ziems are former residents of Redding and French Gulch.

*My grandfather's second wife had a brief life of triumph, struggle and mystery before passing at age 24.*

*Mrs. Vidal was formerly Miss Thelma Hastings of French Gulch and is a daughter of Mrs. Paul Ziem, former resident of Redding, by her first marriage.*

While the story quickly solves itself and her marriage to my grandfather soon after this event proves Thelma was successful in escaping her first husband, I cannot help but feel sympathetic towards her. While I've truly no way of knowing her role in the doomed marriage, I assume she suffered at the hands of some type of abuse. The same type, sadly, that she would likely experience with my grandfather only a short time later. My suspicions are supported by a divorce announcement in which Thelma charges "extreme cruelty" on the part of her first husband.

The fact that Thelma is originally from Northern California forces me to reconsider the listing for G.R. Hammond in Fresno. Remember the conflicting evidence with the 1920 census listing in San Francisco and also considering my grandfather and Thelma identify as residents of Richmond, California – near the bay area – give cause to once again cast-off northern California as a false lead, one of hundreds that I've mainly ignored in this story.

I am pleased to find an *Ancestry.com* member has included Thelma in her family tree. I contact "JHernandez9361" asking for any information on Thelma May Hastings. With her 1934 death, I know it extremely unlikely that my contact was acquainted with Thelma, but I held out hope that her story, and her sad fate, may have been the stuff of family lore and that I may access some of the details. A day later I receive a response explaining, "she is my husband's fourth cousin, related through the Berryessa family." The information not really adding to the story of my grandfather, I press a little further, providing some details of my search and how information about Thelma may fit in. Again, I receive a polite reply, but one void of any useful details. Well, it was worth an effort.

After some extended time searching, I am able to discover an obituary for an erroneously identified "Velma Ziem" printed in the May 3, 1934 edition of *The Oakland Tribune*. The given name was nothing more than a typo, but the surname printed was of note. While I was mildly interested her birth name, "Hastings" was not used, I took more note that – despite the fact that Thelma's death was less than two and a half years after their marriage – the surname "Hammond" did not appear. The brief announcement shared that "Miss Velma May Ziem, 24, died at her home Tuesday night after a long illness." I recognized the address as that of her mother and stepfather. Immediately following, it listed her mother, two sisters, and a stepbrother as the mourners. I'm not really surprised at the omission of my grandfather's name, accepting unusually short marriages as *status quo*. I take the opportunity for a quick mental review of his brides: my Oma, Clara Stanley, Bertha Erhardt and now Thelma May Hastings.

After completing vital information requests for three California states and almost two months of waiting, I am pleased one day to discover a large manilla envelope in the mailbox, stamped, "County of Contra Costa Vital Records." Carefully tearing open the top flap, I discover a death certificate for my grandfather's second known bride. I was still quite curious what could cause the death of a twenty-four-year-old woman. I didn't expect the expiration could be attributed to any action of my grandfather, but my mind was given certain concessions and freedoms to run wild. While it was true he was omitted from the obituary, I fantasized this could have been because the family was unhappy with him rather than him being out of the picture. Could my grandfather's drinking have resulted in something like a fatal automobile accident? Could he have done the unthinkable, his violent, drunken outbursts finally going too far?

Now with certificate in hand, I quickly scanned for highlights: "Thelma May Hastings, also known as Ziem and Hammond;" "Divorced from Roy Hammond;" "Cause of Death: pulmonary tuberculosis." Of course, I'm relieved her death couldn't be attributed to my grandfather. More so, I'm struck by the sad life of Miss Hastings, including a childhood in a broken home, two young, likely abusive marriages before a prolonged death in her early twenties.

Both vociferous Internet searches and inquiries to relevant government agencies fail to conjure any official divorce document. I mark this as a shame, considering the plethora of details I learned in the Bertha Erhardt divorce file. At the same time, I count myself fortunate to be spared the specifics of their short union. Given the situation, it's not unlikely there was never a legal divorce recorded. This could be due to cost, general neglect or possibly because their marriage was never legal in the first place, a detail fully explained a little later.

In any case, it seems my grandfather had moved on. Under the headline of "Marriage Licenses" in the November 11, 1935 edition of the *Reno Gazette-Journal*, I find buried amongst almost one hundred other names, a listing for "Gordon Roy Hammond and Helen D. Smith, both of Santa Monica."

Subsequent searches of Santa Monica and California in general fail to expose any corroborating documents. The left side of my brain argues this fact cannot be proven and thus should not be included in my grandfather's story. The right side of my brain is amused and suggests what I eventually accept: it probably was him.

Continuing to happily toil away on *Newspapers.com*, I find a curious announcement in the Tuesday, January 18, 1938 edition of *The Salt Lake Telegram*. Under the title of "Divorces Asked," it lists, "Bertha Hammond from Gordon Roy Hammond, desertion." The listing was not found in my earlier searches as I believed my grandfather to be well out of Salt Lake City by 1938. Had he returned to his former city, possibly in a successful reconciliation with his first bride? Having been so successful in the past with the State of Utah Department of Vital Records, I cross my fingers and make another request, this time for any divorce documents from 1938. Again, the state of Utah does not disappoint, and I find another legal filing in the sad saga of Bertha Erhardt versus Gordon Roy Hammond.

Dated January 17, 1938 Bertha charges that the defendant, Gordon Roy Hammond, "has for more than fifteen years prior to the commencement of this action, willfully deserted and abandoned the plaintiff, which desertion has been without just cause or provocation." Immediately I consider the conflicting 1922 announcement published in *The Salt Lake Tribune* stating my grandfather was charged with providing five dollars a month in a "decree of separate maintenance." Reviewing the article now, I realized it doesn't specifically state a divorce has been granted. Delving into the 1922 divorce papers, the second such filing and the first in which my grandfather acts as plaintiff, I realize it merely states the same, decreeing my grandfather provide monthly maintenance but making no mention of an official divorce.

While I'm no legal expert, I take this to mean that my grandfather's marriage to Thelma May Hastings was never actually official. These 1938 divorce papers prove Bertha was alive and presumably well at the time of my grandfather's 1931 California marriage to Thelma. For that matter, was his 1947 Seattle marriage to my Oma ever legal? With credit to the *1942 Salt Lake City Directory,* I am successful placing Bertha in Salt Lake City until that year but not thereafter. If she was able to survive another five years, I would take that to mean my grandparents' union was never official. But again, I'm no legal expert, nor do I consider it very meaningful amongst the details in my grandfather's strange life.

Now sixteen years removed from their most recent legal action, Bertha once again confirms that she is "entirely without money or property with which to pay the costs or for the service of the papers in said action." Recalling fragments of my social studies classes in high school, I conclude that times must have been difficult for a single, working woman in the 1930s. At the same time, I reflect that, even sixteen years removed from the purported traumatic years with my grandfather, it seems Bertha has been unable to create a comfortable or sustainable lifestyle for herself. In any case, I know that I'm certainly not in any position to judge a person living in a long-ago time period of which I know very little.

Further in the 1938 missive, Bertha declares, "she is in possession of no information whatever concerning the whereabouts of said defendant." She further alleges, "that he has departed from the State of Utah," because she has "inquired of friends and relatives and by letter of various means...to locate him but has been unable to do so." The submission that she has sought his whereabout through friends seems reasonable. My grandfather was reportedly a charming man so lasting friendships wouldn't be too difficult to imagine. The statement that she has searched through relatives certainly piques my interest. Does this mean Bertha has queried her own relatives? Her mother? Her sister? Bertha's mother, Anna, was listed as a widow of "Charles" in several city directory entries, which could mean he was

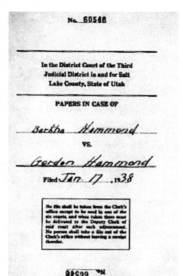

*My grandfather's 1938 divorce papers paint a disparaging picture including bigamy.*

deceased or was living apart.  Was my grandfather a friend of Bertha's father, Charles?  Was this the relative she contacted?

I also considered that my grandfather may have taken on an adoptive family while in Salt Lake City.  After all, the first evidence I have of him assuming the "Gordon Roy Hammond" identify is his marriage in Utah.  Had he taken on some type of surrogate family providing him with his new identity?  I also considered that, perhaps, "friends and relatives" was simply a type of common or legal phrase, meaning she had informally spoken to a number of people who knew him in Salt Lake City.

Recalling my grandfather listing "Frank Hammond" on both his 1917 World War I draft card and his social security application, I perform a search for any owner of that name residing in the Salt Lake City area at the time of my grandfather's habitude, specifically 1914 to 1921.  In the *1920 United States Federal Census*, I find only one such "Frank Hammond."  I learn that the individual in question was born in Chicago, before a stop in Spokane, Washington and eventually a move to Salt Lake City.  While there are some

313

parallels, this Frank Hammond's 1895 birthdate seems to rule him out as a potential "father-figure" to my grandfather.

Also, I scour the records for a Charles Erhardt, estranged father of Bertha, who may have maintained some type of relationship. Having steadfastly researched this name prior, I am unsurprised to discover no new information.

Finally, at the end of the 1938 divorce proceedings, some closure. I read, "the plaintiff is entitled to a decree of this court dissolving the contract of marriage heretofore and now existing between the plaintiff and defendant and that each be resolved of the obligations thereunder." Lastly, the court offers "that the plaintiff is entitled to the restoration of her former name, which was Bertha Gearhart." Momentarily, my mind is enraptured with the prospect that I've been researching Bertha's incorrect maiden name. A moment later, I relegate the "Gearhart" name to nothing more than an innocent typo, proven so by the several documents I've found for "Bertha Erhardt," and also her own signature at bottom of page.

Having long left Utah, I wonder if my grandfather is ever aware that his marriage to Bertha is officially over, much less if he even cares. The situation parallels his marriage to my Oma which lasted only a few short years but was never legally concluded. At minimum, with this 1938 divorce, I can once again safely assume his 1947 marriage to my Oma is legitimate. I cannot say the same for his 1931 marriage to Thelma May Hastings and I am able to mark my grandfather as "bigamist," whether he knew it or not.

Brief in-person or absentee interactions with Thelma May Hastings, Helen D. Smith, possibly, and even Bertha Hammond tell the story of a man both chasing and running from women during this time. Like Celia Lewis suggested, no real surprises.

# The Last, Final Chapter of Mr. Roy Hammond

**Sunday, April 21, 1968, 10:57 p.m. 8168 Hudson Street, Vancouver, British Columbia, Canada.**

*Don - I don't feel much like writing. I have had the blues for the past month. I don't seem to be able to shake it. Don, how would you like to take a few days off at the end of the week? I will have some money then. If you think Toronto is too far, how about just going to Osoyoos? I got a letter from Olga a few days ago and she asked me to ask you to pay them a visit. I've got a lot to talk to you about that's very important. I should have done this the last time you were in Vancouver. Don, have you heard from Shirley lately? Don, if you will do this for me I will consider it an Xmas gift from you or a birthday present. Don, how is the weather where you are at? Is it wet in the woods. Don, please write to me right away. I'll go nuts if I don't hear from you, and, Don, before I forget it, let me know if you would like some pocketbooks to read. Well, I guess I will close with all my love and best wishes. Don, when you can answer this letter, do you want me to phone your mother and say hello for you? Well, Don, please answer right away and think this trip to Osoyoos up. I know we will enjoy it. I can't say in words how much I have missed you. Oh, say, I almost forgot to tell you that Lola was up here about a week ago from Seattle. She asked about you and I told her you were up in the Queen Charlotte Islands or Franklin River, the other side of Port Alberni. Well, I can't think of anything else to say. Please answer right away. With all my love, I remain, your loving father, Alfred.*

During my initial discovery of my grandfather's "Gordon Roy Hammond" identity on the social security number record, the suggested documentation to the right of the *Ancestry.com* screen directed me to a 1942 World War II draft card. On the card, completed on February 15, 1942, I read that "Gordon Roy Hammond" is living at "1607 – 14th Avenue, Seattle Washington." He lists "Sam Laurie" as his employer at "Home Utilities, 919 Pike Street." While a Google search is fruitless, I envision Home Utilities to be a direct-to-buy purveyor of household gadgets, my grandfather likely peddling "door-to-door." He provides a familiar physical description of himself, 5'8", two-hundred and eight pounds with grey hair and his signature blue eyes. Curiously, he lists a scar on his right cheek of which neither my father nor aunt report awareness. Aside from the physical, further corroborating evidence appears with his birth details, November 23, 1897 in Buffalo, New York. Lastly, the signature itself bears the familiar slanting "R" with the

*A 1942 draft card provides a reason my grandfather
abandoned his secret identity and returned to Canada.*

generous middle loop that I recognized from the letters and other documents I collected in his pen.

Initially, I smirk at the generous eight-year gift he provides himself from his actual birthyear of 1889. Amusement gives out to wonder, as I read the header of the card: "Registration Card: Men born on or after February 17, 1897, and on or before December 31, 1921." If I assume my grandfather returns to Canada in late 1942 to avoid being drafted into World War II, it's an irony that had he given his true birthdate it would have precluded him from service due to old age. I can only assume he was unable to report any earlier birthdate based on prevarications recorded in previous government documents. Oh, what a tangled web we weave.

Now placing him in Seattle, Washington in 1942, I turn my attentions to the *1940 United States Federal Census* hoping for confirmation and further information. As I enter the search information I am privy to, I cross my fingers that I'm not left empty-handed such as the case in the *1930 United States Federal Census*. Almost immediately I find a potential match:

Name: Roy Hammond
Age: 42

317

Estimated Birth Year:1898
Address: 1121 Minor Avenue
Birthplace: New York
Marital Status: married
Residence in 1935: Seattle, King, Washington
Occupation: Salesman, Publishing House
Household Members: Vennice Hammond (34), Betty Hammond (14)

His given name is in accordance with the draft card, 1942 legal affidavit, and other documents showing he favored "Roy" in his final years before eventually returning to his given name, Alfred Victor. Additionally, the birthplace and birthdate fit the fictional identify he has constructed. Lastly, his stated profession again suggests door-to-door sales of the print variety, a profession he was involved in during his latter years in Vancouver. Most, if not all, the details seemed to match-up.

I'm most intrigued about the presence of a child, Betty Hammond. If true and Alfred did father a daughter in 1926, there's a chance one of Betty's children would still be alive, if not Betty herself. I recognize I'm jumping ahead of myself and accept it's just as likely my grandfather joined mother and daughter to become a stepfather. Neither possibility is ruled out definitively.

Pleased, I wonder if similar entry would appear in the *1930 United States Federal Census*. After all, it's possible my grandfather's brief, likely non-legal 1931 California union to Thelma May Hastings was nothing more than a quick trip south and he was in Seattle the whole time. Alternatively, I may find information in a 1930 census on the same Roy, Vennice and Betty Hammond that eliminates my grandfather. I limit the parameters to Washington State and complete another check of the *1930 United States Federal Census*. And I finally seem to have found my elusive grandfather's 1930 listing:

Name: Roy Hammond
Age: 33
Estimated Birth Year:1897
Address: 6077 2nd Street, NW
Birthplace: England
Marital Status: married
Residence in 1925: Seattle, King, Washington
Occupation: Restaurant
Household Members: Celia Hammond (33), Betty M. Hammond (3)

Again, the birthdate seems like a match and I'm optimistic, even though it doesn't include Roy Hammond's fictional birthplace of New York. Roy's listed profession is "restaurant worker" which seems of similar vein of entry level position of which my grandfather may find himself an employee. Concerning his female partner, I hypothesize that Celia may be a middle name of Vennice or vice versa. However, there is also the small matter of a nine-year birthdate discrepancy, with Vennice of the 1940 census reporting a 1906 birthdate and Celia of the 1930 census reporting an 1897 birthdate. Certainly, Vennice and Celia could be different women, but what of the daughter, Betty reported in both census reports being born at basically the same time in 1926 or 1927? With matching name and approximate birthyear, I feel it probable this Betty is one in the same. Is it possible that Celia left my grandfather alone with child at some point in the 1930s, only to have Vennice join the family as wife and eventual stepmother? That would suggest that Betty was my grandfather's child, perhaps one of the two cute blonde girls in my mystery photo. Name. Birthdate. Residence. Daughter. At least several dominoes fell into place, but it would take a little more digging for any firm conclusions.

I decide to focus my initial efforts on specific details of the 1930 census. Working backwards, I learn that the Celia Hammond in the 1930 census is originally Celia Theresa Fleury born March 27, 1897 in Green Bay, Wisconsin. By 1916 she and her parents are living in Seattle, Washington, where seven years later in 1923, Celia marries her husband, listed as Roy Hammond. I learn that their daughter, Sylvia "Betty" Mae Hammond, is born in Seattle three years prior to the 1930 census in 1927. Is it possible that my grandfather is the Roy Hammond living in Seattle between the years of 1923 and 1930? Absolutely. In fact, the dates fit nicely with the bookend locations I have for my grandfather: leaving Salt Lake City in 1922 and marrying in the Oakland area of California in 1931. Of course, this would entail that the marriage to Celia was over by 1931, permitting my grandfather to travel south and marry Thelma May. I continue my search to discover if Celia and her Roy Hammond ever separated. In an entry in the *1940 United States Federal Census*, I find Celia has retreated to the home of her parents, without her husband, Roy Hammond. Of concern, I note that Celia has also brought her daughter, now thirteen years old. In this scenario, Celia has left my grandfather by 1940, leaving my grandfather to take up residence with Vennice. The fact that Betty appears as resident of two separate households is possibly nothing more than a duplication error.

I now switch reports and endeavor to see what I can learn about Vennice Hammond as identified in my original finding in the *1940 United States Federal Census*. Following a not unusual pattern of transposed first and middle names as well as the predictable misspellings, I learn that Vennice Hammond is originally Cynthia Vernice Jensen born October 12, 1908 in Monroe, Utah. In 1925, at age sixteen, Vernice marries William John Silver and the two welcome daughter Betty Bernice Silver in Salt Lake City one year later. Despite the fact that my grandfather could be in Salt Lake City around that time, I accept that this Betty is a child of William John Silver, not my grandfather. Or is she? Seeing as Betty is going by the surname Hammond in the 1940 census, is it not possible that William John Silver was the temporary stepfather arriving on the scene to marry an already pregnant Vernice? I can't rule it out.

At this point, I take stock in my findings. Based on the background research I am able to complete, I am satisfied that Celia Hammond in the 1930 census and Vennice Hammond in the 1940 census are not the same person. Also, with official birth records indicating one Betty Hammond born in Seattle in 1927 and another Betty Hammond is born in Salt Lake City in 1926, I accept that they are also separate children, either of which could be my grandfather's biological offspring. Yes, it was complicated. Which Roy Hammond – if either – was my Roy Hammond?

I ponder this strange set of circumstances, both matching and conflicting, for the better part of the next two days. While this chapter may be read in continuous time, my research opportunities certainly were anything but and I often found myself settling for only minutes at a time and not every day. It wasn't long, though, before I felt I'd made progress, this time in the form of a family tree on *Ancestry.com*. A woman with the username, "cupidcarol" listed Celia Theresa Fleury in her tree.

Instantly enamored with her cheeky alias, I jumped into the pages of her impressive family tree. Immediately, I click on Celia Theresa Fleury and find her daughter Betty. However, the name of Betty's father is not Roy Hammond, but rather Thomas Watkins. Does this mean the Roy Hammond listed in the 1930 census is simply a stepfather, arriving on the scene only years after the birth of Betty or is it possible "cupidcarol" has listed Thomas Watkins as he was the one who stepped up to raise Sylvia Betty after my grandfather left?

It's a disappointment, but not a surprise, that Betty is listed as deceased in the family tree, although a specific year is not provided. While the name appears only as "private" in the tree, it appears that "cupidcarol" may be Betty's daughter. I decide to cease my hypothesizing and contact the woman directly.

*Hello: I am very interested in "Sylvia Betty Mae Hammond," born 1927, in your family tree. I see that in a 1930 census, it seems her father is a "Roy Hammond." I believe that Roy Hammond may actually be my grandfather. Do you have any information about Sylvia? Sincerely, Ron Williams*

Within the hour, I receive a succession of brief replies.

*"Hello, Roy Hammond is my grandfather as he was my mom's dad."*

*"Who was your dad?"*

I congratulate myself that I was correct in guessing "cupidcarol" was Betty's daughter. At the same time, I am intrigued she refers to Betty's father as Roy Hammond instead of Thomas Watkins as listed in her family tree. The responses soon continue.

*"Roy Hammond was the name he used in the United States, and he was born in England. The name he had there was Thomas Watkins."*

I was floored. At once I was both one hundred percent convinced this was my grandfather, and at the same time one hundred percent confused at the name Thomas Watkins. My mind races with possibilities but confusion temporarily takes hold and I'm unable to amalgamate the details into my story. Does the mention of an alias prove "cupidcarol's" Roy Hammond is my own Roy Hammond? Does this prove or eliminate my grandfather as the biologically accurate parent? While I'm thinking, my newest electronic pen pal continues typing.

*"Have you taken a DNA test?"*

This last comment causes me some pause. If "cupidcarol" is, in fact, my grandfather's granddaughter, she would appear as a pretty close match in my father's DNA connections. While I already know the result, I check his matches to ensure. No "cupidcarol." Still convinced by the unique "Roy Hammond" alias, I now consider that my grandfather must only have been stepfather to "cupidcarol's" mother, still a discovery, nonetheless. I offer a response:

> *Hello: Thanks for the response. The information you've provided me likely eliminates my grandfather as the biological father of Sylvia Betty Mae Hammond. My grandfather was born Alfred Victor Williams in 1889 in Worcestershire, England. He immigrated to Canada in 1906, but moved to the United States soon after and adopted the name, Gordon Roy Hammond. I am trying to fill in some blank years with his life. I know he was in Seattle in the early 40s, which is why your mother's family came up on my radar.*
>
> *My dad, Donald Roy Williams, took a DNA test that I manage for him. I don't think he is a match to yourself. The fact that both my Alfred Victor Williams and your Leslie Thomas Watkins took on the name of "Roy Hammond" leads me to believe they are one in the same and actually a stepfather to your mother.*
>
> *Thanks, Ron Williams*

"Cupidcarol" responds confirming that her DNA results also prove the man born Leslie Watkins and eventually becoming Roy Hammond is her biological grandfather, thus eliminating my own grandfather. Simply put, the Roy Hammond married to Celia Hammond in the 1930 census is not my grandfather. I still can't help but wonder, though, at the coincidence of two separate English men immigrating to North America and taking on the alias, Roy Hammond. I consider this may have been a type of generic alter-ego, similar to a "Joe Smith" of today. My searches of the Internet don't turn up any confirmation of my theory and I soon abandon it altogether.

Though I'm convinced, through DNA, that there is no relation, I find I'm unable to fully abandon this second, separate Roy Hammond, especially when I note on "cupidcarol's" *Ancestry.com* page that the man eventually moved north to Vancouver, Canada. Sure enough, in the *1936 Vancouver City Directory,* I am able to find the following listing:

Watkins, Thos L (Celia T) 6272 Windsor Street.

While there is no listing in 1937, Watkins and his wife reappear in a nearby residence in the 1938 and 1939 versions. Finally, on *Newspapers.com*, I'm able to discover the following obituary printed on February 4, 1948 in the very same *Vancouver Sun* newspaper that would employ my grandfather. Under the heading, "RCAF Veteran Among Four Sudden Deaths," I read, "Thomas Leslie Watkins, 48, who suffered a heart attack in his room in the Cecil Hotel, 1336 Granville, at 6:10pm Tuesday, died before medical aid could reach him." Though the article makes no mention of Watkins' "secret identity," I wonder at the coincidence of a man sharing my grandfather's "Roy Hammond" moniker dying in a Vancouver hotel, not ten minutes away from the very similar, Astoria Hotel, my grandfather had recently vacated. Being so near in proximity, and likely both fond of drink, I find myself wondering if they ever crossed paths. If so, I'd love to have heard their conversation.

In truth, my efforts to study the entry in the *1930 United States Federal Census* were, in part, to eliminate what I felt was the weaker lead. Details I found in the *1940 United States Federal Census* including place of birth and occupation better matched my grandfather. As well, I had to stretch a little to place my grandfather in Seattle in 1930, as I knew he had married in California in 1931. Based on the 1942 draft card, there was little difficulty placing my grandfather in Seattle the years prior. It was high time for another check of the trusty city directory. In the interest of brevity and an attempt to preserve your patience, I'll get directly to the point in reverse order.

1942 - Hammond, Roy slsmn, 1607 14<sup>th</sup> Ave.
1941 - GR Hammond, 1527 Terry Apt 4.
1940 - Roy Hammond, 1121 Minor Ave, slsmn publishing
1939 - Roy G Hammond (Vurnice) slsmn. 1703 15<sup>th</sup> Ave.
1938 - Roy Hammond (Vernice) 329 Fairview Ave, apt. 15
1937 - nothing.
1936 - Roy Hammond (Betty V) 1158 11<sup>th</sup> Ave.

I note that the 1942 address matches the information my grandfather entered in his World War II draft card. As well, the 1940 entry matches the address I have on the 1940 census report. Based on matching addresses, name, and occupation, I am convinced that this is my grandfather. It seems that for at least five years, my grandfather and Vernice considered themselves, Mr. and Mrs. Hammond.

What my findings didn't tell me, however, was if Betty was in fact my grandfather's child. If you recall, this Betty is born as Betty Bernice Silver in 1925 in Salt Lake City, Utah, the surname implicating that her biological father is Vernice's husband at the time, William Silver.

I briefly consider the likelihood that my grandfather first made acquaintance with Vernice while he was in Utah, entertaining the wild theory that my grandfather may have been Betty's biological father, estranged for a time in which Vernice marries William Silver. In the 1938 divorce papers, Bertha Erhardt declared that my grandfather had been estranged from her for more than fifteen years.

If you recall, I am unable to ascertain the precise whereabouts of my grandfather between the years of 1922, when it's his turn to serve first wife, Bertha, with divorce

*The 1940 census record listing Betty as my grandfather's child. Could she have been one of the girls in the photo?*

papers in Salt Lake City and 1930, when he appears in San Francisco. It's certainly possible he is in Salt Lake City in 1925 to father a daughter.

Again, through the *Ancestry.com* messenger service, I am able to make contact with a delightful woman named, Charlene Rene Babbel, who explains that "Cynthia Vernice Jensen was [her] great grandmother whom [she] didn't know, but her daughter, Betty Bernice Silver was [her] grandmother that [she does] have memories with." When I share that my grandfather led a type of transient lifestyle, she shares that her great grandmother "fit in with that kind of lifestyle too." She explains, that in 1943, while living with her sister in San Francisco, Vernice died at thirty-four years old "due to an alcoholic lifestyle." It's a sad irony that she and my grandfather shared the same geographical tour: Utah, Seattle, San Francisco.

Back on *Ancestry.com*, I find a May 11, 1942 Washington State Corrections Record documenting the arrest of thirty-four-year-old "C.V. Hammond," a resident of the Port Angeles Auto Court, for being "drunk." Cynthia, who is described as 5'8" and 150 pounds and having a "ruddy" complexion receives a ten dollar fine for her actions. A sad precursor to her death only eight months later.

Lacking any DNA leads from my father's own DNA test, I accept that my grandfather's role with Betty was likely stepfather. Whether or not Betty is one of the cute blonde girls in the mysterious photo discovered in my grandfather's wallet is a question I will likely never be at liberty to answer.

By the time of Cynthia's 1942 arrest, however, my grandfather is long gone, listing a "Mary J. Cowley" as his next-of-kin on the 1942 Draft Card. According to Charlene, her grandmother, fifteen-year-old Betty, is married for the first time that very year. I assume that my grandfather is out of her life also.

Once again, Celia Lewis's words strike me: "It's likely that your grandfather's early life was no different than what we know of his later life." Young brides. Short relationships. Alcoholic destruction. Menial jobs.

His time in Seattle almost understood, I wonder of Mary J. Cowley. In the *1938 Seattle City Directory*, there are seven viable options, but no exact match to a "Mary J. Cowley." I am able to find listings for Mary Cowley, Mary I. Cowley, Mary (wid. Tim) Cowley, Mary M. Cowley, Mary V. Cowley, Mary M. Crowley, M. Crowley, Mary Crowley, and Mary Crowley. I supposed I had to focus on the "J." Both to my surprise and good fortune, I was able to discover a February 9, 1937 obituary in *The Seattle Star* for Mary E. Richardson, listed as the mother of a Mary J. Cowley. The Seattle location combined with the correct middle initial, convinced me I had the correct Mary. To anyone researching family history, an obituary can be a goldmine of useful information and this one delivered, to an extent. I had the name of a mother, and possibly Mary's original surname, as well as the name of a sister, Mrs. Vera Pooler, and an address connected to the family, 1824 18th Avenue. Faintly recognizing the address on 18th Avenue, I quickly check my notes from the Seattle directories, where I see the address on 18th Avenue attributed to a "Mary I. Cowley." Is the discrepancy nothing more than a common typo? With no way of ascertaining for certain, I continue my investigation on *Ancesstry.com* in agitated uncertainty.

With details in hand, I learn that the "Mary J. Cowley" listed in the obituary is actually Mary Isabell Davison, born 1876 in Michigan. She married Herbert Cowley in 1895, soon adding two sons, Courtland and Robert. In 1910 Mary is a married, thirty-four-year-old mother living in Los Angeles,

California; however, by 1920, and still listed as married, she is back with her parents, no sign of her beloved Herbert. I track Mary to 1930, where, at age fifty-four, she is living with only her mother but now referring to herself as widowed, which I understand, either means Herbert is dead or has left her. It seems that sometime between 1930 and 1937, Mary and mother, move to Seattle and into the home of Mary's sister. Mother and two daughters, all widows living under one roof, appear in the 1937 phone book at 1824 18th Avenue.

Could this really be the Mary J. Cowley that my grandfather lists as his "next of kin" in the 1942 draft card? My best clue, the potentially honest typo of "Mary J. Cowley," is tentative at best. However, there appear no better options in any of my usual sources. Mary Cowley is listed at her sister's house, 1824 18th Avenue, only until 1942. This suggests she possibly moved out of her sister's residence in 1942, to be with my grandfather. I further learn that the address on my grandfather's 1942 draft card, 1607 14th Avenue, matches the Vantine Lodge. Were Alfred, or Gordon Roy, and Mary shacking up for a short time?

Again, I consider my grandfather's predilection to younger women. In 1942, my grandfather's actual age is fifty-two, Mary would have been sixty-six, not my grandfather's usual preference. In the end, I can't be certain that this is the Mary Cowley listed on my grandfather's draft card. Even if it is, I'm unable to ascertain if she is an acquaintance or some other relationship. He did select her as the person who would definitely "know his address," whatever that means.

Realizing I have inched ever so close to my grandfather's November 1942 return to Toronto, Ontario, I look for any last remaining traces of Gordon Roy Hammond in Seattle, Washington. I see no trace of any "Roy Hammond" in both the 1943 and 1944 city directories, confirming that the "Roy Hammond" listed in prior years must be my grandfather. I do, however, find an item of interest in the February 19, 1943 issue of *The Seattle Star*. Under the headline of "Board 7 Lists

Missing Men," I read "Draft Board No. 7 today listed the following men as 'delinquent' a draft board spokesman saying the men had failed to give notification of change of address or had committed other irregularities." Far down the long lists I spy the name, "Gordon Roy Hammond," who, at the time, happens to be living comfortably at 351 Ashdale Avenue, in Toronto, having just returned to his birth name and reunited with his England family. Oh, the irony.

And thus comes to an end my grandfather's Seattle days, both the last of his American occupation and Gordon Roy Hammond alias. While pleased I'm able to track him and solve the "Seattle mystery," I'm hardly surprised at the details.

It seems that my grandfather lands in Seattle around 1936, a few months removed from a brief engagement to Helen D. Smith and the unsuccessful, brief union with his twenty-year-old beauty queen, Thelma May Hastings. Almost immediately, he takes up residence with Vernice Silver, also some twenty-years his junior, who shares a penchant for drink. There, he tries his hand at parenting, temporarily becoming, to some degree, a stepfather to Betty. Some five years later, he is again, likely, on his own selling home supplies door to door, but mainly worried about evading service in World War II, which seems the likely reason for his retreat back to Toronto, Ontario, a move that makes him nostalgic for his English home and relatives.

# Epilogue

**October 7, 1968, 3:31 p.m. Vancouver General Hospital, 920 West 10th Avenue, Vancouver, British Columbia, Canada.**

*Alfred is admitted into Vancouver General Hospital today. It's the fourth time in the past three years that he has been required to stay a night or more under the orders of his physician, Dr. H.G. Weaver. What Alfred fears more is that this trip will not end in any return back to his home.*

*In truth, heart disease has been slowing him down for some time. Then, about two years ago, he began suffering repeated attacks of cerebral thrombosis, with blood clots limiting supply to his brain and causing him to pass out for extended periods of time. Now, sadly, the senility is becoming more of a burden resulting in daily problems with memory and thought.*

*As he lay in bed, his confused mind jumps between past places, Kidderminster, Toronto, Utah, Seattle, Vancouver; partners, Bertha, Thelma May, Vernice, Clara, Elizabeth; and identities, Gordon Roy Hammond, Roy Hammond, Alfred Victor Williams. And it's true, he tries to focus on the present, including visits with his kids and Don's new girlfriend, Melody.*

*Yes, he has regrets, but he had adventures also and plenty to reminisce.*

So, here we are at the end of my little tale. I do hope you've enjoyed reading it as much as I've enjoyed telling it. In the introduction, I assured I was "very satisfied I was able to solve the mystery," and I shared the optimistic promise that readers wouldn't feel "robbed, tricked or disappointed." I do hope I've fulfilled my promise, if not in full, then in part.

In May of 2023 as I began writing this story, I realized I hadn't heard from Greg Stanley in a while. A couple of months earlier I obsessed over what I considered the probability that we were both grandsons of Alfred Victor Williams. My grandfather was living with Greg's grandmother, Clara, as husband and wife in the year Greg's father, Al, was conceived. When Clara did marry Patrick Stanley, the man Greg considered his grandfather, she was already pregnant. Lastly, the younger two Stanley siblings, twins, matched Patrick Stanley's height and stood over six feet tall. Greg's father, Al, at only 5'7" matched perfectly my grandfather's shorter stature. I suppose I had lost track of the weeks and failed to follow up, subconsciously expecting Greg would reach out the moment the results were available. Surely the time had come. I turned to our preferred method of contact, Facebook Messenger:

*Hey Greg, how's it going? Any news on the DNA test?*

*Ya, I got my DNA results back and we're not a match.*

Both Lana and I were utterly floored. Given the extenuating conditions mentioned above, we were so sure we'd found an offspring of my grandfather. Whether I was simply surprised or actually disappointed, I backed off from the Stanley family, uncertain of what effect I'd had on these nice people. After a time, my conscience weighing heavily throughout, I reached out to Greg once again.

*Hey Greg - I guess it's been a month since you received the DNA results. I've been thinking a lot and I really want to apologize if I upset you or your family. From your family's perspective, I guess it wasn't a good feeling to wonder if your father and your uncles had a different dad. Also, this may have caused further upset as I understand your grandmother was a wonderful lady. Anyway, I just wanted to offer my sincere apologies if I caused any unnecessary bad feelings within your family...I can tell that you are all great people.*

Almost immediately, I received his frank response.

*Hey Ron - There is no need to apologize about anything. It was a very interesting and nerve-wracking period for me, but I wouldn't have done it if I didn't think there was a possibility that there would be more family out there that I haven't met.*

*As for the rest of my family, nobody really knew that I did the test except my one uncle. He wasn't too concerned about the results whether they be positive or negative that we are related. If anything, this experience has given me someone I can maybe go for a beer one day with if I'm ever in the lower mainland again and get to know you!*

And for one last time during this journey, I am touched by the kindness of my fellow man.

During our meeting with Michelle, another kind person who provided a psychic reading with my departed grandfather, she shared his cryptic response to our curiosity: "good luck finding me...it won't be easy." In the end, I think I was able to do just that. At the beginning, I knew nothing of my grandfather's first fifty-seven years. I pause now for the final time to reflect upon what has been learned:

Alfred Victor Williams was born November 23, 1889 in Kidderminster, Worcester, England. In 1906, at the age of sixteen, he immigrates to Toronto, Ontario, Canada and takes residence with his first cousin, William Turley. In 1910 Alfred is likely on West 21st Street in Manhattan, New York living as a boarder and working as a salesman. By 1914, he has adopted the name, Gordon Roy Hammond and marries Bertha Erhardt in Salt Lake City, Utah. The marriage apparently saves him from serving in World War I, but is short-lived due to mistreatment, and 1920 sees Alfred lodging on Market Street in San Francisco earning as an asbestos worker.

Most of the 1920s unknown, a now middle-aged Alfred emerges in 1931 near Oakland, California where he marries former beauty queen, Thelma May Hastings, twenty years his junior. Thelma passes away as a widow of sorts in 1934, two years prior to Alfred, now simply going by Roy Hammond, emerging in Seattle, living with Vernice Silver, also twenty years his junior, and her daughter Betty. Most likely marred on both sides by alcoholism, this union breaks up by 1942 when Alfred is forced to register for the World War II draft. It's this event that likely drives him back to Toronto, Ontario in November where he takes up residence with his aunt and uncle, reclaims his true identity, and rekindles a relationship with his England family. Working as a hospital orderly, he begins an affair with Clara Stanley, a married woman twenty-three years his junior, before a divorce ruling causes them to flee west to Edmonton in July of 1944. After this union too proves short-lived, Alfred arrives at the Astoria Hotel on East

Hastings in Vancouver, soon engaged to my Oma, a hotel maid again twenty years his junior.

In a 1943 letter, Alfred's Uncle George writes, "you have seen a bit of life and you will see more travelling." In the same year, Alfred's sister-in-law, Eva, writes that she "would like to be able to visit the interesting places you talk about in your letters." I can now imagine the places he described: the arctic, snow-white winter land of Ontario, the rugged plateaus and mountain ranges of Utah, the bustling metropolis of New York City, the remarkable Golden Gate bridge of San Francisco and of course the awe-inspiring natural beauty of Niagara Falls. Incredible? Yes. Exotic? Certainly. The entire story? Not quite.

Of course, I'm careful to only permit a pause at this point in my research and discovery. On a recent podcast, I hear an actual genealogist, a contrast to the novice attempt at family research I've presented here, posit that all genealogical pursuits will soon be made an exercise in futility as the world's DNA bank continues to grow, the promise that it will one day expose all ancestors, histories and skeletons in the closet. Whether future discoveries come through an expanded DNA rubric or from documents that continue to be rolled out year after year, month after month, there's plenty I anticipate.

What is my grandfather's DNA connection to Shirley Erwin, the mysterious close cousin with ancestors in England and ties to Ontario in the early 1900s? How did my grandfather, with a history of menial, often temporary jobs, amass the funds in 1948 to pay cash for his first Vancouver home? Why did he feel it necessary or perhaps desirable to marry my Oma in Seattle? Where was he for a majority of the 1920s?

Then I consider the still larger questions, lingering in my somewhat satisfied mind. Who were the two girls whose photo he kept in his wallet until his 1968 death? While all research avenues have led to dead ends, Lana, for one, is certain there must have been prior children. Unconvinced myself, I can't ignore the many relationships I became privy to and speculate on the volume of relationships to which I remain ignorant.

Finally, the largest question of all. Why Gordon Roy Hammond? Is the strange alias, not so different from the identity adopted by fellow Englishman Thomas Watkins, a random choice or is there meaning behind it? Either way, it seems to have been born at the same time he fled Canada for the United States. Were these changes an attempt to rid of past baggage or necessary for his very survival? There has to be a reason he took on a new identity, especially one that very likely precluded him from communicating with his father, mother, and brothers for essentially his entire adult life. I wonder that I'll ever know his reasons.

In the end, he bestowed the name, "Roy" not "Alfred" on his only son. I take that to mean it's whom he identified himself to be...Roy.

For closing, I consider this man in the entirety of his known life. A man whom I never had the advantage of being acquainted with in any finite way. What to make of him?

I've certainly shared some shortcomings of his character and there's never any acceptance for violence against woman. But I also accept that I'll never know his own struggles and horrors, what tragedies motivated his behaviors and the painful memories that drove him to drink.

Finally, I consider the final earthly reminder of Alfred Victor Williams, the very cold, metal grave marker my own father bent to kiss. And I know why I wrote this story.

For my dad.

# Acknowledgements

I t's difficult to know where to begin when I gratefully consider the magnitude of help and support I received while both researching and writing this book.

During the research stages, my mother conducted regular research endeavors that helped with several obstacles. My father used his skills on the telephone to order record checks and contact various officials.

My Aunt Shirley offered memories and comments throughout all stages of the project. As well, she generously shared her box of possessions that contained so many clues necessary to this story.

My wife, Lana, was instrumental at all stages of the project. I can't thank her enough for lending her critical mind and creative suggestions when I was fraught with some puzzle creating a roadblock in my curiosity. As a sounding board, she provided her insight more than a few times and was absolutely essential to the finished product.

Kylie Hughes provided excellent services as an editor and proofreader. The enthusiastic energy and diligent focus she offered added a degree of clarity and accuracy to the final text.

For the second time in my very brief writing career, Paul Palmer-Edwards outshone expectations by creating cover art that was both aesthetically pleasing and perfectly appropriate. He is also responsible for improving on my original, poorly written subtitle.

Also, I offer gratitude to my children, Jack, Ben, Tommy and Scott for their unwavering interest and encouragement. Along with Lana, it is their commitment to life that both inspires and motivates me to live my life.

Ron Williams' passion is unravelling the stories of our people through reflection and memoir. Having recently converted to a born-again genealogist, Ron is fascinated with those who came before us, especially his own family. In addition to genealogy and the written word, Ron's passions include cooking for friends and family; enjoying fine ales; exploring late nights, early mornings, and unknown neighborhoods. Ron holds a degree in English Literature from Simon Fraser University and proudly teaches high school composition in his hometown of Port Coquitlam, a suburb just outside Vancouver. Proud husband to Lana, and father to Jack, Ben, Tom, and Scott, Ron is a product of the '70s & '80s who always has time to talk music. Check out Ron's website, www.ronwilliamsmemoirs.com. Comments are welcome and responses imminent!

Printed in Great Britain
by Amazon

58376598R00198